Eleanor Roosevelt

**Recent Titles in
Women Making History**

Eleanor Roosevelt

A LIFE IN AMERICAN HISTORY

Keri F. Dearborn

Women Making History
Rosanne Welch and Peg A. Lamphier, Series Editors

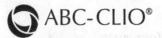 ABC-CLIO®

An Imprint of ABC-CLIO, LLC
Santa Barbara, California • Denver, Colorado

Library of Congress Cataloging-in-Publication Data

Names: Dearborn, Keri F., author.
Title: Eleanor Roosevelt : a life in American history / Keri F. Dearborn.
Description: Santa Barbara, California : ABC-CLIO, [2022] | Series: Women
  making history | Includes bibliographical references and index.
Identifiers: LCCN 2021059590 (print) | LCCN 2021059591 (ebook) | ISBN
  9781440873928 (hardcover) | ISBN 9781440873935 (ebook)
Subjects: LCSH: Roosevelt, Eleanor, 1884–1962. | Presidents'
  spouses—United States—Biography. | Women social reformers—United
  States—Biography. | United States—Politics and government—1933–1945.
Classification: LCC E807.1.R48 D44 2022 (print) | LCC E807.1.R48 (ebook)
  | DDC 973.917092 [B]—dc22
LC record available at https://lccn.loc.gov/2021059590
LC ebook record available at https://lccn.loc.gov/2021059591

ISBN: 978-1-4408-7392-8 (print)
      978-1-4408-7393-5 (ebook)

26 25 24 23 22   1 2 3 4 5

This book is also available as an eBook.

ABC-CLIO
An Imprint of ABC-CLIO, LLC

ABC-CLIO, LLC
147 Castilian Drive
Santa Barbara, California 93117
www.abc-clio.com

This book is printed on acid-free paper ∞

Manufactured in the United States of America

Contents

Series Foreword

We created this series because women today stand on the shoulders of those who came before them. They need to know the true power their foremothers had in shaping the world today and the obstacles those women overcame to achieve all that they have achieved and continue to achieve.

It is true that Gerda Lerner offered the first regular college course in women's history in 1963 and that, since then, women's history has become an academic discipline taught in nearly every American college and university. It is also true that women's history books number in the millions and cover a wealth of topics, time periods, and issues. Nonetheless, open any standard high school or college history textbook and you will find very few mentions of women's achievements or importance, and the few that do exist will be of the "exceptional woman" model, ghettoized to sidebars and footnotes.

With women missing from textbooks, students and citizens are allowed to believe that no woman ever meaningfully contributed to American history and that nothing women have ever done has had more than private, familial importance. In such books we do not learn that it was womens' petitioning efforts that brought the Thirteenth Amendment abolishing slavery to Abraham Lincoln's attention or that Social Security and child labor laws were the brainchild of Frances Perkins, the progressive female secretary of labor who was also the first woman appointed to a presidential cabinet.

Without this knowledge both female and male students are encouraged to think only men—primarily rich, white men—have ever done anything meaningful. This vision impedes our democracy in a nation that has finally become more aware of our beautiful diversity.

The National Bureau of Economic Research said women comprise the majority of college graduates in undergraduate institutions, law schools, and medical schools (56 percent in 2017). Still, women's high college attendance and graduation rates do not translate to equal pay or equal economic, political, or cultural power. There can be little argument that American women have made significant inroads *toward* equality in the last few decades, in spite of the ongoing dearth of women in normative approaches to American history teaching and writing. Hence, this series.

We want readers to know that we took the task of choosing the women to present seriously, adding new names to the list while looking to highlight new information about women we think we know. Many of these women have been written about in the past, but their lives were filtered through male or societal expectations. Here we hope the inclusion of the women's own words in the collection of primary documents we curated will finally allow them to speak for themselves about the issues that most mattered. The timeline will visually place them in history against events that hampered their efforts and alongside the events they created. Sidebars will give more detail on such events as the Triangle Shirtwaist Factory Fire. Finally, the chapter on Why She Matters will cement the reason such a woman deserves a new volume dedicated to her life.

Have we yet achieved parity? We'll let one of our subjects—the Honorable Ruth Bader Ginsburg—remind us that "when I'm sometimes asked when will there be enough [women on the supreme court]? And I say when there are nine, people are shocked. But there'd been nine men [for over 200 years], and nobody's ever raised a question about that."

Preface

On December 7, 1941, Eleanor Roosevelt typed changes to her radio script. The Imperial Japanese Navy had bombed the U.S. naval base at Pearl Harbor, Hawaii. By 2:30 p.m. Eastern Standard Time, newscasts were breaking into scheduled radio programming to report an act of war. Americans gathered around their radios hungry for information. There was no television, no immediate visual images. Radio was the latest technology transmitting up-to-the-minute details to a country in shock. That evening a voice came over the radio speaking to the nation. It wasn't the president. It wasn't a military leader. It was First Lady Eleanor Roosevelt.

With her calm, familiar voice, she was the first national figure to reassure the country. "The cabinet is convening and the leaders in Congress are meeting with the president," Eleanor Roosevelt said in her radio address of December 7, 1941. "The State Department and the Army and Navy officials have been with the president all afternoon . . . By tomorrow morning, the members of Congress will have a full report and be ready for action."

Then she spoke directly to the nation's women, reminding them she was also a mother with a son currently on a Naval destroyer. Two of her other children were in cities along the Pacific coast, which now were considered to be in the "danger zone." She empathized with the "clutch of fear at your heart," but encouraged an anxious public to "rise above these fears."

It was supposed to be her Sunday evening interview program, *Over Our Coffee Cups*, but this was not a normal Sunday—a foreign government had attacked Americans on home soil. A formal declaration of war and crafted statements from the president would come in the following days.

Eleanor Roosevelt was making history as a First Lady, as a woman, and as a public figure. She was rallying the nation over the radio airwaves to meet a war greater than the world had ever seen. She had written the words herself and she delivered them with cool courage. "We know what we have to face and we know that we are ready to face it," she said. "Whatever is asked of us, I am sure we can accomplish it. We are the free and unconquerable people of the United States of America."

Though she appeared to effortlessly address the millions of listening Americans, Eleanor Roosevelt had not always been confident and well spoken. She knew what it was to be afraid and to feel alone, to suffer great disappointment and deep personal loss. There were times in her life when depression and thoughts of inadequacy nearly overwhelmed her. Yet, she was determined to pick herself up and become stronger. As Eleanor Roosevelt wrote in her book *You Learn by Living* (1960, 29–30): "You gain strength, courage and confidence by every experience in which you really stop to look fear in the face. . . . You must do the thing you think you cannot do."

Eleanor Roosevelt is one of the most published and written about figures in American history, yet her complete story is still being uncovered. The goal of this book is to bring together past perspectives with newly accessible documents and investigations of Roosevelt's historical impact. It also is an endeavor to consolidate insights about the network of women she influenced.

Eleanor Roosevelt's life spanned dramatic social, cultural, and technological changes. She was not only intricately connected to her time in history but also played an integral role in shaping the United States we know today. Integrated into her story in this book are sidebars on cultural topics that shaped her, women who inspired her, and how she influenced the modern world.

For decades after her death, Eleanor Roosevelt controlled the narrative of her role in history. She was a media pioneer. From the written word to television, she understood how image could define or destroy a public figure. In writing her multiple autobiographies and books, she constructed the persona of "Mrs. Franklin D. Roosevelt"—a well-crafted image of a devoted mother and deferential wife, a shy woman thrust into a public life. It was an image that best supported the legacy of her political partner and husband, President Franklin Delano Roosevelt. It also depoliticized her later efforts on behalf of human rights and the United Nations. The crafted persona, however, does not always accurately depict the real woman.

It is easy to think of Eleanor Roosevelt frozen in time as the gray-haired, grandmotherly First Lady at the end of World War II, but she was also a child who lived through tragedy and public scandal. She was the niece of one of America's most popular presidents, Theodore Roosevelt, and part of a family of strong, politically-engaged women. Over her lifetime she built a network of female friends and activists that would quietly change government and society from within the male power structure.

In recent years, Eleanor Roosevelt's personal correspondences and private documents, radio broadcasts, and television transcripts have become easily accessible to the public. These documents have provided greater depth to her story. We can all read the angry, optimistic, consolatory, and eventually hopeless letters of the Roosevelt family trying to save Eleanor's father from his downward spiral into alcohol and opiate use.

Eleanor's personal letters to lifelong friend Isabella Selmes Ferguson Greenway King reveal active political discussion and involvement long before she would admit she was interested in politics and the public sphere. It was no accident that Isabella and many of Roosevelt's other friends and cousins were among the first generation of women elected to government office.

These intimate communications also reveal that Eleanor didn't conquer her fears and trials on her own. She had a circle of female friends who encouraged and supported her.

The revelation of previously sealed private correspondences with newspaper reporter Lorena Hickok invites reconsideration of Roosevelt's intimate relationships. Whether or not she had a physically romantic relationship with Hickok, the trust between them transformed Eleanor Roosevelt into a serious author and expanded her role in the White House during her husband's presidential administration.

Eleanor Roosevelt's relationships with other women, both known lesbian and straight women, were a source of knowledge, energy, and passion that drove her to advocacy. The fact that so many of these relationships remained unknown for decades prompted biographer Blanche Wiesen Cook to lament that Eleanor Roosevelt's actual intimate life and political influence "has been lost in an historical lie." We may never know the full extent of these personal relationships, but as historians unwind these connections, they are revealing how a core of women connected to Eleanor shaped Franklin D. Roosevelt's New Deal policies and transformed government's role in American society.

Does the sexual orientation of these women matter? No, it is their intellectual brilliance and groundbreaking actions that matter. But if you are a gender-fluid individual and have felt there were never any historical role models for you to look up to, it is important to know there have been others like you in history.

Delving into Eleanor's personal papers may strip away her icon image, but it enables us to understand a woman of flesh and blood, complete with flaws and complexities. Eleanor Roosevelt was not the perfect wife and mother. She could be jealous and self-righteous. At times, her husband's extramarital relationships crushed her self-esteem. She began her life with racial and cultural prejudices and evolved social empathy and racial tolerance over time.

Revealing our heroes and heroines as imperfect humans is imperative. It empowers us all to see the possibilities of leadership and innovator in ourselves.

As often as possible, Eleanor Roosevelt speaks for herself in this book. Her words can be heartbreaking, contradictory, but more often, inspiring. Investigating Roosevelt's media footprint can help us rediscover the voice of a woman actively trying to teach Americans tolerance and informed political activism. Her words on racial and social justice sound as though they have been ripped from our own time. Far from being a political novice, she reveals herself as a media professional, boldly questioning Soviet leadership on nuclear armaments at the height of tensions between the United States and Russia.

Fortunately for the world, saving potentially historical documents was a Roosevelt family obsession. Included in this book are primary source documents that capture specific moments in a historic life, correspondences that reveal true political influence, and Eleanor Roosevelt's greatest social achievements.

Eleanor Roosevelt worked at keeping herself informed. She embraced change, nurtured her intellectual curiosity, and advocated for a better world for all people. Let this book be an introduction to the complicated and rich life of a unique woman. May you discover in Eleanor Roosevelt something of your own experience. If she could cultivate bravery and become a powerhouse for good, so can we.

Thank you to my editors Dr. Rosanne Welch and Dr. Peg Lamphier for sending me on this journey of discovery. I appreciate your confidence in me and your support.

To my parents Robert Dearborn and Maxine Fruin Dearborn: Thank you. You have always valued my desire to write and never suggested that life had limits because I was female.

The greatest love and appreciation to my husband Michael Lawshé and canine companion Bodie. You accepted Eleanor Roosevelt into your lives and didn't mind when she took precedence over dinner or afternoon walks.

Please note that throughout this volume, Eleanor Roosevelt is referred to as both "Eleanor" and "ER."

Introduction: Why Eleanor Roosevelt Matters

Search "Eleanor Roosevelt quotes" on the Internet and you will find scores of inspiring phrases, like:

"[G]o out and do things . . . Don't believe what somebody else tells you, but know things by your own contacts with life. If you do that you will be of great value to the community and the world." (Eleanor Roosevelt, June 3, 1938 commencement speech to the Todhunter School graduating class)

"The only way to get rid of one's chains is not by complaint or lamentation. It is by knocking them off." (Eleanor Roosevelt, *The Autobiography of Eleanor Roosevelt*, 1961)

"It is today that we must create the world of the future . . . In a very real sense, *tomorrow is now*." (Eleanor Roosevelt, *Tomorrow Is Now*, 1963)

In a world before social media, Eleanor Roosevelt (ER) was an influencer. Using every form of media available to her, she communicated intimately with Americans, especially women. Her motive wasn't self-aggrandizement; she used her voice to educate, inspire, and persuade for a more equitable world. More importantly, behind every quotable phrase was a lifetime of practical action and purpose. She understood the power of engaging the public with trustworthy information and embraced new technologies to shape American opinion and influence governmental policy.

Eleanor Roosevelt secured a place in history as the wife of U.S. president Franklin Delano Roosevelt (FDR) (1882–1945). Standing beside him, she was the longest serving American First Lady (1933–1945) and championed the American people through two national crises: the Great Depression and World War II. Her position as First Lady, however, is just a slice of her legacy.

Eleanor Roosevelt is one of the most influential women in American history. She not only lived through but also participated in some of the most critical moments of the twentieth century—World War I, the 1918–1919 influenza pandemic, the Great Depression, the 1943 Detroit race riots, World War II, the first use of a nuclear weapon against humanity, the beginning of the Cold War between the United States and the Soviet Union, and the establishment of the United Nations. She played a leading role in labor reforms for women and children, the inclusion of women in American politics and government, pioneering journalism on the radio and television, and laying the foundation for antidiscrimination legislation and the modern feminist movement.

Her story is especially relevant today because she experienced and actively fought to alleviate many of the same challenges we face in the early twenty-first century: extreme economic inequality, communities challenged by substance abuse, a global pandemic, racial divisions, international persecution of refugees and ethnic groups, and threats to human rights.

Eleanor Roosevelt lived in a transitionary time—a period of great cultural, social, and technological change. As a teenager, she felt the sorrow of the British Empire as she watched the funeral procession for Queen Victoria. She marveled at how one small woman had such an impact on so many lives. Roosevelt herself would influence lives around the world and far into the future, especially through her work at the United Nations.

While we traditionally think of history as an ever-progressing upward line, we might figuratively think of it as an ever-climbing spiral. Women and people of color frequently earn rights and social position, only to experience backlash, which erodes some of those gains. Three times, Eleanor Roosevelt rallied against economic downturns that forced women out of the workplace. Economic depression also fed isolationism and populism in the 1930s, giving rise to European Fascism and the German Nazi Party. Similarly, economic disparity in the twenty-first century is promoting isolationism and a fear of people who seem different. The rise of popular nationalism and white supremacy would also be familiar to Eleanor Roosevelt. Her life offers insight and strategies for speaking truth to hate. She observed that "we are united by our aspirations and divided only by our fears" (Roosevelt 1963, 85).

The spiral of history also brings positive upswings. Political and social movements cycle back around to reclaim losses and build on the foundation of past efforts. Eleanor Roosevelt's story is especially relevant today because she and her generation of politically active women initiated the gender parity in politics that finally enabled the election of Kamala Harris as the first female vice president of the United States in 2020.

As an effective influencer, Eleanor Roosevelt helped shape our modern world. She was a political player who educated women for their new role as voting citizens and laid the foundation for greater female participation in politics. She redefined the role of women in public life and opened the door for women to attain positions of power and influence. She was a voice for the underrepresented, a champion of visionary change, and she built a foundation for civil rights and antidiscrimination legislation. Having experienced the devastation of two great wars, she championed the creation of the United Nations and led the effort to create the *Universal Declaration of Human Rights*, which established a baseline for humane treatment of people around the world.

EFFECTIVE INFLUENCER

Eleanor Roosevelt speaks to us today—through her words and deeds—because we can see ourselves in her desires and vulnerabilities. As a child, she experienced the death of her mother and also her father's addiction to alcohol and opiate drugs. By age ten, she was an orphan. While family wealth meant she would never suffer poverty, it didn't make her feel safe or replace a parent's unconditional love. Her early years were scarred by a fear of inadequacy and failure.

Overcoming fear and loss didn't happen in a single magical moment. She struggled with self-doubt throughout her life. "About the only value the story of my life may have," Eleanor Roosevelt wrote in her autobiography, "is to show that one can, even without any particular gifts, overcome obstacles that seem insurmountable." She is a role model not only because of her successes but also because of how she approached failure.

Like most of us, she was a naturally shy person. It took her years to hone her communication skills. Through draft and rewrite, she became an accomplished author. With practice and training, she learned to speak in public. She ignored criticism that women's voices were too shrill for microphones and became a pioneering communicator in the new mediums of radio and television. Supported by facts, she spoke from her heart, captivating audiences and motivating them to participate and find purpose.

One of her unique abilities, as an influencer, was listening. With empathy, she heard the concerns and needs of others. She seriously considered other points of view and bravely reevaluated her own preconceptions. Appreciating the needs of others enabled her to serve as an unprecedented conduit of change. She conveyed the voice of the American people—irrespective of their race, religion, ethnicity, physical ability, or sex—to the rooms of power where decisions were made.

For twenty-seven years, her ideas and thoughts were in people's homes six days a week through her newspaper column "My Day." She interacted with the public through her monthly magazine column "If You Ask Me"—answering questions ranging from the personal to the political. She engaged directly with people, responding to over a million private letters and crisscrossing the country on speaking tours for over twenty years. She conveyed her experiences and insights through 25 published books and over 500 articles. She informed American thought on subjects ranging from motherhood and subsidized housing to the challenges facing rising nations—like India—and the threats posed by an unsustainable military arms race. She spoke publicly at press conferences, on various radio programs, and ultimately on television.

Through her media platforms, she inspired other women to question societal norms and discover their own best selves. She encouraged Americans to think about uncomfortable topics: racism, gender inequality, poverty, and social injustice.

Born into a world where well-behaved women did not speak about politics in public, she became the most published and heard female political voice of the twentieth century. For decades, the depth of her influence was veiled by the 1950s backlash against female empowerment, which labeled the aging diplomat and former First Lady as a busybody grandmother. Male historians overlooked her innovative efforts on radio and television. They disregarded the long-term impacts of her direct communication with the public about serious governmental policy questions, including those concerning nuclear weapons and the United Nations.

Eleanor Roosevelt remains an effective and influential voice because her personal experiences resonate with our modern challenges. She offers an insider's knowledge of how government works and how personal and institutional change can be manifested.

"The American Dream can no more remain static than can the American nation," she warned. "[W]e cannot . . . take an old approach to world problems. They aren't the same problems. It isn't the same world. . . . we must emulate that pioneer quality in our ancestors that made them attempt new methods for a New World" (Roosevelt 1961, 408).

A POLITICAL PLAYER

Eleanor Roosevelt was thirty-six years old in 1920, when American women won the right to vote. She wasn't active in the Suffrage Movement herself. She and her Roosevelt aunts and cousins never felt a need to rally for a woman's right to vote. As members of New York's high society, they were already uniquely placed to influence men of power.

ER observed how her uncle, Theodore Roosevelt (1858–1919), the twenty-sixth president of the United States, would walk from the White House to confer with his sister, Anna "Bye" Roosevelt Cowles (1855–1931), on upcoming legislation or pressing international issues. Roosevelt women participated in private political discussions and built personal alliances with the men who ran the Republican Party and the nation.

When the Nineteenth Amendment to the Constitution secured women the vote, Eleanor joined the first generation of American women to embrace their political voice and actively participate in the political process. She adopted the philosophy of Carrie Chapman Catt, founder of the League of Women Voters (LWV). Women needed to learn about political candidates, the legislative process, and issues so that they could fulfill their responsibility as informed voting citizens. It was a belief that guided every public communication Eleanor Roosevelt initiated for the rest of her life. Education was one of her four pillars of democracy.

ER chaired the LWV's trailblazing effort to identify important pending legislation, analyze both sides, and summarize the legal terminology into understandable nonpartisan language. Modern voter information guides stand on the foundation created by Eleanor Roosevelt and the League of Women Voters. The women collected data that proved that voters—female or male—who understood how legislation or a candidate's stances impacted their daily lives were more inclined to vote and to make informed choices.

Eleanor Roosevelt soon felt legislation and policy were too important to not take a specific stance. She accepted a leadership role in the Women's Division of the Democratic Party and demanded parity with the men. She quickly realized, however, that equal responsibility and office space didn't assure equal respect or voice. If women were going to truly play a role in national and state politics, they needed to network and build coalitions. In a 1928 article for *Redbook* magazine, she wrote, "women must learn to play the game as men do." Women had to be leaders, themselves. They had to learn negotiation and accept reasonable compromise. Women had to be able to deliver a voting constituency.

She learned to draft legislation and plan winning strategies. Roosevelt cofounded, wrote for, and edited the first political newsletter for women in the Democratic Party: *Women's Democratic News*. She was shaping how women became politically active in the Democratic Party. She employed education as an element of every political campaign she worked on or advised, including presidential campaigns. Through her various media outlets, she framed political issues in easy-to-understand, fact-based, teachable moments to educate voters.

She helped initiate political inclusion. The Women's Division established a speaker's bureau of informed women who could publicly interact with local constituents about issues, programs, and candidates. During President Roosevelt's administration, First Lady Roosevelt helped create a national network of volunteers, including African American women in the South, who became local experts on New Deal programs. These women not only informed their communities about New Deal agencies and opportunities, they also evaluated government services, identified weaknesses, and reported back on policy implementation. Many of these women used their expertise to become community leaders and elected public officials.

"One of the important duties of the President," Eleanor Roosevelt observed in her autobiography, "is to be the educator of the public on national problems." A leader who can explain challenges and propose solutions is more likely to encourage public participation and partnership. As First Lady, Eleanor Roosevelt had a marked influence on her husband's administration. President Roosevelt employed an educational methodology in his communications to the country during the Great Depression and World War II. The president initiated public discussion and Eleanor's network of women continued the discourse. Government-funded work programs like the National Youth Administration (NYA) couldn't help anyone if communities didn't know that college grants and job training programs were available. Food rationing during the war received a better public response after the First Lady and female representatives presented information on why it was necessary and how it would work in American homes.

Eleanor Roosevelt used the power of her words to influence political opinion for the rest of her life. She showed women how to lead. She played the game and taught American women to be political players, too.

REDEFINING THE ROLE OF WOMEN

To many historians, Eleanor Roosevelt represents one of the first modern women of the twentieth century. During World War I (1917–1919) and the ensuing influenza pandemic, she volunteered at U.S. Navy facilities and with the American Red Cross. Like many women working in the place of men who had gone to war, the young wife and mother realized for the first time that she had solid skills. She was a gifted organizer and manager. She found purpose working outside of the home.

First Lady Eleanor Roosevelt earned her own income. She built careers for herself as an author, educator, public speaker, businesswoman, and broadcaster. She advocated for women's right to work and receive equal pay. She pressed for women to be included in New Deal employment programs and actively created job opportunities for thousands. She personally demonstrated that women were as capable as men by going to places where women did not typically go: coal mines, construction sites, and battlefields.

Eleanor Roosevelt began her activist career championing poor immigrant women in the labor movement. She found strength and empowerment combining her efforts with that of other women. Her greatest successes grew out of collaboration. She developed a genius for identifying innovative individuals and connecting them to people who could give their skills and vision opportunity.

Eleanor Roosevelt recognized brilliance in Frances Perkins (1880–1965) and her drafted prototypes for unemployment insurance and old-age pension plans. She introduced Perkins into Franklin D. Roosevelt's circle. Perkins became one of FDR's most trusted advisers and the first woman to hold a presidential cabinet position. Working together, Secretary of Labor Perkins and Eleanor Roosevelt conveyed reform ideals from the women's labor movement into New Deal government programs.

Similarly, ER brought Rose Schneiderman (1882–1972), a Jewish immigrant seamstress and president of the Women's Trade Union League, into the Roosevelt administration. Immigrant garment workers didn't need charity; they needed equal opportunity. ER realized that if the government was going to truly help the working poor, policy makers needed to hear directly from those individuals. As president, FDR named Schneiderman to the previously all-male National Labor Advisory Board.

Eleanor Roosevelt credited the scholarly Esther Lape (1881–1981) and her life partner, lawyer Elizabeth Read (1872–1943), as her primary instructors in law, international issues, and social justice. She brought their Progressive views on the World Court and a national health system into the Roosevelt White House. While FDR failed to act on a national health program, Lape and ER continued promoting the idea over thirty years to a series of U.S. presidents. Their influence provided incremental steps on the path to establishing Medicare and Medicaid in 1965, and eventually The Affordable Care Act of 2010.

Lape and Read were lifelong influences on Eleanor Roosevelt and introduced her to a community of accomplished professional women, who were also lesbians. Eleanor loved both men and women. While she was compelled to keep her intimate relationships secret, her experiences with the LGBTQ community informed her view that women were capable of succeeding in any field or position to which they aspired—from furniture maker to chairperson of the United Nations Commission on Human Rights. Tolerance was vital to a thriving society and her second pillar of democracy.

Eleanor Roosevelt was intelligent, innovative, and practical. She realized that standing on an equal footing with men required creating a network of women who supported and empowered each other with connections, data, and diverse expertise. Long ignored by male historians, Roosevelt was the center of a women's network that extended from seamstresses sewing coats in New York's garment district to the first female Federal Appeals Court Judge, from an African American civil rights leader to the nation's most famous female pilot, Amelia Earhart.

Her network also included the press. First Lady Roosevelt's press conferences provided consistent employment for the first cohort of serious female journalists. The weekly event covered issues important to women:

child welfare, education, and female employment. Covering these topics increased mainstream media interest in them. Female officials, like Perkins, were highlighted and acted as primary sources. Giving female experts a platform increased public acceptance of women as professionals in government, science, and academia. As a journalist herself, Eleanor Roosevelt regarded a trustworthy and free press as her third pillar of democracy.

The long-range goal of the women's network was to bring women's voices into every level of government. When the Roosevelt presidential administration began in 1933, Eleanor Roosevelt and Democratic Party leader Molly Dewson (1874–1962) secured appointments for over thirty qualified women in government agencies and departments. These women went on to hire other women to clerical, analytical, accounting, and professional positions within the civil service. Six years later, ER proudly proclaimed there were approximately 55 women in major federal positions and 162,518 women in government agencies.

Network members Caroline O'Day (1869–1943) in New York and Isabella Ferguson Greenway (1886–1953) in Arizona were elected to the U.S. House of Representatives. In Congress, they provided pivotal support for legislation, like the Social Security Act, which originated with Perkins at the Department of Labor.

Eleanor Roosevelt's network shaped Progressive legislation and government policy. They transformed the workplace by establishing worker safety laws, maximum work hours and workweek, and a minimum hourly wage. Women with plans for health care, social reform, conservation, the arts, vocational training, and education gained opportunities to voice their ideas and be taken seriously through Eleanor Roosevelt.

During World War II (1941–1945), Eleanor Roosevelt actively expanded female participation in professional and nontraditional industrial jobs. She worked closely with the NYA which trained young women as medical technicians, radio operators and equipment repair workers, metal lathe operators, and welders—jobs that would become fused with the wartime image of "Rosie the Riveter."

Eleanor Roosevelt advocated for the White House to include women in the U.S. military, not only as nurses and medical staff, but wherever their skills could be employed. She supported the establishment of the Women's Army Corps (WAC) and was instrumental in the creation of the U.S. Air Force's Women's Air Service Pilots (WASPS) and the U.S. Naval Reserve's Women Appointed for Volunteer Emergency Service (WAVES). Military service empowered a generation of women and forever changed the view of what American women were capable of accomplishing.

Following World War II women were again economically and socially pushed out of the workplace. The 1950s spiraled into a period of backlash;

women lost many of the political and social gains that Eleanor Roosevelt and the women's network had struggled to achieve.

When President John F. Kennedy (1917–1963) took office in 1961, seventy-six-year-old Eleanor Roosevelt chastised him for only appointing nine women into his administration and none to his Cabinet. She urged him to place more women in policy-making positions. Her activism compelled Kennedy to appoint a Presidential Commission on the Status of Women. Why were women not running for high political office? Why were so many college-educated women not using their degrees for employment? Why, in Eleanor Roosevelt's words, was the American woman not making the most of the rights her grandmother secured for her? ER knew investigation and data were necessary to quantify the challenges facing women and to provide the evidence to inform change.

President Kennedy appointed Eleanor Roosevelt to head the Commission on Women. Her declining health limited her participation, but her skill came in setting goals and putting together qualified people to get a job done. Kennedy concurred with the prevailing attitude that a woman's primary responsibility was in the home. The Commission's report would reveal that in reality women made up a third of the American workforce. They worked without adequate access to childcare and without equal pay for equal work.

The Commission found women wanted to work in higher-paying professions but were denied opportunity. Ruth Bader Ginsberg graduated first in her class from Columbia Law School in 1959, yet no major law firm would hire her and they told her directly that it was because she was a woman.

Though Eleanor Roosevelt died before the report was completed, its findings led to the inclusion of protections against discrimination on the basis of "sex" in the employment section of the 1964 Civil Rights Act. It also prompted the establishment of the National Organization for Women (NOW) to advocate for equality in the workplace. The foundation had been laid for the 1960s wave of feminism.

A VOICE FOR THE UNDERREPRESENTED

Eleanor Roosevelt believed women placed a greater value on the social welfare of other people than men did. Gradually male politicians would learn that if they wanted support from female voters, they would have to show greater concern for social issues. It is a philosophy that continues to shape American politics.

Eleanor Roosevelt was part of a transitional generation of high-society women. Initially, they used their status, privilege, and wealth to charitably help the less fortunate, but gradually, they stepped out from behind patriarchy to publicly use their own voices, writings, and actions to enact far-reaching social change.

In the aftermath of World War I, Eleanor Roosevelt was a whistleblower revealing inadequate funding to provide mental health care to injured veterans. She brought together medical professionals, government officials, and charitable organizations to dramatically improve mental health treatment. The effort rippled change across the country. The act of directly helping others empowered her and gave her life purpose.

Eleanor Roosevelt was an idealist who embraced Carrie Chapman Catt's motto from the 1921 New York LWV Conference: to participate within the nation's established political structure, but "to be one of the minorities which agitate and educate and shape ideas today which the majority will adopt tomorrow." Eleanor Roosevelt was an early advocate of ideas that have since become mainstream—federal food and housing assistance, government programs for children's health, and public support for the arts. She also agitated for change that continues to be controversial—community-funded childcare, two years of national service for every American, and national health care.

Working on the American (Bok) Peace Prize competition, Eleanor Roosevelt learned that even the most utopian enterprise begins with an idea. Global peace was a complicated and fanciful dream, yet each submitted plan offered a possible road map toward that goal.

Eleanor Roosevelt's life demonstrates that even idealistic ventures can be achieved working one small step at a time. In 1910, President Theodore Roosevelt called for a "League of Peace" to avoid warfare between nations. Thirty-six years, multiple failed attempts, and two World Wars later, Eleanor walked into the first session of the United Nations General Assembly. She lived the reality that no wide-eyed ideal was impossible if people were committed to its attainment. Social Security, unemployment insurance, and antidiscrimination laws all began as idealistic convictions.

Eleanor Roosevelt traveled to impoverished regions of the United States and lobbied for specific federal responses. Because of her initiative, government oversight of American territories and Native American Reservations was transferred from the militaristic War Department (today's Department of Defense) to the Department of the Interior. Where she saw poverty and homelessness, she proposed utopian housing projects, like "Arthurdale," to lift coal-mining families out of generational poverty. Where she saw unemployment, she helped create jobs for women in medical research, health care, libraries, schools, and the arts.

While Eleanor Roosevelt became an important voice for civil rights, her attitudes on race were not always what we would, today, consider to be enlightened. Many of her original thoughts on racism were entrenched in the belief that it was the white man's burden to care for the lesser people of color. But ER was willing to learn and grow. Her attitudes on racial equality evolved and were greatly influenced by her longtime friendship with Mary McLeod Bethune (1875–1955), founder of the National Council of Negro Women and vice president of the National Association for the Advancement of Colored People (NAACP). Bethune made ER aware of racial inequities in government programs. Social Security initially excluded domestic workers and farm laborers, a large percentage of whom were African Americans. It was a form of institutionalized racism.

If government officials didn't understand how African Americans were being discriminated against, how could they correct the problems? Through Eleanor Roosevelt, Bethune's circle of African American leaders gained access to President Roosevelt. Bethune was appointed Director of the Division of Negro Affairs for the NYA, where she expanded work programs and opportunities in minority communities.

Eleanor Roosevelt fought diligently for anti-lynching legislation but failed to find political support. It would take multiple revisions to make Social Security inclusive. In fact, some of ER's most successful civil rights efforts came not through policy or government programs, but through her own personal demonstrations of tolerance and her ability to compel people to reevaluate their own prior beliefs.

In 1939, when the Daughters of the American Revolution barred African American opera singer Marian Anderson from performing in their auditorium, Eleanor publicly discussed her decision to resign from the organization in her newspaper column "My Day." Behind the scenes, she helped facilitate Anderson's concert in front of the Lincoln Memorial, which would become an iconic moment of the Civil Rights Movement.

In 1941, Eleanor Roosevelt persuaded President Roosevelt to establish Executive Order 8802 stating that it was "the policy of the United States that there shall be no discrimination in the employment of workers in defense industries or government because of race, creed, color, or national origin." The order also provided for a Committee on Fair Employment Practices to pursue violations. It was a first step toward a vision of race equality.

Eleanor Roosevelt employed EO 8802 to press for the creation of the African American 99th Fighter Squadron and the all-female African American 6888 Central Postal Directory Battalion of the Women's Army Corps. These specially trained units provided opportunity and bolstered a generation of African American professionals who would advocate for civil rights.

Eleanor Roosevelt spoke frankly about race. "We have no common race in this country," she wrote in Collier's magazine in October 1943. "Every citizen in this country has a right to our basic freedoms, to justice and to equality of opportunity." We must be willing to "grant to others the free-doms that we wish for ourselves." ER knew that democracy requires inclusivity.

Eleanor Roosevelt's social reforms were often too revolutionary for the time or not completely successful in their implementation. Still, she made a historic difference in peoples' lives by championing underrepresented groups and expanding opportunities for women and people of color. Her actions helped lead the Democratic Party toward progressive social reform and give voice to communities of color within FDR's administration. Her efforts working with the NAACP, black labor unions, and female leadership in the African American community played a pivotal role in changing African American political affiliation from the Republican Party of Abraham Lincoln to the Democratic Party of Roosevelt.

Eleanor Roosevelt "believed in the power of ideas to transform society" (Cook 2016, 570). The National Youth Administration that she helped guide shaped a generation of Americans to believe that the government should work to improve the lives of its people. A young Lyndon B. Johnson (1908–1973) acted as a NYA regional director in Texas building public parks and schools. President Johnson would carry forward Progressive ideals and pass meaningful civil rights and voting rights legislation, establish anti-poverty programs, and realize Medicare.

ESTABLISHING THE UNITED NATIONS AND HUMAN RIGHTS

The twentieth century was filled with more violent global warfare than mankind had ever known; Eleanor Roosevelt lived through those conflicts and experienced them more personally than many Americans. She sat at the bedsides of young men returning from World War I, their bodies broken and their minds scarred. She witnessed the aftermath of trench warfare; the French countryside which she had loved as a teen was pulverized into a sea of mud.

As with so many American women, World War I gave her the most compelling reason to vote: to stop future wars. Peace activism was at the heart of Eleanor Roosevelt's personal politics. She believed that human survival demanded peace; conflict could be avoided if all of humanity was treated as having equal value.

She embraced her uncle Ted's vision for a "League of Peace"—an international organization of nations who agreed to mediate conflicts through legally binding treaties of arbitration. Theodore Roosevelt was an internationalist, as were Eleanor's aunts. Living and studying abroad, Eleanor spoke multiple languages. Her network of female contacts extended across Great Britain, Europe, and Australia. Her internationalist viewpoint shaped her writings, speeches, and her influence in Franklin D. Roosevelt's White House. Some of her deepest philosophical rifts with her husband involved the World Court and his abandonment of the League of Nations.

As tensions between governments increased around the world in the late 1930s, Eleanor quietly worked in opposition to the Roosevelt administration's position of neutrality. She brought voices warning about Fascism and Hitler's atrocities to the attention of FDR and the country. When she failed to change minds toward action, she focused her efforts on refugees.

Eleanor Roosevelt knew in her bones how it felt to be the outsider, the unwanted, and the powerless. Behind the scenes she worked with Frances Perkins to extend work visas for Jewish scientists and scholars to stop their deportation back to Nazi-controlled Europe. She used her media reach to build an infrastructure of humanitarians who tried to bring refugee children to safety in the United States. They continued their efforts despite opposition from anti-Semitic members of President Roosevelt's State Department. Eleanor became the last hope for many refugees.

When the United States joined the war effort against Hitler's Germany, Eleanor Roosevelt was the primary influence advising President Roosevelt to put his political clout behind an allied force of United Nations. With her encouragement, FDR held firm against a limited alliance of superpower countries and cemented the mandate to establish the United Nations.

During World War II, instead of sending his vice president, FDR asked First Lady Roosevelt to travel to war zones in Great Britain and the South Pacific. She became FDR's diplomatic representative to foreign governments and his eyes on the ground. She felt, however, that her more important job was being the face of home to half a million American military personnel. She comforted those who would never return home and deepened her resolve for world peace.

Surreptitiously, she was drawn into the Manhattan Project—the development of America's first nuclear weapon. She understood the enormity of the project and the global threat it posed. She was one of the first high-profile Americans, outside of the military or government, to visit postwar Japan and bear witness to the atomic bomb's destruction at Hiroshima. She used her media influence to sound the alarm about nuclear weapons and, as a journalist, pressed world leaders on controlling their use. Her calls for armament control helped initiate the movement against nuclear weapons.

After the war, when President Harry S. Truman (1884–1972) appointed her as a U.S. delegate to the first session of the United Nations (UN) General Assembly, Eleanor Roosevelt became one of the most influential Americans on the international stage. She used her celebrity status to highlight the small cohort of female UN delegates and called for greater female participation in governance worldwide.

When the UN Human Rights Commission elected her to chair the committee drafting the *Universal Declaration of Human Rights*, she applied her entire life experience to the job. While the world struggled through threats of conflict, Eleanor Roosevelt led a committee of women and men with different worldviews, languages, religions, politics, and social priorities to find common ground. Many felt the former First Lady was the only person who could have accomplished the immense task and successfully secured the UN General Assembly's approval.

Eleanor Roosevelt conveyed to the world that human rights began "in small places, close to home," in neighborhoods, schools, countrysides, and workplaces. "Such are the places where every man, woman and child seeks equal justice, equal opportunity, equal dignity without discrimination" (Roosevelt 1953). The *Universal Declaration of Human Rights* turned a spotlight on human rights abuses around the world: apartheid in South Africa, totalitarian governments around the world, and Jim Crow laws in the United States. Roosevelt's work on the UN Human Rights Commission bolstered the American Civil Rights Movement and continues to aid people around the world struggling to lead lives of dignity.

Eleanor Roosevelt used every media platform available to her, including television, to nurture success for the United Nations. Working with the American Association for the United Nations, she demonstrated to Americans how their participation in the United Nations benefited the United States and the world. She championed young people gaining firsthand experience in issues and negotiation through model UN role-playing. To this day, model UN programs are the incubators for women leaders entering the male-dominated world of national security and international diplomacy. Eleanor Roosevelt traveled the world teaching the value of the United Nations and international relationships.

HER INFLUENCE CONTINUES

Eleanor Roosevelt's story demonstrates the transformative impact a single individual can have on society and the world. She voiced her opinions and advice to three American presidents—her husband Franklin D. Roosevelt, his successor Harry S. Truman, and John F. Kennedy—and to a future president, Lyndon B. Johnson. She served as a role model to many American First Ladies, from Bess Truman to Hillary Clinton. Yet, some of her greatest impacts came through interaction with a single individual—helping them or offering them opportunity. She made history and empowered others to do the same.

Eleanor Roosevelt wasn't the best or the bravest; she wasn't the smartest or the most creative. She could be judgmental and disapproving, especially toward her close family. She was a flawed and imperfect woman, which makes her a true and real role model and heroine. She had empathy for other people's experiences and suffering. She was an organizer and network builder, a national influencer, and an international consensus builder. Her political actions, workplace advocacy, and social reforms continue to influence our daily lives. She believed in the possibility of a better world and championed innovative ideas to make it happen.

Whether you can relate to Eleanor Roosevelt's personal losses, her fear or self-doubt, or her need to help others, her story empowers us all to nurture our bravery and find purpose. At the First Anniversary Luncheon of the Eleanor Roosevelt Memorial Foundation in 1964, First Lady Claudia "Lady Bird" Johnson reminded us all that we have the power to emulate Eleanor Roosevelt if we are willing "to pluck out prejudice from our lives, to remove fear and hate where it exists, and to create a world unafraid to work out its destiny in peace."

SOURCES

Cook, Blanche Wiesen. 2016. *Eleanor Roosevelt, Volume 3: The War Years and After, 1939–1962*. New York: Viking Penguin.

Roosevelt, Eleanor. 1953, March 27. "Where Do Human Rights Begin." In *Courage in a Dangerous World: The Political Writings of Eleanor Roosevelt*, edited by Allida M. Black, 190. New York: Columbia University Press, 1999.

Roosevelt, Eleanor. 1961. *The Autobiography of Eleanor Roosevelt*. New York: Harper Perennial.

Roosevelt, Eleanor. 1963. *Tomorrow Is Now*. New York: Penguin Random House.

1

Surviving a Tragic Childhood
(1884–1894)

A clanging alarm bell rang out through the thick fog. Screams rose like unseen specters from people trapped below in the torn hull of the ship. Eleanor Roosevelt was just two and a half years old. Terrified, she clung to the ship's steward as her parents climbed into a lifeboat and were lowered over the side into the dark Atlantic Ocean.

Waves rocked the lifeboat. Stern voices ordered her to let go so she could be lowered into the lifeboat. Frantic with fear, she struggled. Finally, Eleanor was held over the ship's railing and half handed, half dropped, down into her father's waiting arms.

Though she and her family were rescued, the terror of the experience etched itself into her young mind. A fear of water, a fear of boats, and a fear of not meeting other people's expectations would haunt her. She wrote of her childhood: "I was always afraid of something: of the dark, of displeasing people, of failure" (Roosevelt 1961, 12).

A GILDED BEGINNING

Anna Eleanor Roosevelt was born on October 11, 1884. She was named after her mother Anna Hall Roosevelt and in honor of her father's older sister, Anna Roosevelt, who went by the nickname "Bye" or "Bamie." With so many Annas in the family, the newborn became known by her middle name, Eleanor.

At the height of the Gilded Age, her parents were at the center of New York City's affluent upper class. With her French nurse and imported German bisque-china doll, Eleanor Roosevelt's life began in privilege.

The Roosevelt family, like the Randolph and Livingston families, was "old money"—their economic fortune was rooted in colonial America prior to the Revolution. To them, the billionaire Astors, who built their wealth on the frontier fur trade, were newcomers.

Following the Civil War, rapid economic growth and business monopolies concentrated wealth in a new class of multibillionaires. Their fortunes were made in steel, railroads, shipping, crude oil, and banking. Carnegie,

GILDED AGE TO SPACE AGE

Eleanor Roosevelt was born into a world of gaslight, telegraph lines, and horse-drawn carriages. She lived to switch on electric lights, host her own television program, and witness astronaut John Glenn orbit the Earth.

The Gilded Age (1870–1920), into which she was born, is named for the excessive wealth of a limited few, but it was also a period of investment in new ideas and inventions. Patents were submitted to the U.S. Patent Office in ever-increasing numbers. Many technological innovations, which are part of our everyday lives, were initiated during this pivotal period in history.

Automobiles, telephones, radio, and motion pictures were born. Mechanized adding machines and typewriters transformed office work.

Even buildings were changing. Stone and brick construction had limited structures to ten floors. Mass production of steel enabled the first skyscrapers and necessitated the development of the elevator. The year before Eleanor's birth, the Brooklyn Bridge became the nation's first steel suspension bridge. The New York City of her childhood was transformed by steel.

Electricity was also reshaping home appliances and industry. Washing machines, irons, and sewing machines were electrified. Electric streetlights, streetcars, trains, and subways were changing cities.

The speed of a galloping horse thrilled young Eleanor. Once she had a driver's license, she always preferred careening down the road behind the wheel of her own car. She loved to fly and became the first Acting First Lady to cross the continent and travel the world in an airplane. "The great difference between the world of the 1880's [sic] and today," she wrote, is "the extraordinary speeding up of our physical surroundings" (Roosevelt 1961, xi).

Further Reading

Roosevelt, Eleanor. 1961. *The Autobiography of Eleanor Roosevelt.* New York: HarperCollins.

Rockefeller, Vanderbilt, Mellon, Morgan, and Crocker were the families of "new money."

When Eleanor Roosevelt was a baby, less than 1 percent of the country's families held 99 percent of the nation's economic wealth. Her parents were part of that 1 percent. This small group of wealthy urban upper-class families from the Eastern seaboard was referred to as "the Establishment." They drove industry, banking, and politics. Their influence ran the nation.

For those with money, it was a time of lacquered black carriages driving through Central Park at sunset. Women in imported silk gowns and men in top hats were out to be seen. There were extravagant masquerade balls, evenings at the newly built Metropolitan Opera House, and late-night dinners served on gold-rimmed plates. New York City was growing rapidly and establishing itself as one of the world's most influential cities. To compete with Paris, London, and Rome, New Yorkers were rapidly creating their own cultural centers, building monumental buildings and mansions, and anointing their own aristocracy based on financial wealth.

Mark Twain and Charles Dudley Warner titled a novel *The Gilded Age* in reference to a thin golden exterior of excess that masked a society's deep failings—corruption, greed, social and economic inequity. During the economic boom of the late nineteenth century, extreme prosperity for a few depended on millions of rural farmers, recently emancipated African slaves, and new immigrants toiling in extreme poverty.

FAMILY HERITAGE

The Roosevelts descended from the original Dutch families who first settled the village of New Amsterdam in the 1640s. The city would be renamed New York under the British, and as it grew, so did the family's prosperity. Eleanor's branch of the Roosevelt family made its fortune importing and selling stained glass and plate glass for windows. They compounded their fortune by investing in real estate and banking.

On her mother's side, she was directly descended from American founding fathers: Archibald Bulloch (1730–1777) and Robert R. Livingston (1746–1813). Both men served in the Continental Congress; Bulloch represented the colony of Georgia and Livingston represented New York. Livingston served on the committee to draft the "Declaration of Independence," but neither man signed the document because they were recalled to their colonies before its ratification. Bulloch became Georgia's first governor and Livingston was made chancellor of New York. As New York's highest-ranking judicial officer, Livingston administered the oath of office to President George Washington. He continued his public service as U.S. minister to France and negotiated the Louisiana Purchase for President Thomas Jefferson.

Beginning life from such a position of affluence and family prestige provided Eleanor Roosevelt with a world of opportunity, but it did not guarantee a life of influence or protection from tragedy.

THE TWO MOST IMPORTANT INFLUENCES

In 1951, Eleanor Roosevelt wrote an article for *LOOK* magazine about the seven most influential people in her life. She included her parents, Elliott Bulloch Roosevelt (1860–1894) and Anna Hall Roosevelt (1863–1892). Such a disclosure about the influence of parents was expected during the family-centered 1950s. Eleanor, however, told a tale of one parent who empowered her with courage and another who scarred her with self-doubt. Both perceptions, however, were shaped by the memories of a little girl.

Eleanor Roosevelt idolized her father and regarded him as the guiding force in her life. "He was the center of my world," she wrote in her memoirs, "and all around him loved him" (Roosevelt 1961, 5).

Elliott Roosevelt's siblings considered him the most gregarious and outgoing of the family. He had his mother's Southern charm and his father's piercing blue eyes. He offered the same generous smile to the doorman as he did to Mrs. Astor, the queen of New York society. Eleanor believed that her father regarded all people as individuals and that he was empathetic and compassionate toward everyone. She would spend her life trying to emulate these traits.

What Eleanor Roosevelt seldom recounted or chose not to remember was the dark side of her father's personality, which included depression, self-doubt, and anxiety. These traits impacted her as well.

Many historians depict Eleanor's father as the black sheep of his family, a perpetual failure among highly successful siblings. Some discount him as a playboy who lived on charm, alcohol, and excess, and ultimately brought shame to his family with his self-destructive behavior. Others blame his downfall on sibling rivalry. They describe Elliott as the golden-haired favorite son and athletic rival to his older brother Theodore. Theodore Roosevelt Jr. would become one of the United States' most loved presidents. In Ted's success, some biographers see the cause for Elliott's downfall. But none of these interpretations separate Elliott Roosevelt the man from Elliott Roosevelt the individual trapped in substance use.

Elliott Roosevelt belonged to a close-knit and influential family. His father, Theodore Roosevelt Sr. (1831–1878), is typically credited with shaping the lives of his children. He was a dominant figure in New York City during the 1870s. He amassed enough of a fortune from the family plate-glass business to devote most of his time to being a father, Presbyterian Church elder, and respected philanthropist. He provided New Yorkers access to art and science by helping to found the American Museum of Natural History and the Metropolitan Museum of Art.

Elliott's mother, Martha "Mittie" Bulloch Roosevelt (1834–1884), was a petite Southern belle from Georgia. Though she is depicted as naïve and pampered by her husband, Mittie Roosevelt was a strong-willed woman. She vocally supported the Confederacy throughout the Civil War, despite living in New York City and being married to a staunch abolitionist. She taught her children to question majority opinions and value viewpoints other than their own. While her political opinions were racially bigoted, Mittie's inclusive philosophy inspired her children to reach across racial and economic divisions. The Roosevelts would impact American politics and the Progressive Movement well into the mid-twentieth century. Mittie also taught her offspring how to weave a good story. Two of her children and a number of her grandchildren, including Eleanor, would become authors.

All of Elliott's siblings would play an important role in his daughter's life. His sister, Anna, or "Bye," was four years older than the other three children. The epitome of a big sister, Bye supported her siblings in times of need. Theodore Jr. was the oldest son, followed sixteen months later by Elliott, and then a year and a half later by Corinne (1861–1933). The closeness in age between Ted and Elliott made them steadfast playmates, wrestling opponents and, later, hunting companions. For most of their lives, they were close friends.

As in most affluent Victorian homes, nurses cared for the Roosevelt children. When the time came for a teaching governess, however, their mother's older unmarried sister, Anna Bulloch (1833–1893), came to fill the position. All of the children were educated in history, the arts, literature, the sciences, and European languages. It was not unusual for the Roosevelts to discuss the poetry of Johann Wolfgang von Goethe in German and to speak only in French at the dinner table.

Eleanor's grandfather also funded a variety of medical institutions. Bye had been born with a deformed spine, possibly caused by polio or tuberculosis in the bone. The new field of orthopedics transformed her life. Theodore Roosevelt Sr. helped found the New York Orthopedic Hospital and was determined to make treatment of diseases and deformities of the bones and joints available to all, regardless of their ability to pay. He also supported the Bellevue Training School for Nurses and the Roosevelt Hospital started by a cousin.

As a board member of the Children's Aid Society, Theodore Sr. advocated for the city's newsboys and shoeshine boys. He helped establish the Newsboys' Lodging House—a place where indigent boys living on the streets could spend the night and receive two meals for five cents (a penny more than the cost of the *New York Times* newspaper the boys were selling).

He believed it was his Christian duty to help these poor children, but he also believed it was each child's responsibility to live a virtuous life and to work hard to improve their situation. Theodore Sr. impressed this philosophy on his own children. He took them to volunteer at the Newsboys' Lodging House, where they passed out food or holiday items to the newsboys. Such interactions had a lasting influence; all of the Roosevelt children continued their father's philanthropic works.

As children, Theodore Jr., Elliott, and Corinne all suffered from asthma. Their father believed travel and outdoor exercise were the best remedy for ill health. And indeed, changing environments improved the children's asthma. Coal gas, used in early gas lighting in the family's brownstone home, may have aggravated their respiratory conditions. Travel removed them from the toxins and may have improved their symptoms. All of the family came to believe that travel was the best health tonic.

The family spent a year touring Europe. They celebrated Christmas in Rome and explored Mount Vesuvius. Theodore Jr. and Elliott boiled eggs in the volcano's heat and were thrilled when Ted jabbed his walking stick into a pool of lava and it burst into flames. Italy was the perfect adventure for ten-year-old Elliott.

At fourteen, Elliott experienced a series of fainting spells and seizures. While family sources suggest epilepsy, there is no medical evidence to support such a diagnosis. Physicians at the time diagnosed a nervous condition. After several travels to quiet his nerves, Elliott was finally allowed to attend a college preparatory boarding school.

He thrived at first, making good grades and participating in a wide range of sports. He wrote to his father reporting he was doing well and mentioned he was taking his "anti-nervous medication" (Lash 1971, 33). At the time, laudanum (morphine dissolved in alcohol) was a standard treatment for headaches and nervousness. At age fifteen, Elliott Roosevelt was most likely being initiated into his lifelong problem with alcohol and opiates under the direction of a trusted family physician.

In the world of the Roosevelts, substance use disorder only happened to poor unfortunates, people of inferior moral fiber. They believed that educated people of good social standing, who were chosen by God to hold positions of power in the world, couldn't become addicted to substances. They possessed the moral fortitude to say "no" to temptation. Elliott closed his letter requesting his father to send more of his medicine.

Within a few months, he collapsed at school. No one questioned how much anti-nervous medication he had consumed. No one knew to be concerned about the side effects or addictive nature of the medication.

When Ted had been sickly and frail, living an outdoor life in the Dakotas had rebuilt his body and strengthened his health. Elliott was sent off to live as a cowboy in the remote Texas hill country. He became an

America's First Opiate Crisis (1870–1920)

America's first opiate drug crisis grew out of the Civil War (1861–1865) and the availability of morphine. Sap from the opium poppy (*Papaver somniferum*) naturally contains over fifty alkaloid chemicals, which physiologically impact the human body.

An *opiate* is a drug compound derived from natural opium. Morphine, cocaine, and heroin are opiates. Modern *opioids*—like fentanyl, oxycodone, and hydromorphone—are synthetically constructed chemicals, which replicate opium-based compounds.

Morphine was the first alkaloid refined from opium. Its heightened pain-killing abilities enabled patients to survive complicated surgeries. Unfortunately, it also triggered chemical dependency in the brain, making it highly addicting.

Both the Union and Confederate armies handed out morphine and laudanum for pain management and to reduce death from dysentery. Opiates cause constipation as a side effect; daily doses prevented diarrhea from intestinal illnesses. Armies of soldiers returned home dependent on morphine; substance use disorder was initially called the "Soldier's Disease."

Morphine was unregulated and became an ingredient in products treating everything from asthma and nervousness to menstrual cramps and infant teething pain. Heroin was synthesized from morphine in 1874 and sold in lozenges as a "cough suppressant." Cocaine elixirs were used to treat malaria and individuals with alcohol and morphine dependencies. Manufacturers believed processing opiate compounds increased their strength but removed the addictive properties. They were wrong.

Historians calculate that by 1890, sixty percent of individuals addicted to opiates were middle- and upper-class women, like the mother character in Eugene O'Neill's autobiographical play *Long Day's Journey into Night*.

The epidemic peaked in 1895, the year after Elliott Roosevelt died. Within four years, aspirin was developed, providing an inexpensive and nonaddicting pain reliever.

President Theodore Roosevelt appointed the first commissioner to investigate the nation's opiate crisis and supported the Pure Food and Drug Act of 1906. Pressured by voters, the Harrison Narcotic Act of 1914 strictly regulated opiates.

Further Reading

Courtwright, David T. 2001. *Dark Paradise: A History of Opiate Addiction in America*. Cambridge, MA: Harvard University Press.

experienced rider and expert shot. He admired the military officers and cattlemen who befriended him, but they probably also introduced him to hard alcohol; he was seventeen.

After nearly a year in Texas, Elliott returned home to find his beloved father in extreme pain and rapidly declining due to intestinal cancer. Ted was away at Harvard. Theodore Sr. was only forty-six years old.

The death of Theodore Roosevelt Sr. in February 1878 was a turning point for Elliott Roosevelt. When his father was alive, earning his respect had been a driving force. Ted buried himself in his Harvard studies, more determined than ever to build a life and career that would honor their father. Elliott focused on living in the moment.

Each of the Roosevelt children inherited approximately $125,000 ($3.2 million in 2020 dollars); half of this was bequeathed directly and the other half was placed in a trust fund. Instead of going to college, Elliott decided to leave sorrow behind and travel the world. He delayed his sailing only to serve as best man at Ted's wedding to Alice Hathaway Lee.

As Elliott left on an international adventure, did either of the young men envy the other? Possibly. Sibling rivalry had been encouraged as a way to develop competitive spirit and excellence. Ted and Elliott competed against each other in sports, sometimes to excess and injury. But on or off the game field, their respect for each other was genuine. When Ted published his first book, *Hunting Trips of a Ranchman*, in 1885, he dedicated it "to the keenest of sportsmen and truest of friends, Elliott Roosevelt."

Over his years of travel, Elliott acquired an ease integrating with strangers. Now he was a handsome, wealthy, young American. He easily entered the elite social world of British aristocrats in London and the crown colony of India.

The duality of India filled his letters and diary. He was overcome by the poverty, the "ocean of misery and degradation," human bodies and "the Immortal Souls of Beings in God's image . . . brought so low" (Lash 1971, 38–39). He looked at the British control over India and recognized a people under governmental "protection" they did not want. As a child, he had heard stories from his mother and aunt about the African slaves working their plantation in the South before the Civil War, and he had heard his father's arguments against slavery. As he witnessed human subjugation it appalled him.

At the same time, he found the life of luxury addicting. Servants waited on his every need. His days were filled with hunting and playing polo. He wrote to his sister Bye: "it would be very nearly perfect in its way. Not, I think, 'our way' for that means life for an *end*. But this for the mere pleasure of living is the only life" (Lash 1971, 39). It wasn't a life of purpose, as his father and brother championed, but life for its own enjoyment.

When Elliott Roosevelt returned to society after sixteen months abroad, he possessed the self-confidence of a world adventurer. He was only twenty-two, but all of New York knew he had faced a tiger in India, shot it, and sent the skin back to lie before his mother's fireplace. He had lived as a cowboy out West, stalked elephants in Sri Lanka, and traveled through the exotic Asian ports of Singapore and Hong Kong. Charming with refined manners, but ruggedly handsome, he had a sense of humor that made him easy to like and an air of danger that made him intoxicating. New York heiresses swooned at his debonair risk-taking and the young "swells" starting up a club to play the exotic newly imported game of polo sought his experience and expert horsemanship. In the fall of 1882, Elliott Roosevelt was one of the most eligible bachelors in New York City.

ANNA REBECCA LUDLOW HALL

In the social season of 1882, Anna Ludlow Hall's beauty turned heads. Her delicate frame and tiny corseted waist created a perfect hourglass figure. She wore her hair in the latest fashion: piled soft curls framing her creamy white complexion. Anna Hall personified the image of Gilded Age femininity: a lovely angelic creature unencumbered by the reality of work or the necessity of income.

New York socialite Peter Marié singled her out as an example of ideal feminine beauty and commissioned her portrait. The golden highlights in her soft brown hair and the reserved innocence in her pale blue-gray eyes created a style of demure womanhood that other debutantes tried to emulate, making her a fashion trendsetter. All noticed what she wore, how she did her hair, the fan she carried, the flowers she did or didn't wear.

While her external appearance was tranquil elegance, her home life was chaos. Her father, Valentine Hall, was a reformed alcoholic who found salvation through puritanical religious practice. He demanded strict obedience and controlled all aspects of his household. To mold the perfect upright posture in his daughters, he reportedly had them walk a distance several times a day with a wooden rod behind their backs and braced in the bend of their elbows. He also deemed it unnecessary to educate his daughters. Anna and her younger sisters attended their father's daily religious teachings and learned a bit of French from a nurse with formal training in etiquette and music.

The Halls had comfortable financial wealth and through her mother, Anna descended from America's form of aristocracy—founding father Robert R. Livingston. The Livingstons owned vast tracts of land in New York's Hudson River Valley. Anna was seventeen, and the eldest of six children, when her father died. Her mother, Mary Livingston Ludlow Hall (1843–1919), had no experience managing a household or finances. She had had no voice in disciplining or educating her children. With the death of her husband, Mrs. Hall withdrew to her rooms, slipped into depression, and left Anna to try and stabilize the family. Though she made an effort,

Anna found managing her younger siblings and the household accounts overwhelming. She escaped by becoming a debutante.

When Elliott Roosevelt first saw Anna Hall, her regal beauty matched his romantic ideals. He pursued her through the New York social scene of luncheon parties, tennis matches, and balls. They appeared the perfect couple: the lovely socialite and the dashing adventurer invited to all of the elite social events of the city's 1882–83 season. Yet when Elliott proposed, Anna hesitated.

She knew he had a taste for champagne that occasionally led to excessive social drinking. Some sources contend she was concerned about his mood swings, occasional depression, and anxiety. On several occasions during their courtship, Elliott stayed locked in his room for days and later apologized for being "blue and disagreeable" (Lash 1971, 46). He had also taken several serious riding falls, suffering injury to one or both legs. At which point he sought pain relief for these injuries is unknown, but opiates were working their way back into his life, if indeed they had ever left.

Most accounts of Anna Hall, including those made by her daughter Eleanor, describe the young woman as frivolous and shallow. However, Anna's letter to Elliott in the summer of 1883, prior to their wedding, reveals a young woman seriously attempting to establish a relationship built on open and truthful communication. "I shall indeed always tell you everything and shall not be happy unless I feel that all your troubles, joys, sins and misfortunes are to be mine too. Please never keep anything from me for fear of giving me pain" (Roosevelt 1932, 149). Anna didn't disregard Elliott's troubles, she wanted to share them and relieve some of his burden.

Finally, despite her concerns, Anna said "Yes." Elliott Roosevelt and Anna Ludlow Hall married on December 1, 1883. The New York newspapers described it as "one of the most brilliant social events of the season." Carefree and jubilant, the young couple engaged in a world of tennis, yachting, carriage rides by moonlight, and elegant dinners with friends. Yet, as Eleanor would write about her parents' marriage, "tragedy and happiness came walking on each other's heels" (Roosevelt 1961, 5).

A RAY OF HOPE AMIDST TRAGEDY

Eleanor Roosevelt was born into a family gripped by sorrow. Three months after her parents' wedding, her father took over as head of the household while his older brother Theodore, a rising young politician, served as a New York State assemblyman in Albany. Close to delivering their first child, Ted's wife Alice had stayed behind in New York City. It was a happy time; Elliott and Anna were expecting their first child as well.

On February 12, 1984, Alice gave birth to a daughter. Elliott telegraphed his brother that the baby had arrived and both mother and child were doing well. Within hours, however, the situation changed. Pregnancy had hidden Alice's symptoms of kidney failure. At the same time, their mother Mittie had come down with typhoid fever. Theodore dashed home just in time to say goodbye to his mother and to hold his dying wife in his arms. Both women perished within a span of twenty-four hours.

The family was rocked with grief. Theodore resigned from the assembly, left his newborn daughter in the care of his older sister, Bye, and fled to the wilds of North Dakota to escape his despair. As for Elliott, who had pictured himself as his mother's protector, her death at age forty-nine sent him into freefall. He fell ill with a recurring "fever," possibly malaria, which had plagued him since his ventures in India two years earlier. He sank into a deep depression.

Throughout Anna's pregnancy, Elliott worried for his young wife and their unborn child. When Eleanor finally arrived and both mother and daughter remained healthy and safe, he held his daughter high in the air, pronouncing her a "miracle from Heaven" (Roosevelt 1961, 5). It was the beginning of an enduring bond. Whatever the state of his mental or physical health, Elliott always lavished his daughter with unconditional affection.

MOTHER AND DAUGHTER

Eleanor Roosevelt never felt close to her mother. Where her father saw an infant's innocent charm, Anna allegedly saw a nose that was too long and a face that was too wrinkled. Some historians disregard Anna as cold and aloof, while others paint her as merely more interested in parties than children. The distance between mother and daughter, however, was probably more complicated than the memories of an eight-year-old Eleanor.

Anna Hall Roosevelt was only twenty-one when Eleanor arrived. She had been a fashion and style influencer since her social debut at age seventeen. Her beauty and figure had given her social power and prestige. Without any available form of birth control, she had little choice regarding motherhood. Anna became pregnant within three months of being married and gave birth to Eleanor before her first wedding anniversary.

While Elliott had known close relationships with both of his parents, Anna had had no nurturing role model; her father was an authoritarian and her mother was detached. As an upper-class woman, she did as expected and handed her baby over to a servant to be cared for. Eleanor had a French nurse and learned her first words in French.

Anna may have envied her husband's social freedom, his activities unhampered by parenthood. He continued to spend his days at business meetings in the city's finest restaurants and weekends playing polo. As a new mother, Anna and her infant daughter spent most of the spring and summer at her mother's rural estate, a hundred miles north of New York City and a world away from afternoon teas and carriage rides with friends.

Anna wrote to Elliott complaining that she had lost her appetite, fatigue overwhelmed her, and she struggled against wanting to sleep all the time. She blamed him for her anxiety and inability to return to her normal activities. From a modern perspective, her complaints are symptomatic of postpartum depression, which may have contributed to her inability to bond with her baby.

Eleanor believed that her mother disapproved of her simply because she wasn't pretty. Anna valued physical beauty; it was part of her own identity. Eleanor's light golden hair was fine. Her young face was round with a broad mouth that turned down at the corners. Her features may not have risen to Anna's standards of beauty. Any of these factors, or all of them, may have contributed to Anna's distanced relationship with her daughter.

ABANDONMENT

Elliott seldom worked and leaned into pleasure—playing polo, arranging English-style foxhunts, and drinking. Increasingly concerned about his excessive lifestyle, his siblings urged Anna to change his environment and travel. In the spring of 1887, the couple booked passage to England on the SS *Britannic*. Anna's sister Elizabeth, affectionately called "Tissie," and a nurse came along to help care for two-year-old Eleanor. In a dense fog 350 miles offshore, the SS *Celtic* rammed their ship. Six passengers were killed in the initial collision and an equal number were washed overboard as they scrambled to be evacuated.

Traumatized, young Eleanor froze with fear, unable to let go of the steward so she could be lowered into the lifeboat. She misinterpreted her parents' anxious orders as anger. Once safely ashore, Eleanor's parents immediately booked passage on another ship. When little Eleanor refused to get on board, her parents left her behind with relatives. In her child's understanding of events, displeasing her parents resulted in abandonment.

Eleanor was entrusted to her very loving Great Aunt Gracie; her father's aunt Anna Bulloch had married banker James King Gracie. Aunt Gracie had helped raise Elliott and his siblings; now she filled the hole in their lives left by their mother's early death.

Aunt Gracie found Eleanor vulnerable and helpless. She wrote to Elliott's sister Corinne: "She asked two or three times in the train ... where her 'dear Mamma was, & where her Papa was, & where is Aunt Tissie?' I told her 'They have gone to Europe.' She said 'where is baby's home now?'" (Cook 1992, 49).

Though her great-aunt tried to reassure her, the traumatic experience left its scars. When they passed a large body of water, little Eleanor became anxious and fearfully protested: "Baby does not want to go into the water. Not in a boat" (Cook 1992, 49).

For nearly six months, while her parents toured Europe, Eleanor lived a quiet and secure life. Aunt Gracie described her as having "such a gentle, generous, affectionate nature. It is impossible not to love her" (Peyser and Dwyer 2015, 14).

Ted's daughter had been named Alice in memory of her mother. She was still in Aunt Bye's care. The two parentless cousins developed a childhood friendship. Gradually, with the support of loving aunts, little Eleanor became confident enough to play on the beach at Oyster Bay. Anna wrote home expressing how she missed her young daughter, but her sentiments never seemed to have reached Eleanor.

EARLY MEMORIES

When her parents returned, Eleanor was not the center of their lives. Elliott plunged back into his sporting life, purchasing property on Long Island to build a country estate. "Half Way Nirvana" would be near Meadow Brook polo club and a short ride from Ted's quiet summerhouse, "Sagamore Hill" on Oyster Bay. Anna reestablished herself in New York's high society by starting up an amateur theatrical group and organizing charity balls.

Home for young Eleanor remained amorphous. She spent great amounts of time with relatives and, by her own description, was not a happy child. When her father was present, he focused his attention on Eleanor in a way that made her feel special and unconditionally loved. She remembered happily dancing and spinning with carefree abandon in his dressing room as he rose in the morning. He encouraged her to perform little dances for his riding friends. They would applaud and laugh, and her father would lift her high into the air, lavishing her with praise.

At Half Way Nirvana horses, dogs, and life swirled around Elliott Roosevelt. Eleanor was with her father the first time she rode a horse. In a school assignment titled "My First Joy," she recalled the speed, the freedom, and mostly the security of her father, adding up to the perfect moment of joy for a five-year-old girl.

Her early memories of her mother were exactly the opposite; they were moments of inferiority and humiliation. One event in particular burned into Eleanor's memory. She stood meekly in a doorway with her finger in her mouth, peeking into a room where her mother sat with a friend. Anna noticed Eleanor and called her "Granny" because of her serious expression. Young Eleanor wanted to "sink through the floor in shame" (Roosevelt 1961, 9). She felt the name "Granny" denigrated her.

Eleanor considered her mother the most beautiful woman she ever knew and compared watching her dress to go out for the evening to watching a princess prepare for the ball. She admired her mother's elegance, "grateful to be allowed to touch her dress or her jewels or anything that was part of the vision" (Roosevelt 1961, 7).

Where she felt inclusion with her father, Eleanor perceived judgment from her mother. The elegant woman in the flowing gown with gloves pushed up to her elbows seemed unapproachable. Eleanor would always feel she was never pretty enough, never accomplished enough, never personable enough for her mother to like her.

Eleanor fondly remembered time spent at the Newsboys' Lodge. Elliott took his daughter to volunteer at Thanksgiving, dishing out dinner or handing out gift items to the poor working boys. Eleanor long remembered how her father engaged with these children, listened to their stories, and sincerely cared about them as individuals. He impressed upon her that all people mattered regardless of their background.

Her mother also participated in these charitable acts. Anna and Eleanor volunteered one Christmas while Elliott was away, in the midst of an alcoholic episode. Additionally, Anna raised funds for other charitable endeavors of the Roosevelts, but Eleanor did not remember her mother's contributions.

CYCLES OF RELAPSE AND RECOVERY

Throughout Eleanor's childhood, her father was treated with morphine for illnesses and injuries. In August 1888, he seemed healthy and the family stayed with Uncle Ted and his second wife, Edith Carow Roosevelt (1861–1948), at Sagamore Hill. Cousin Alice (1884–1980) was now living with her father and stepmother. The two little girls put together small tea parties—early training for the two women who would independently become two of the longest reigning hostesses in Washington, D.C.

Weeks after Eleanor's fourth birthday, her father broke his ankle. Whether the injury occurred while riding or—as a young Eleanor believed—in connection with a charity circus, the bone had to be reset to heal correctly. Years later, Eleanor recounted how the sounds of her father's anguished cries in the other room tore at her heart. She described herself as "dissolved in tears" and believed that "[f]rom this illness my father never quite recovered" (Cook 1992, 53).

For young Eleanor, it was a tragic turning point in her father's life. In reality, it was a link in his growing chain of chemical dependency. Elliott was again prescribed opiates.

The road ahead for the Roosevelt family read like Robert Louis Stevenson's book *The Strange Case of Dr. Jekyll and Mr. Hyde*, which had been published just two years earlier. Substance use disorder caused Elliott Roosevelt to swing back and forth between contradictory behaviors. Eleanor would impress into her memory the charming gentleman and loving father preserved in a photograph: Elliott, in his three-piece suit, gazing at his golden-haired daughter while she held his gold pocket watch—the symbol of a successful man of the Gilded Age. The family shielded her from the man who became unpredictable, self-destructive, and potentially violent. No photos of this Elliott exist, only words dashed in letters and hidden in diaries.

Eleanor's brother Elliott Jr. was born in the fall of 1889. Anna begged her husband to give up champagne; she realized alcohol was poison to him. She worried his drinking caused him to agitate his ankle and therefore made it more difficult for him to give up the morphine and laudanum. Her own health had not completely recovered from giving birth to the new baby. Headaches and postpartum depression were compounded by her husband's long absences. Still, she wrote to Elliott that she could not help him if he would not confide in her.

By the summer of 1890, Elliott's siblings were desperately trying to convince him to find a new physician. They implored Anna that a trip abroad was the only way to separate him from negative influences.

HAPPY DAYS ABROAD

Eleanor turned six years old in Europe. For the first time in her life, her father was present on a daily basis. The early months of travel were bliss. On the Venice canals, her father polled their gondola, crooning along with the other singing boatman and enchanting Eleanor. The scene remained fresh in her mind her entire life. In *This Is My Story*, she described it as a magical moment, which filled her with "intense joy." There is no mention of her mother being present.

Father and daughter built more happy memories navigating a small sailboat from Naples toward the island of Capri. The bay was as blue as the sky. Eleanor dared not tell her father how the water frightened her. Besides, she felt safe in his company. Newly pregnant and ill with morning sickness, Anna plays no part in this memory either.

Twenty years earlier, Italy had inspired a love for adventure in a ten-year-old Elliott. Now, he was reliving a happy time from his own life and trying to recreate the same experiences for his daughter. He took Eleanor up Vesuvius; they tossed pennies into the volcano's molten magma and retrieved them encrusted with lava.

They went riding over the hillsides of Sorrento. The difference was that Eleanor was six years old, not ten. The only time she could remember disappointing her father was on a narrow mountain trail outside Sorrento. When the group of men on horseback and one little girl on a donkey came to a sharp descent, she became afraid. Experienced riders were sliding as they went down the steep trail. Eleanor recalled: "I turned pale, and preferred to stay on the high road. I can remember still the tone of disapproval in my father's voice" (Roosevelt 1961, 6). What she sometimes left out in recounting the story was that her father rode off and left his six-year-old daughter behind.

Throughout her life, Eleanor would look back at that moment on the donkey and chastise her young self for giving in to fear. For her, it became an allegory about finding one's bravery; attempting things you don't think you are capable of doing. She didn't acknowledge that her father was not there to help her overcome her fear.

An exhausted six-year-old Eleanor traveled down the slope of Vesuvius fighting back tears of fatigue. She didn't want to reveal her weariness and disappoint her father again. Instead, she learned to hide her true emotions.

THE CYCLE RETURNS

The sun-filled days of Italy settled into despair in Vienna. Eleanor's father spiraled back into substance use. Her mother wrote home for help and Aunt Bye arrived from New York. She convinced her brother to enter a facility to treat his alcohol dependency.

Over the next six months, as her mother's pregnancy advanced, her father recovered and then relapsed. There would be happy days sledding through the forest and then anxious nights when he wouldn't return.

Eleanor remembered little of this time. Her mother and Aunt Bye protected the children from the storm raging around them. Her father was not only experiencing problems with substance use but also having an extramarital relationship with a married American tourist. Simultaneously, Uncle Ted wrote from New York that a young woman named Catherine "Katy" Mann was threatening to reveal that she was pregnant with Elliott's child. Mann had been a housemaid in Anna and Elliott's home before the family left for Europe.

Letters and cables raced back and forth across the Atlantic Ocean. One moment Elliott was threatening to financially abandon his wife and children; the next moment he was threatening suicide. Anna was briefly hospitalized after a violent altercation. Bye fought to stabilize her brother's diminishing health, committing him to consecutive spas and asylums. Unfortunately, the supposed cures for alcohol dependency frequently included cocaine or other opiate treatments. (In Primary Documents, read *Theodore Roosevelt Letter to Anna "Bye" Roosevelt, June 7, 1891*.)

In the midst of this turmoil, they sent young Eleanor to a French convent school for girls. In her mind, it was a punishment. The nuns frightened her. The girls spoke only French. Eleanor felt abandoned and forcefully separated from her father, another mark against the memory of her mother.

She became desperate for attention. When another student swallowed a penny and became the center of attention at the convent, Eleanor made up a story about swallowing a penny too. She was a little girl pushed to the side while the adults in her life were consumed in conflict. The nuns saw through her ruse and dismissed her from the school for lying. Eleanor felt that her mother and aunt punished her like a criminal. She didn't understand that the two women were immersed in Elliott's deceptions. In young Eleanor's mind, only her father lovingly embraced her and soothed her anguish.

Sixty years later, Eleanor would write that her mother "had such high standards of morals that it encouraged me to wrongdoing; I felt it was utterly impossible for me ever to live up to her!" (Roosevelt 1951, 54). Young Eleanor may have believed her mother's "high standards" were impossible for her father to live up to as well. This belief allowed her to blame her mother for her father's downfall.

Each time her father was sent off to another facility, Eleanor equated it with her own exile. Her mother was punishing him. What she couldn't understand was how her father's behavior threatened every aspect of her life. He was having sexual relationships with multiple women, which potentially threatened her mother with a sexually transmitted disease. In a time before antibiotics, syphilis and other venereal diseases were often incurable and posed serious health consequences. Also, Elliott was rapidly spending his inheritance, which threatened his children's financial future and the family's social position.

Katy Mann gave birth to her child, and this resulted in a paternity lawsuit. Evidence that Elliott was the child's father included a locket given as a gift, testimony from other household servants, and the child's appearance. Ted wrote to his brother in a letter dated June 14, 1891 that Katy Mann "could get testimony that you were often wild and irresponsible either from being out of your head or from the use of liquor or opiates." Offering the young woman funds to secure the child's future was the right thing to do and the only way to avoid scandal. Funds were pooled from Elliott's inheritance, from Ted, and from other Roosevelt family members to provide a trust fund for the child, Elliott Roosevelt Mann. The sum was equivalent to $280,000 in 2020 dollars.

Shortly after, Anna gave birth to a son, Hall Ludlow Roosevelt (1891–1941), and returned home with the children. Elliott remained under treatment in a French facility. "It is all a nightmare of horror," Ted wrote to Bye (May 23, 1891). The family offered to assist Anna in having Elliott declared legally insane due to alcoholism and therefore unable to act on his own behalf, or to support her in divorce, both dramatic actions for a family of their social standing.

COMING HOME

For Eleanor, sailing back to New York meant abandoning her father. She begged to stay behind.

Over the next six months, Anna shielded Eleanor and the two young boys from the growing scandal. Newspaper headlines proclaimed "Elliott Roosevelt Mad" and "Elliott Roosevelt Demented by Excesses" (Cook 1992, 67). Anna refused a divorce. Theodore and Bye sued to gain control over Elliott's financial assets, but the lawsuit lingered in the courts as some Roosevelt relatives refused to believe the action was warranted.

Anna became plagued by migraine headaches. For the first time, Eleanor felt her mother needed her. In the twilight of her mother's curtained room, she eased her mother's discomfort by soothingly rubbing her forehead. These quiet moments became Eleanor's only positive memory of her mother.

In January 1892, Theodore traveled to France and confronted his brother. After several days of back and forth, Elliott relented. In a letter dated January 21, 1892, Ted wrote to Bye: "He signed the deed, for two thirds of *all* his property (including the $60,000 trust); and agreed to the probation." Roosevelt historian Joseph P. Lash estimated Elliott's financial holdings at the time to be $175,000. (As per the calculations of the U.S. Government's Bureau of Labor Statistics, the total would be equivalent to nearly $5 million in 2020.) Elliott agreed to end his extramarital relationship and go into treatment at the Keeley Clinic for alcohol and drug addiction in Illinois. He submitted to a two-year separation from his family, during which he would have to prove he could stay sober and be gainfully employed. Corinne's husband provided him with a position evaluating property in rural Virginia. Ted added, "I told him we would do all we legitimately could to help him, that our object now would be to see him entirely restored to himself, and so to his wife and children."

Eleanor didn't know that her mother still believed her father could be cured. Anna offered to welcome Elliott back after one year of sobriety. What Eleanor heard were whispered discussions in the night between her mother and her aunts. "I acquired a strange and garbled idea of the troubles around me," Eleanor wrote years later. "Something was wrong with my father and from my point of view nothing could be wrong with him" (Roosevelt 1961, 8).

LETTERS

Amid the daily uncertainty, Eleanor's education had not been a priority. She was nearly seven years old and could speak French and some German, but she had never been taught to read. Pressured by Roosevelt relatives, Eleanor's mother hired a well-regarded teacher and set up a small classroom on the third floor of their home in New York City. A small group of girls—daughters of Anna's friends—joined Eleanor in class.

Anna tried to be more present for her children. She devoted an hour in the late afternoon specifically to them. "My mother made a great effort; she would read to me and have me read to her," Eleanor wrote (Roosevelt 1961, 9). After her two younger brothers had gone to bed, she frequently stayed with her mother. For a time, she slept in her mother's room. Yet, Eleanor continued to feel separate, believing her mother preferred the two little boys.

Anna never confided in Eleanor, never tried to explain why her father lived hundreds of miles away. The letters Anna received from Elliott became increasingly inconsistent; he could be loving or chastising, morose or euphoric, leaving Anna lonely and angry. She was twenty-nine years old, in a social limbo, and uncertain of her future.

Eleanor resented her father's exile. His letters became her lifeline. She quickly learned to read and write so they could correspond. On paper, she saw the perfect loving father. She cherished him and committed to protecting him.

If Anna had wanted to separate father and daughter, she could have denied Eleanor access to her father's letters or refused to mail Eleanor's letters to him. She never did. Eleanor began acting out defiantly against her mother, throwing tantrums in public and refusing to answer the teacher's questions when her mother brought guests up to observe the class.

A CRUMBLING FAMILY

A little more than a year after they returned from Europe, Anna underwent surgery for an unknown condition. Elliott pleaded that he should be at his wife's side. Anna, however, no longer wanted him present. Her mother, Mary Hall, forcefully requested he stay away. During her recovery Anna contracted diphtheria—a deadly bacterial respiratory disease. As Elliott wrote, demanding to see his wife, Anna died.

At eight years of age, Eleanor couldn't completely understand the finality of death. Her relationship with her mother was now frozen in the understanding of a child. There were no opportunities for teenage arguments or adult conversations; no chance to understand each other better.

While she credited her mother with teaching her poise, Eleanor believed her mother fostered her lack of self-confidence and extreme shyness. She never appreciated that some of her ability to persevere during difficult times came from her mother.

While she knew something terrible had happened, the only thing Eleanor really understood was that now she would be reunited with her father. Before her death, however, Anna conveyed her wishes that her mother, Mrs. Hall, should raise the children. The Roosevelt family did not contest; they believed Elliott was incapable of parenting his children. Without any familial support, Eleanor's father conceded custody.

Living with Grandmother Hall was not the result Eleanor had expected. She vividly remembered her father coming to see her at her grandmother's house in the city. He was dressed all in black. "He held out his arms and gathered me to him," she recalled. She sat on his lap as he explained that her mother had died. "[S]he had been all the world to him," he said, "and now he had only my brothers and myself, that my brothers were very young and that he and I must keep close together." He spun a tale where Eleanor "would make a home for him again" and the two of them would travel (Roosevelt 1961, 9). They would have many adventures together—everything she longed to hear he told her over and over.

To reassert his family ties, Elliott posed for portraits with his three children. Eleanor stood beside her father with a somber gaze, while the two boys were wide-eyed toddlers. Within a few months, Elliott Jr. died. He was not quite four years old when he contracted scarlet fever, followed by diphtheria.

Elliott Roosevelt's grief retriggered his substance use. Though Eleanor received gifts from her father—a pony and a cart—visits from him became fewer. Elliott wrote that he regretted not being able to teach her to ride, but he expected Eleanor to practice. She needed to become a good horsewoman so they could ride together. As always, his words created scenarios of an idyllic future.

Less than a year after the death of Anna and their son, Elliott Roosevelt was in a downward spiral. When he sat for a photograph to send to his children, his gold watch was gone. The once-athletic man slouched and used a cane. His gaunt face and somewhat sunken eyes made him appear older than his thirty-three years. Three fox terriers substituted for his children.

In the city, Eleanor generally saw her father once a month. Together they would walk his dogs through Central Park. One time as they strolled down the street, he asked her to hold the dogs while he went into one of his clubs. Six hours later, she was still waiting. Her father had become intoxicated. A kindly doorman arranged for a carriage to take her home.

By Eleanor's ninth birthday, her father's behavior had become completely unpredictable. Neither family knew where he would appear. Walking through Central Park with her governess, Eleanor might catch sight of him. If he saw her, he would sweep her up into his carriage and drive his black horse "Mohawk" on a spirited run between carriages in the park, both thrilling and terrifying Eleanor.

Despite his negligence and risk-taking behavior, her father remained the dashing hero in her story. His letters kept them closely connected. On the last day of his life, he wrote that he loved her and her little brother.

On the evening of August 14, 1894, Elliott Roosevelt died. His valet confided to the family that Elliott had been taking stimulants. Throughout the day, he hallucinated about talking with his children. At one point, he climbed out a window. Despite newspaper stories about an attempted suicide, there was no evidence that he was aware of his actions. In addition to the opiates, he had been consuming vast amounts of alcohol.

Eleanor, not yet ten years old, was in Maine when news came of her father's death. She had lost the compassionate and loving father who had entertained her with stories of his daring safaris. The soft voice that forgave her "shortcomings" and gave her reassurance had fallen silent. Grandmother Hall felt a funeral was no place for a child. There would be no moment of closure, no farewell.

SOURCES

Cook, Blanche Wiesen. 1992. *Eleanor Roosevelt, Volume 1: 1884–1933*. New York: Viking Penguin.

Lash, Joseph P. 1971. *Eleanor and Franklin: The Story of Their Relationship Based on Eleanor Roosevelt's Private Papers*. New York: W.W. Norton & Company, Inc.

Letter from Theodore Roosevelt to Anna Roosevelt. 1891, May 23. Theodore Roosevelt Collection. MS Am 1834 (316). Harvard College Library. Theodore Roosevelt Digital Library. Dickinson State University. https://www.theodorerooseveltcenter.org/Research/Digital-Library/Record?libID=o281340

Letter from Theodore Roosevelt to Anna Roosevelt. 1892, January 21. Theodore Roosevelt Collection. MS Am 1834 (297). Harvard College Library. Theodore Roosevelt Digital Library. Dickinson State University. https://www.theodorerooseveltcenter.org/Research/Digital-Library/Record?libID=o280913

Letter from Theodore Roosevelt to Elliott Roosevelt. 1891, June 14. Theodore Roosevelt Collection. MS Am 1834 (961). Harvard College Library. Theodore Roosevelt Digital Library. Dickinson State University.

https://www.theodorerooseveltcenter.org/Research/Digital
-Library/Record?libID=o286324

Peyser, Marc, and Timothy Dwyer. 2015. *Hissing Cousins: The Untold Story of Eleanor Roosevelt and Alice Roosevelt Longworth*. New York: Nan A. Talese, Doubleday.

Roosevelt, Eleanor, ed. 1932. *Hunting Big Game in the Eighties: The Letters of Elliott Roosevelt Sportsman*. New York: Charles Scribner's Sons.

Roosevelt, Eleanor. 1951, June 19. "The Seven People Who Shaped My Life." *LOOK*, pp. 54–56, 58.

Roosevelt, Eleanor. 1961. *The Autobiography of Eleanor Roosevelt*. New York: Harper Perennial.

2

A Teenager Finds Her Voice
(1895–1903)

"I wept long and went to bed still weeping" (Roosevelt 1961, 10). The news of her father's death shattered Eleanor Roosevelt's vision of her place in the world. Where was her home? Who constituted her family? What was her future? She couldn't believe her father was dead. Without him, who loved her?

When the tears stopped, Eleanor walked the wooded pathways of her grandmother's estate in silence. Mrs. Hall worried that her granddaughter had experienced too much sorrow and would face the social scars of her father's scandals. She sequestered Eleanor and her young brother away from New York society and tried to limit the influence of their Roosevelt relatives.

Most of Eleanor's young life had been spent waiting for her father's return. Without closure, she convinced herself that his absence was merely an extension of the separations she had always known. By her own account, she became lost "in a dreamworld in which I was the heroine and my father the hero" (Roosevelt 1961, 13).

Referencing her father's letters, Eleanor made up scenarios of their adventures together. With her cheek pressed against the neck of her pony, she let its earthy smell transport her back to riding across the Italian countryside. Walking the overgrown pathways, she imagined stalking big game beside her father in India. Was the snap of a twig the footfall of a tiger?

When scenes written by her father became stale, she escaped into fictional worlds with the help of the household library. Together, she and her imaginary father played out scenes from Sir Walter Scott's poem "The Lady of the Lake," or from one of his favorite Charles Dickens stories.

Eleanor read and reread her father's letters. They reinforced his loving devotion and fixed his image in her mind. She could still feel the strength of his reassuring hand on her shoulder and hear his comforting words whispered in her ear. She lived the next few years in a fantasy, with her father as an imaginary companion. One word at a time, she discovered lessons in his letters to rebuild a fragile foundation of self. She kept her father alive, in her thoughts and in her heart, as her confidant and friend in a world where she felt like an outsider.

LIFE WITH GRANDMOTHER HALL

The world of Mary Livingston Ludlow Hall followed a predictable pattern. Winter was spent in the city. Spring through fall, the family lived at "Oak Terrace," their estate north of Tivoli in the Hudson River Valley. During the summer heat, Mary Hall retreated to the seaside in Maine.

Oak Terrace was a large brick house with high ceilings. Large heavy mirrors maximized the flickering light from candle-lit chandeliers. Walking up the stairs to the bedrooms each night was an exercise in bravery. A handheld candlestick provided the only illumination as Eleanor forged into the darkness.

The woods and fields of Tivoli hadn't changed much since the colonial era. There were pathways to ride, trees to climb, and quiet niches where Eleanor could hide away with a letter or a book. The views of the Hudson River flowing past the Catskill Mountains were lush green in the spring and splashed with red and gold in autumn. Oak Terrace offered tranquility.

Just as the year had a specific social calendar, each day played out with an expected rhythm. Morning baths were cold. Grandmother believed cold water stimulated good health. Occasionally, Eleanor used her friendship with the housemaid to sneak hot water. The entire household, including the servants, attended a morning prayer led by Grandmother Hall. Then, the older woman would retreat to her rooms.

Eleanor's three-year-old brother, Hall, spent most of his day with a nurse. Aunt Tissie had married and moved to her own home, but two other aunts and two uncles lived in the house.

Aunt Edith, known as "Pussie," and Aunt Maude were unmarried and beautiful, but as debutantes with a social calendar they had no time for a sad little girl. The men of the house, Valentine and Edward Hall, were serious tennis players. They had placed second in the U.S. National Tennis doubles championship two summers earlier. "Vallie" had won men's doubles in 1888 and 1890, but at twenty-five, his career had already peaked. Uncle "Eddie" shared Eleanor's love for literature, especially Dickens. Her Hall uncles taught her tennis and riding, but their attention was focused on their own pursuits.

On the large estate, it was easy to wander off unnoticed. Eleanor often spent the day on her own, reading, exploring, and finding solace in her private world.

As winter approached the family returned to their brownstone in the city. A butler supervised the staff. A cook made their meals. A housemaid did housework and dressed the women. A nurse looked after Hall and Eleanor, while a laundress washed the family's clothing and linen.

The staff included Eleanor in small tasks: washing dishes, ironing, and light sewing work such as hemming and darning. These tasks helped her feel useful. She spent more time with the servants than with family members.

In the city, Eleanor received daily lessons from a tutor or learned languages from a French- or German-speaking maid. Sometimes on Saturday afternoons, another child was invited to play and stay for supper. Her Roosevelt cousins, Aunt Corinne's children—Theodore "Teddy" Robinson (1883–1934) and Corinne "Corinney" Robinson (1886–1971)—found ways to get out of visiting Eleanor at the Hall house. The dim rooms with large pieces of furniture looming in the shadows seemed threatening. Besides, Eleanor wasn't much fun; she seemed sad and overly serious.

ROOSEVELT RELATIVES

While her father was alive, Eleanor was included in the larger Roosevelt clan. Most Saturdays, Great Aunt Gracie had taken the three oldest Roosevelt grandchildren to explore the city. Alice Roosevelt, Teddy Robinson, and Eleanor were all close in age. Great Aunt Gracie purposefully brought the cousins together to strengthen their sense of family. She instilled a connection to their Roosevelt grandfather's legacy by taking the threesome to the museums and charitable institutions he had founded. Especially at the Orthopedic Hospital, Aunt Gracie reinforced the Roosevelt adage: a life of purpose helps other people.

Aunt Gracie had watched the Union Army ransack the Bulloch's Georgia plantation during the Civil War. She had lived a slice of history that was quickly fading from memory. Eleanor loved watching the older woman's elegant hands rest quietly in her lap while she told riveting tales of the Deep South. To Eleanor, Aunt Gracie was the definition of a lady: she was flawlessly dressed, always giving of herself, and empathetic. Aunt Gracie's passing weakened Eleanor's link with her father's family.

The summer after her father's death, Eleanor and her brother visited Uncle Ted and his family at Sagamore Hill. Theodore Roosevelt's summer home on Oyster Bay, Long Island, was alive with boisterous cousins. Cousin Alice and Eleanor were eleven and ten, respectively. Uncle Ted and his second wife, Edith, had four children together—Theodore III (eight years old), Kermit (six), Ethel (four), and baby Archibald. (Their fifth child, Quentin, would be born in 1897.)

The great rambling three-story house looked like a cross between a summer cottage and a grand hunting lodge. There was no pretense; people lived and played in this house. Warm wooden paneling invited you into Uncle Ted's library lined with bookshelves. Unlike the Hall home, Aunt Edith's sitting room was airy and decorated with comfortable furniture. Even the large blue-and-white Chinese porcelain jars on the mantel were used to conveniently store tennis balls for a quick match on the lawn.

Activities at Sagamore Hill immersed Eleanor in joyous play. Uncle Ted led the children in various sports on the sprawling lawn. He loved children and many family insiders believed Eleanor to be his favorite niece. Perhaps he saw his beloved brother in her or perhaps, as Eleanor's aunt Corinne believed, this quiet, somewhat awkward and tentative child, with intelligence and empathy but a lack of self-confidence, reminded him of himself. Eleanor seemed to need Ted's attention in a way his own daughter, Alice, did not.

Most mornings, Uncle Ted led the string of children on a hike. Initially, Eleanor was reluctant to follow, but she later became an enthusiastic participant. She loved the bird-watching hikes, camping, and good-natured competition. Sagamore was alive with dogs and horses and if she closed her eyes, she could believe her father had joined them. Uncle Ted made a lasting impact on his young niece. He convinced her to reach beyond what she thought herself capable of doing. One afternoon, he and the boys jumped off the boat dock into the bay. Eleanor stood alone, admitting she couldn't swim. Uncle Ted refused to accept her answer. He cajoled her to jump in and try.

Afraid, but unwilling to disappoint her uncle, Eleanor jumped in. She "came up spluttering" and to her horror, one of her cousins casually dunked her under causing her to become "very frightened" (Roosevelt 1961, 19). This time, however, she didn't have to be brave on her own; Uncle Ted was there. Before the visit had ended, she had learned to swim a bit and become less fearful of the water.

Even as girls, Eleanor felt somewhat intimidated by her cousin Alice. Alice seemed more clever and sophisticated. Theodore's daughter had more opportunities to interact with a wide range of people and had parents who introduced her into new social situations. For her part, Alice was a bit jealous of her father's attention toward Eleanor. Early on, Alice understood that she and Eleanor had a similar hole in their lives: the loss of a parent and the need to fill that loss. But Eleanor had her father's letters and Alice had nothing from the mother who had died after childbirth. Theodore Roosevelt never spoke of his first wife, not even to his daughter; they shared a loss which neither seemed able to verbalize.

Theodore's attention toward Eleanor aggravated the growing strife between father and daughter. Going forward, Alice and Eleanor maintained a complicated relationship that ranged from friends to adversaries.

Playing tag, chasing through the haystacks in the barn, and children squealing with Uncle Ted on their heels became the fun-filled childhood Eleanor had missed. Sagamore Hill was a sanctuary of freedom and adventure within the secure world of Theodore Roosevelt. Challenges to personal bravery and opportunities for self-discovery were everyday occurrences. A raucous game could evolve into a thoughtful discussion on any topic from literature to nature. So different from her typical daily life, this large family dynamic both overwhelmed and enthralled Eleanor. Here, she might have finally found a place to fit in.

Unfortunately, the Roosevelts did not dispute Mary Hall's full custody of Eleanor and her younger brother. In the wake of Elliott Roosevelt's death, Aunt Bye moved to England to act as hostess for a Roosevelt cousin in the diplomatic corps. Uncle Ted became consumed with his new position cleaning up the New York City police, and Aunt Corinne and her family moved to New Jersey.

Grandmother Hall was perfectly happy to have the Roosevelts play a decreasing role in her grandchildren's lives. The Roosevelts lived too large, had problems with alcohol, and were becoming too involved in politics. New York's elite upper class elected politicians or financially controlled them; they considered engaging in politics socially degrading.

Aunts Bye and Corinne worried about Eleanor. Was she receiving an adequate education? Maybe she would be better off at a boarding school than at the dreary Hall residence? However, these strong women only expressed their concerns to each other. Aunt Bye sent Eleanor a complete collection of Shakespeare's plays and sonnets for her eleventh birthday, but being across the sea made it difficult to give Eleanor what she needed most: affection and a warm embrace.

INFORMAL LESSONS

Most of Eleanor's early education came intermittently through tutors and servants. While the Roosevelt women believed in educated females, Grandmother Hall had a more conservative outlook. She believed upperclass women should be trained in social graces and the arts; academic knowledge polluted a young woman's femininity.

An elegant piano held center stage at the Hall home in the city. Aunt Pussie was an accomplished pianist. Eleanor loved listening to her play and watching her perform for visitors. She also longed for the admiration that Pussie received through her musicality. For a child seeking love and acceptance, the thought of an audience of admirers was compelling. Eleanor fantasized about being a singer but agreed to piano lessons.

Notoriously flamboyant, Aunt Pussie wasn't much of a teacher, but her love for the arts had a lifelong influence on Eleanor. Pussie introduced her young niece to the theater, the opera, concerts, romantic poetry, and ballet.

With limited adult supervision, Eleanor's early exploration of literature was self-driven. Guided by her father's letters, she chose books from the Hall library that he suggested. She read the same international authors the young Roosevelts had cherished: the adventure tales by Alexandre Dumas, the moralistic works of Victor Hugo, and the German poetry of Heinrich Heine and Johann Wolfgang von Goethe.

As Eleanor's world became more confined to her grandmother's household, she embraced her father's words to watch over her brother. The two of them were alone in the world; she became Hall's protector and supporter. Seldom, however, did she have anyone to cheer her on. In her journal, she wrote that she never felt she succeeded in doing what she set out to accomplish.

THE UGLY DUCKLING STAGE

As Eleanor Roosevelt reached adolescence, it became apparent that she had not inherited the petite physical features of her mother or any of the Hall women. Tall for her age, with a thin figure, her long gangly limbs made her appear awkward and clumsy. Self-conscious of her height, she tended to slouch. Eleanor expected criticism and even when it didn't come, she felt unattractive and unable to measure up to the feminine perfection of her mother and aunts.

It didn't help that Grandmother Hall dressed her in clothing more appropriate for a little girl. Teenagers of the 1890s were wearing dresses hemmed to mid-calf, but Eleanor was wearing skirts that ended at her knee. The high hemline accentuated embarrassing thick black stockings and old-fashioned shoes buttoned to the ankle. The outdated clothing drew attention to a shy girl, invited cruel comments, and accentuated her awkward proportions.

Eleanor had fewer and fewer opportunities to interact with other children. She did, however, attend dancing classes in the city. Like all upper-class girls, she was expected to learn social dancing so she could participate at balls and society events. It was one of the rare opportunities she had to interact with boys her own age.

Grandmother Hall took an unprecedented step and sent her granddaughter to ballet class. At the turn of the century, ballet was regarded as theatrical and beneath the status of an upper-class girl. Most likely, Aunt Pussie or Aunt Maude had convinced Grandmother Hall that ballet would teach Eleanor to have grace and control over her body. Eleanor loved ballet and even learned to dance *en pointe*. But while the other girls in the class went on to dance on stage, publically performing was socially unthinkable for Eleanor.

While she became more comfortable with her height, she remained self-conscious about her protruding front teeth. She tended to look down at the floor or to cover her mouth when she smiled. Grandmother Hall believed a woman of good breeding and virtue would naturally have lovely teeth. In her view, the reduction of an overbite (like Eleanor's) or the straightening of teeth were the kind of actions resorted to by an actress or a notorious woman.

A number of Roosevelt relatives decried Mrs. Hall's inaction regarding Eleanor's appearance, especially her teeth. Orthodontia, a new specialty in dentistry, became commonplace only in 1910. Some in the upper class, however, were already turning to orthodontia to improve their children's dental health and perfect their smiles. Sarah Delano Roosevelt sought out an orthodontist to straighten the teeth of her son, Franklin.

At fifteen years of age, Eleanor was taller than most women but still a naive girl. She had few encounters with boys and felt uncomfortable in most social situations. The words "ugly duckling" were whispered frequently. With every social experience, she felt she was reliving her mother's disappointment. She was plain in a slice of society that expected something exemplary.

Each year, Eleanor was invited to Aunt Corinne's Christmas party. It was a multiday house party for her children—Teddy, Corinney, and two younger boys. As the children became teenagers, the annual event brought together a broad clan of young Roosevelt cousins and friends. The year Eleanor turned fourteen, she felt obligated to attend. The days were filled with activities outside her comfort zone. She looked foolish ice-skating and didn't know how to sled.

As the girls dressed for the dance on the last night, Eleanor's cousins urged her to borrow one of their dresses for the evening. Grandmother Hall had packed a child's party dress—a knee-length white frock with little blue bows on the shoulders. Uncle Theodore had just been elected governor of New York. Cousin Alice was wearing a floor-length gown. Eleanor's dress was juvenile and embarrassing, but she didn't have the self-esteem to believe she deserved better. Despite her cousins' suggestions, she resigned herself to wearing the humiliating dress. Cousin Corinney and her mother felt sympathy for Eleanor.

It is hard to know what Cousin Alice was feeling. Depending on when she was telling the story, Alice Roosevelt either felt sympathy for Cousin Eleanor who was standing uncomfortably alone at the dance or wanted to exert her personal power with a secret to hold over her misfortunate cousin. Alice found a distant cousin who was a bit older, taller, and willing to do her a favor. She sent Franklin Delano Roosevelt over to ask Eleanor to dance.

From Eleanor's perspective, Cousin Franklin had rescued her. She would never forget his kind gesture.

CHANGING FAMILY DYNAMICS

Life with her Hall relatives remained precarious. As Eleanor entered young adulthood, her uncles were in crisis. Their tennis careers were declining. The Hall brothers were spiraling into the same alcohol addiction that had swallowed up her father.

From the moment Eleanor's mother had died, the Roosevelt aunts had discussed boarding school as an option for Eleanor and her brother. Now, letters hinted at concerns for Eleanor's personal safety in the Hall household.

Rather than approach Mary Hall directly, Bye Roosevelt reached out to her former teacher Mademoiselle Marie Claire Souvestre (1835–1905). Elliott and Anna had once visited the headmistress at her new school in England. Bye remembered that Anna had been impressed and expressed her desire for her daughter to attend the school. Strategically, Aunt Bye wrote to her mentor. Souvestre sent a letter to Mary Hall inquiring about Eleanor and expressing her fondness for her late daughter. She established a correspondence with the overwhelmed grandmother.

When Mrs. Hall consulted the Roosevelt aunts, they enthusiastically supported sending Eleanor to Mlle. Souvestre's Allenswood academy. Their young niece would obtain an education and be removed from proximity to her uncles.

ALLENSWOOD

Eleanor Roosevelt had little to say on the decision to send her to Allenswood, but she regarded it as one of the pivotal experiences of her life. The education she acquired created a foundation for independent thought and self-confidence.

Traveling to England required taking a ship across the Atlantic. Eleanor summoned up all of her bravery to step on board. Tissie was her chaperone and Eleanor followed her aunt's example by spending most of the crossing in her stateroom.

Located a short train ride southwest of London, Allenswood was nestled among ancient oaks. The massive ivy-covered Victorian mansion had a safe and centered atmosphere. The private school for young ladies filled the building's three stories with communal rooms, private bedrooms, and servants' quarters.

Eleanor admired Aunt Bye, who had studied with Mademoiselle Marie Souvestre. Still, Eleanor was thousands of miles from the only home she had known. Her experience in the French convent school had been terrifying. She thought of herself as a shy girl who did not make friends easily. As soon as Aunt Tissie said "Goodbye," Eleanor felt lost and alone.

She was used to rules of etiquette, but each day at Allenswood had a defined structure and a list of strict rules. The most difficult rule was speaking only in French. Girls from English- and Germanic-speaking countries were especially challenged.

As the students gathered in the dining hall on her first day, Eleanor feared not fitting in. She felt far more comfortable with adults and gravitated to the empty seat across from Mlle. Souvestre.

Typically, the head table was reserved for Mademoiselle and the school's top students. Only the most experienced students felt comfortable conversing in French with the headmistress. All eyes watched Eleanor take the empty seat. Everyone feared that the new girl had committed a serious misjudgment. But to their surprise, Eleanor began casually chatting with Mlle. Souvestre in French. The years she had spent with French nurses and maids served her well.

In that moment, Eleanor's life changed. Mlle. Souvestre admired her boldness and the other girls respected her bravery. For the first time in her life, Eleanor Roosevelt felt appreciated for her capabilities and talents.

There were challenges that came with this new life. She had never been required to perform daily chores or attend to all of her own personal needs. At Allenswood, she had no nurse, no personal maid. Mending her own clothing and changing her bedsheets was now her responsibility.

Morning walks took place no matter the weather. Sometimes the damp felt unbearably cold. Still, the young women walked in their uniform long blue skirts and tailored jackets. The school was adjacent to Wimbledon's lawn tennis courts. Groups of Allenswood girls, with their matching straw "boater" hats trimmed with a white-and-green ribbon, could be seen strolling past the championship courts.

For the first time in her life, every hour of Eleanor's day was accounted for. Classes were held in the morning. Lunch was followed by two hours of structured exercise.

She took up the school's favorite team sport, field hockey. Playing on a team, Eleanor built friendships and learned to work with others. Her novice efforts were awkward, but over her three years at the school she gradually worked her way to the first team. It was an accomplishment she proudly treasured for the rest of her life.

Afternoons were filled with study and musical practice. Everyone dressed for dinner and after the meal there was more study or occasional dance instruction. Frequently, a small group of girls were selected to join Mlle. Souvestre in her petite salon for poetry reading and discussions.

There was no free time to wander, but Eleanor found security in knowing what to expect each day. "This was the first time in my life," she wrote, "that my fears left me. If I lived up to the rules and told the truth, there was nothing to fear" (Roosevelt 1961, 24). She settled into being her own person. She needn't try to please her mother or grandmother. She needn't meet the expectations of her aunts or high society. She needn't protect her father or parent her brother. Responsible only for herself, Eleanor felt reborn and earned a new nickname: "Totty."

Mlle. Souvestre demanded that each girl stood on her own individual merits. Totty made friends who loved her for herself. They didn't care about the scandal of her parents or the prestige of her relatives.

MADEMOISELLE MARIE CLAIRE SOUVESTRE

Allenswood was not the demure finishing school Grandmother Hall expected. Mademoiselle Marie Souvestre's short, sturdy physique and soft white hair in a neat chignon bun may have appeared grandmotherly, but the tailored linen suit and cigarette held between her forefingers were the accoutrements of an educational rebel. Her school's library brimmed with books of philosophy, history, and politics, works that questioned and challenged young minds. She sought to empower and embolden her female students with unquestioning self-assurance. They would stand uncompromising, like the replica of the Greek *Winged Victory* statue that perched on her desk.

Souvestre was the daughter of the renowned French social moralist, playwright, and novelist, Emile Souvestre. Her literary family moved within the circle of French intellectuals. She was a political progressive and early feminist. For her, it was imperative that young women of influential families be trained as independent critical thinkers who would have long-term cultural, social, and political impacts on their societies.

During Eleanor's term, her fellow students came not only from England and the United States, but also Germany, Holland, and Australia. They were daughters, sisters, and nieces of influential British and American politicians, literary figures, and industrial leaders. Eleanor met the nieces of novelist Henry James and the sister of British prime minister Neville

Chamberlain. Mlle. Souvestre deplored anti-Semitism and Jewish girls were included in the school. Allenswood was at the center of an international network of young women who would lead global social change into the twentieth century.

Mlle. Souvestre's affection for her former student, Bye Roosevelt, helped establish Eleanor directly under her wing. The headmistress was known for gathering a collection of favorites around her. These girls had opportunities to sit with famous and important visitors when they joined Souvestre for dinner. Eleanor earned inclusion in this inner circle—initially due to her family connections—and became Souvestre's protégé.

In Souvestre's history class, Eleanor learned to form questions, do research, and write critical arguments by virtue of hard work. There was no scope for bluffing her way through. The fiery Frenchwoman's eyes could gaze right into Eleanor's soul. Her best option was to "dig in" and do the work. When she discovered points of view or developed questions that others had not considered, Mlle. Souvestre applauded her triumphs.

Allenswood challenged Eleanor to think in complex ways and value her own intelligence. She wasn't the best student in all subjects, but her algebra teacher wrote on her spring term report card: "works hard & steady." Mlle. Souvestre encouraged Eleanor to be bold, academically and in her day-to-day life. When Eleanor visited Paris with her aunt over the holidays, Souvestre suggested her young protégé take the opportunity to have a formal dress made; a dress she could wear to dinners and school functions. Tired of seeing Eleanor in hand-me-downs, the headmistress knew a well-dressed woman would be taken more seriously than a poorly dressed one.

Eleanor found the City of Lights alive with excitement, and its essence rustled through her new dark red gown. Wearing her first French gown made her feel glamorous and confident. She could stand tall and feel beautiful.

TRAVELING WITH MADEMOISELLE

Mlle. Souvestre enjoyed Eleanor's company. Over spring and summer breaks, Eleanor acted as a traveling companion. Touring Europe as a Roosevelt, Eleanor had stayed in elite resorts or with family relations. With Souvestre, she traveled among the middle class; she met and interacted with local people. Together, the woman over sixty and the student of sixteen toured village churches and galleries. They strolled down waterfronts and visited Mademoiselle's artist and literary friends.

Eleanor learned to speak French as it applied to local foods and wines. She lived the culture and the language in small cafés and marketplaces.

She learned to enjoy the uniqueness of a location and its people. She would look back later in life and realize "it all served to make you a citizen of the world, at home wherever you might go" (Roosevelt 1961, 31).

Souvestre taught Eleanor how to travel independently. She entrusted her with packing and unpacking their trunks, deciphering train schedules, purchasing tickets, and handling travel details. Eleanor's self-confidence blossomed.

At times, Souvestre surprised her young friend. Eleanor's travels to the Swiss Alps and Germany with her Aunt Tissie had been entirely pre-planned. Souvestre, however, often disembarked a train unexpectedly to visit a site or a friend. Eleanor discovered spontaneity could be exciting and joyful.

When they arrived in Florence, Italy, Eleanor was reading Dante. Souvestre handed her a guidebook and trusted her to go off for the day on her own. No adult had ever shown such confidence in her. She walked the ancient streets Dante had walked. There were moments when she became lost, but she learned to ask for help. She found people were helpful and treated her with respect. She felt empowered and adult.

From Florence to Paris, Eleanor explored on her own and came back at the end of the day to discuss her discoveries and experiences with Mlle. Souvestre.

LIVING THROUGH HISTORY

Eleanor's three seasons at Allenswood immersed her in international events. Mlle. Souvestre encouraged her students to be articulate global citizens. Eleanor was learning firsthand about the influences and interconnections of governments and nations.

During her first year at Allenswood, Great Britain's efforts to drive Dutch colonists from South Africa escalated into the Second Boer War (1899–1902). Mlle. Souvestre relentlessly championed the common person underrepresented by their government. She was an anti-imperialist and opposed Britain's aggressions toward Afrikaans-speaking white South Africans. It was a controversial position to hold just miles away from the British seat of government.

Souvestre allowed her English students to celebrate victories against the Boers, but she simultaneously engaged her American and foreign students in thoughtful discussions on the rights of small nations and the greed of imperialism. Gold and diamonds drove Great Britain's desire for South Africa. None of Souvestre's discussions, however, focused on the rights of Black South Africans.

There were other underdogs in the world as well. Following the Spanish American War (1898), the United States had taken control of Puerto Rico,

Cuba, Guam, and the Philippines. The Americans were now a global power with an imperial foothold in Central America and the Pacific. A global-minded American politician was also on the rise. In the fall of 1900, Eleanor's beloved uncle, Theodore Roosevelt Jr., won election to become vice president of the United States.

Before her uncle was sworn into office, Great Britain and the world faced a historical social change. Queen Victoria had been the British monarch for sixty-four years when she died on January 22, 1901. Under her rule, Great Britain had become the world's largest modern empire. Victoria's sense of propriety had shaped etiquette and style since before Eleanor's parents had been born. The Queen's death marked the end of an era.

Eleanor traveled to London to see Queen Victoria's funeral procession. "I shall never forget the genuine feeling shown by the crowds in the streets or the hush that fell as the gun carriage bearing the smallest coffin I had ever seen came within our range of vision." The Queen's crown and royal symbols rested on the white-draped coffin. A parade of military and governmental officials accompanied the carriage. "I have never forgotten," she wrote, "the great emotional force that seemed to stir all about us as Queen Victoria, so small of stature and yet so great in devotion to her people, passed out of their lives forever" (Roosevelt 1961, 29).

A TURNING POINT

Grandmother Hall demanded Eleanor return home following the 1901 spring term. Family friends had reported seeing the teenager without a chaperon in Paris. But returning home was difficult. The obliging little girl had transformed into an independent-minded young woman.

Eleanor refused to be treated like a child and she no longer had patience for Aunt Pussie's emotional tantrums over her romantic breakups. Pussie pushed back. She hissed that Eleanor was an "ugly duckling" and would never have the male admirers the Hall sisters enjoyed.

When the well-worn insults failed to have the same power they had had in the past, Pussie attacked the memory of Eleanor's father. She pulled out the secret words that had been beyond a little girl's understanding eight years earlier: addict, alcoholic, adulterer. Just how disparaging the words became stayed between the two women. Eleanor would only say her aunt spat "painful and distressing facts about my father's last years" (Roosevelt 1961, 33).

Eleanor refused to stay in the hostile environment. She told her grandmother she wanted to return to Allenswood for a third year. Mrs. Hall set a stipulation, which she felt would keep Eleanor at home: she could return to Allenswood, but she could not sail to England alone. She had to have a chaperone. But Aunt Tissie was already in Europe, Maude was unavailable, and traveling with Pussie was out of the question.

Eleanor was undeterred. She was an experienced traveler. She ran an advertisement in the newspaper, hired a female companion, purchased their fares, and packed her red dress.

FINAL DAYS AT ALLENSWOOD

In her last year at Allenswood, Eleanor became more determined to follow in Mademoiselle Souvestre's footsteps and become a teacher. It was an opportunity to use her intelligence and make her father proud by having a positive impact.

Around the world the gilded view of unregulated capitalism was cracking. In September 1901, a lone gunman, radicalized by the extreme poverty of the American working class, assassinated U.S. president William McKinley. Eleanor's progressive-minded uncle, Ted, succeeded McKinley to become president of the United States.

In their final travels together, Mlle. Souvestre pointedly emphasized the responsibilities and obligations of power. Christmas in Rome found them walking the ruins and considering that they might be standing in the place where Roman senators assassinated Julius Caesar.

In the spring, Mlle. Souvestre took Eleanor to Calais on the northern French coast to spend relaxing days with an older couple. There were walks on the beach and long talks with the Ribots. Only later did Eleanor understand that Alexandre Ribot was the former head of the French parliament and would become the French prime minister. Mlle. Souvestre was impressing upon her student that positions of wealth, status, and power were only important if they were used to help others.

With the spring term of 1902, Eleanor's younger cousin, Corinney, joined the new class. For a few months their paths overlapped, cementing a lifelong bond. Aunt Corinne's daughter wrote to her mother in shock. The dreary cousin she had felt sorry for was one of the most admired girls in the school. "Totty" was the elected captain of the field hockey team.

Eleanor held a position of power and respect at Allenswood. She was the headmistress's favorite, sitting with her at dinner and helping to entertain guests. Each night, Totty dismissed all of the other students from the dining hall. All the girls wanted to be her friend. Corinney had always been the athletic one, the popular one. Alice was the witty, clever one. It was a revelation to see Eleanor in this new light. With Corinney at Allenswood, Eleanor reconnected with her Roosevelt relatives. They embraced her and brought her back into the clan.

A fourth year at Allenswood would have completed Eleanor's education, but she was going to turn eighteen in October. Grandmother Hall insisted she make her debut in New York society.

When Eleanor said farewell to Allenswood, she was an independent young woman fluent in written and spoken French and competent in German and Italian. She had a background in European history and personal experience traveling the continent. She had met influential people and developed the ability to listen and converse on complicated subjects. She had exercised leadership skills and practiced critical analysis of issues. Eleanor Roosevelt had become an accomplished young woman who stood tall to her full six feet and moved with grace and poise.

The school and her mentor had molded her character. She had absorbed habits she would continue with for the rest of her life: morning walks, a tendency toward tidiness, traveling among the local people, and championing supposedly lost causes.

Eleanor's years at Allenswood were happy and Marie Souvestre held a warm place in her heart. She had been the lost cause and Mlle. Souvestre had believed in her. The teacher's portrait always sat at the corner of Eleanor Roosevelt's desk.

THE REALITY OF HOME

Eleanor Roosevelt had changed, but New York's high society and her Hall family had not. Her aunts had expectations of how she should look and behave. A new wardrobe of French gowns had been ordered, without Eleanor's input. The Halls needed her to uphold their social position and secure a wealthy, high-status husband.

Mlle. Souvestre warned her young friend not to let the trivial priorities of social success overwhelm her. The experienced French headmistress feared superficialities would chip away at Eleanor's new confidence.

While Eleanor was unable to see herself as pretty or socially adept, other people regarded her as attractive and enviable. Her long honey-colored hair pinned into a bun gently framed her pale complexion and sky-blue eyes. She was taller than many men, but her cousin Franklin described her slim figure as "willowy." When Franklin recognized her on the train headed toward Tivoli, he eagerly engaged her in conversation.

Over the summer, life at Oak Terrace became tense. Eleanor felt a duty to look after her ten-year-old brother Hall, but life was challenging due to Uncle Vallie's drunken exploits. In angry outbursts, he'd begun shooting at passersby on the road.

As soon as September arrived, Eleanor took Hall to Groton School, a private boarding academy preferred by New York society. She assumed responsibilities as his guardian, writing to him daily, visiting him each term, and communicating with his teachers. With Hall safely at school, Eleanor moved into the city with Aunt Pussie. The social season was about to begin.

A NEW YORK DEBUTANTE

Balls and luncheons held little appeal for Eleanor, yet she felt obligated to live up to family expectations.

Cousin Alice Roosevelt had come out as a debutante the previous January at a ball hosted at the White House. "Princess Alice," as the press was calling her, had become notorious for her biting repartee and challenges to social rules. To her father's distress, she smoked in public and took pleasure rides in automobiles with young men, unchaperoned. The president's daughter was the most high-profile female celebrity in the country. No debutante wanted to compete with Alice Roosevelt.

Three other distant Roosevelt cousins were also debuting in 1902. The society press columns took to calling them "the Magic Five" (Lash 1971, 140). All of the young women were under intense pressure to appear and act in a manner deemed appropriate by a small number of wealthy upper-class matrons. Alice sneered at the rules and her popularity soared. Eleanor tried to please, but always believed she disappointed.

In recounting her debutante season, Eleanor claimed she was a wall-flower, a misfit relegated to sit beside an elderly host at dinner rather than with the eligible young men. She implied that her dance partners were prompted by pity. Those partners, however, recalled a different reality. Franklin Delano Roosevelt, one of his Delano cousins, and three other young gentlemen competed for her attention at balls and events.

Dinner hostesses sat the young Miss Roosevelt beside influential older men because she was one of the few debutantes able to converse on a range of topics. New York buzzed that Eleanor was more like the charismatic president than any of his own children. Whether she wanted to believe it or not, Eleanor Roosevelt was one of the sought-after debutantes of the season. She had her own wealth and was the niece of the president.

Eleanor anguished over the Assembly Ball at the Waldorf-Astoria Hotel. The December event was the formal introduction of debutantes to New York society. Eleanor wrote that she felt alone, danced little, and went home early. Despite her critique of her performance, she was accepted into the highest levels of New York and American society. Invitations were extended for dinners and dances and she made the list for Mrs. Astor's Ball, an accomplishment for any new debutante.

Now that Eleanor had been allowed in society's door, she was happy to leave early. Fortunately, she encountered Robert Munro Ferguson (1867–1922) early in the season. He had claimed her as a dance partner when she seemed alone and introduced her to other potential partners.

"Bob," as all the Roosevelts called him, was the younger brother of a Scottish lord. He had been a Rough Rider under Theodore Roosevelt's command during the Spanish American War and the two men were fast

---

WHAT IS A DEBUTANTE?

Debutante refers to a young woman, typically between the ages of sixteen and eighteen, making her first formal appearance in high society. While New Yorkers regarded themselves as American royalty, in actuality, their social registry originated with the 920 members of the National Horse Show. The multiday equestrian showcase opened the social season in mid-November and set the tone for the year. Which seems appropriate, because the debutantes were about to be displayed, put through their paces, and vied for just like horses.

The opening of the Metropolitan Opera, the following week, sounded the starting gun for the race to social success. Parents or relatives hosted events to introduce the debutante to high-ranking society leaders. The *New York Times* social column for December 12, 1902 reported that "Mrs. Valentine Hall has cards out for several dinners for her granddaughter, Eleanor Roosevelt." Attendees expressed their approval of the debutante by reciprocating and extending her further social invitations.

The Assembly Ball in December was the grand showcase. Debutantes were trotted out in virginal white gowns and reviewed by society hostesses. An inappropriate curtsy could bring a disapproving look and disqualification from the entire race.

On the arm of an escort, each debutante was paraded across the ballroom floor, introducing her to New York's assembled elite. With each step, she was critiqued for beauty, gait, and poise.

Eligible men validated a debutante's merit by adding their name to her dance card. A full dance card signified a popular and, therefore, successful debutante. The finish line, of course, was a socially enhancing marriage.

It was a beauty and wealth contest that used young women as extensions of their family's social power. Could something like this happen today? Absolutely, the Assembly Ball still takes place in the twenty-first century.

---

friends. Bob was Uncle Ted's ranching partner in the Dakota Territory and part of the extended Roosevelt family. He was nineteen years Eleanor's senior and trusted as a chaperone. On Bob's arm, Eleanor could politely leave any boring dance or dinner.

Ferguson was a free spirit, moving with ease between the highest royal society in Great Britain and the ranchers of the Dakota badlands. He introduced Eleanor to a different New York society, the Bohemian artists of Greenwich Village. They were the kind of people Mlle. Souvestre would have championed.

Ferguson also introduced Eleanor to a young woman from the Dakota Territory, Isabella Selmes (1886–1953). The Selmes family had been Uncle Ted's Dakota neighbors. Isabella's father had died when she was nine years old. Theodore Roosevelt considered Isabella like another daughter and supported her mother's decision to bring her to New York. As a debutante, the Selmes girl might find a husband to secure her future.

Isabella and Eleanor hit it off immediately. Both felt like outsiders in New York society and had had similar personal losses. Isabella Selmes was fun and adventurous. Eleanor had a new best friend.

VISITING THE WHITE HOUSE

Through the 1902 holiday season, one young man had become Eleanor's frequent dance partner, Franklin D. Roosevelt. He was tall and charismatic. His wide smile and mischievous eyes made Eleanor smile. The fact that he was a distant cousin, someone she had known all her life, made him less intimidating. He was after all the gallant knight who had stepped in to ask her to dance when she was an awkward teen.

Most of Franklin's life had been spent with Delano relatives and the Roosevelts of Hyde Park, New York. The Hyde Park Roosevelts were long-established members of the Democratic political party. Eleanor's grandfather had broken with tradition to join the Republican Party and support Abraham Lincoln prior to the Civil War. Uncle Theodore heightened that division by entering politics and becoming a Republican president.

Only recently had Franklin become a frequent face at events hosted by the Oyster Bay Roosevelts, including Alice's debutante ball. Cousin Alice enjoyed dancing and partying with Franklin, but she and her half-brothers dismissed him as a mama's boy and a lightweight, physically and intellectually. They joked that "FD" stood for feather duster. Despite his Roosevelt name, Franklin had neither the wealth nor the social prestige of Alice and Eleanor.

Both Eleanor and Franklin were invited to Washington, D.C. to celebrate the turn of the New Year at the White House with the president and his extended family. Aunt Bye hosted them both at her Washington home with her husband, naval captain William Sheffield Cowles. Bye's home was a hub of political debate and discussion. Eleanor loved the vibrancy of the house and its stream of visitors. She delighted in discussions with her aunt. As Bye's house was just a short walk away from the White House, Uncle Ted often dropped in to confer with his trusted and informed sister.

REALITIES OF FAMILY STRIFE

During her Washington stay, Eleanor may have confided to her aunt that she was managing the Hall household. Her grandmother stayed in the country and Pussie was either absent or verbally abusive. Her Hall uncles were chronically intoxicated and had become a physical threat. Historian

Blanche Wiesen Cook details evidence that three additional locks were added to Eleanor's bedroom door.

Bye Roosevelt knew how substance abuse had altered her brother's behavior. She and her sister Corinne tried to convince Eleanor to come stay at one of their homes. Mlle. Souvestre wrote from Allenswood adding her voice to this suggestion. Between them, the Roosevelt aunts even considered legal action to remove Eleanor and her brother from Mrs. Hall's custody.

Eleanor, however, wanted to remain in New York City. She was trying to balance social demands with her sense of self and purpose. She had another life in the city.

MAINTAINING A SENSE OF PURPOSE

Eleanor had been volunteering weekly at the Orthopedic Hospital. Leaving New York would mean abandoning this reconnection with her father and her purposeful volunteer work. Ultimately she moved in with her godmother, Susie Parish, and her banker husband. Cousin Susie was her mother's favorite cousin; the move saved face for the Halls and removed Eleanor from a precarious situation.

Eleanor also met a group of college-educated debutantes who were involved with the Settlement Movement.

Mary Harriman (Rumsey) (1881–1934) was the daughter of a wealthy railroad entrepreneur. While at Barnard College, Harriman started the *Junior League for the Promotion of Settlement Movements* and opened the College Settlement on Rivington Street, on New York's Lower East Side. Harriman and the young women she recruited went beyond donations; they directly assisted people living in poverty. Harriman's junior league idea quickly spread across the country.

At the College Settlement, Eleanor Roosevelt and debutante Jean Reid taught music and exercise to tenement children. Many of their young students labored long days making decorative artificial flowers for hats and ladies' clothing. The dance class provided a rare opportunity for them to play.

New York City had grown to 3.5 million people. Over 2 million of them were jammed together in degrading tenement housing. Many were new immigrants from Europe seeking refuge from famine or religious persecution. Despite the deplorable conditions, these poor Italians, Austro-Hungarians, Irish, Germans, and Eastern European Jews saw the United States as a place of prosperity and possibility.

Eleanor learned the startling reality that only three miles from the mansions of Fifth Avenue, children lived in extreme poverty. Reid took a

THE SETTLEMENT MOVEMENT

The Settlement Movement began in England. Wealthy upper-class university students felt living or going to "settle" in the slums of London was the only way to bridge the cultural gap created by extreme income inequality.

In the United States, the movement focused on social issues. Instead of donors throwing money at what they believed the poor should want, the Settlement House was a place driven by the needs of the community it served.

College Settlement was the first such facility in New York City. Female students from Barnard College settled on the Lower East Side to integrate into the impoverished immigrant community. They provided services requested by working mothers: day care, kindergarten, and after-school programs. Fieldtrips to the shore and organized recreation for children, like the classes Eleanor Roosevelt taught, helped counter the dehumanizing conditions faced by child laborers.

The Settlement provided referrals for charitable aid, medical care, and employment. Community members could meet to discuss issues and develop community-driven solutions. Some Settlements taught English-language or adult literacy. Others offered social clubs and events where families could gather in an alcohol-free environment. All promoted community participation in local change.

College Settlement commissioned a study on working conditions for young girls. They found girls less than seven years old were working twelve- to fourteen-hour days, six days a week, in the garment industry. New Yorkers were shocked and the National Consumers League was founded. Eleanor Roosevelt was participating in the birth of modern community activism.

By 1908, over 100 settlement houses were bringing social reform to American cities. The Settlement Movement laid the foundation for the Progressive Movement. Many of its female leaders would play substantial roles in President Franklin D. Roosevelt's New Deal programs.

---

family carriage to the Settlement House. Eleanor purposefully commuted with the people who lived in the slums. She took the elevated train or the crowded streetcar and walked through the Bowery, alone. Street mongers' carts lined the sidewalks. Garbage, even a dead horse, might lay uncollected for days on the streets. Leaving in the evening, she waited for the streetcar with trepidation as men lurched out of saloons.

She convinced Franklin to escort her home from the Settlement House one evening. Visiting the tenement rooms of one of her students introduced him to extreme poverty. Eleanor claimed the experience made a lasting impression.

Settlement House friends recruited Eleanor into the National Consumers' League. The newly formed organization brought together young Jewish labor reformers and upper-class women like Aunt Corinne. Together they sought to improve working conditions for impoverished workers, especially women and children.

The wealthy women believed they could use economic pressure to positively influence employer behavior. The Consumers' League compiled a "white list" of retailers that treated their employees ethically. They sought to influence women to shop only with white list retailers that adhered to three major tenets: equal pay for equal work, a ten-hour workday, and a minimum wage of six dollars a week.

The Consumers' League sent pairs of women out to collect scientific data on the working conditions of laborers in garment factories and sales girls in department stores. Eleanor had never considered that shop girls might have to work long hours without sitting down or taking a break to use the restroom. She was startled to learn that clothing was made in facilities where air quality jeopardized worker health, machinery maimed, and women's lavatories were unsanitary.

The most troubling data Eleanor collected concerned the children she loved teaching at the Settlement House. Roosevelt recounted that in sweatshops hidden away in tenement households, she "saw little children of four or five sitting at tables until they dropped with fatigue" (Roosevelt 1960, 104). She developed a strong opinion against child labor as she learned how to advocate for others.

Cousin Susie disapproved of Eleanor's investigative work. The Halls and most of New York's upper class had little empathy for the recent immigrants. To the white Protestant families who pinned their status on the founding fathers, Catholic and Jewish immigrants were "lower class." The Irish and the Italians were labeled untrustworthy and only slightly better than the descendants of former enslaved Africans, who were frequently regarded as a subhuman servant class.

Both Eleanor's parents had openly regarded members of the Jewish faith with contempt. Yet, her mentor Marie Souvestre had spoken out against anti-Semitism. Eleanor had walked the streets of Florence, Rome, and Munich. She had met Italians and Germans in their home countries. Now she was engaging with families who, though poor, sought to love and provide for their children like any other parents. Her personal experiences challenged the racism she had learned at home.

LEARNING THE POLITICAL ROPES

The Washington Roosevelts proudly celebrated Eleanor's reform work. Aunt Corinne felt that Eleanor epitomized the Roosevelt ideal of social responsibility, while Alice did not. Uncle Ted appreciated his niece's quiet ease and selfless nature, which contrasted with the demeanor of his challenging daughter.

Invitations for extended visits in Washington came from Aunt Bye. Eleanor found reassurance in her older aunt; Bye always listened fully and offered sound advice. All of the Roosevelt women believed that if Anna "Bye" Roosevelt Cowles had been a man, she would have been president. She was a skilled diplomatic hostess and a master of personal politics.

At her aunt's side, Eleanor experienced the intricacies of making daily rounds to influential Washington officials, policy makers, and their wives. Bye bolstered her brother's administrative agenda and gathered intelligence from supporters and detractors. Through Aunt Bye, Eleanor learned the power of networking. She was also adding contacts to her own network.

AN UNEXPECTED ROMANCE

Eleanor Roosevelt began seeing more of Franklin D. Roosevelt at various society events. The Harvard student was charming, outgoing, and self-confident. He had a natural ease with people, reminiscent of her father. In the spring of 1903, he was flirting with multiple young women; no one suspected that Eleanor Roosevelt would be among them.

Much of their romance evolved through correspondence. Like her relationship with her father, writing to Franklin created a private and excitingly clandestine connection. Written letters, much like modern digital communications, instilled a greater sense of intimacy. People, even family members, who observed the pair did not recognize the developing relationship.

Franklin Delano Roosevelt came from the line of Roosevelts who established themselves as sugar merchants, and then invested in banking and real estate. They owned vast tracts of land in the Hudson River Valley, married heiresses, and lived the life of gentlemen farmers. Franklin's father had been a respected breeder of trotting racehorses.

James Roosevelt (1828–1900) was a widower when he married Sara Delano (1854–1941). She was twenty-six years younger, close in age to his adult son, James "Rosy" Roosevelt (1858–1927).

Sara Delano brought an infusion of wealth to the marriage. Her father and grandfather had made fortunes in shipping, especially through the opium trade in Asia. A bold young girl, she had traveled with her father to China and Europe. She was intelligent, opinionated, and a friend of Bye Roosevelt.

When Sara's only son Franklin was born, he became the center of her life. Through her, his heritage reached back to the founding of the Massachusetts colony. Social status was highly important to Sara Delano Roosevelt and she believed that only the best was good enough for her son. When Franklin's father died in 1900, his mother temporarily moved to Boston to be near her son while he attended Harvard. She opposed his interest in politics, which she considered beneath their status.

In the summer of 1903, Eleanor was included in a group of young people invited to stay at Franklin's family summerhouse on Campobello Island in New Brunswick, Canada. Franklin's mother regarded Eleanor merely as Bye's niece and a mild-mannered sweet young woman.

Sara and her husband had also been friends of Eleanor's father. They had enjoyed Elliott Roosevelt's company so much while crossing the Atlantic on their honeymoon that two years later they had asked him to be Franklin's godfather. While including Eleanor was merely a kind gesture, Eleanor appreciated the opportunity to spend time with someone who had known and liked her father.

While there were moments when Eleanor and Franklin walked the shoreline together, no one suspected a serious relationship between the two young people, especially not Franklin's mother. Franklin was corresponding flirtatiously with several other young women. Eleanor continued dancing with new partners in New York and meeting young diplomats in Washington, D.C.

In November, when Eleanor took her brother Hall back to Groton for the fall term, Franklin met her there. As they walked along the riverbank, he proposed and she said "Yes."

SOURCES

Lash, Joseph P. 1971. *Eleanor and Franklin: The Story of Their Relationship Based on Eleanor Roosevelt's Private Papers*. New York: W.W. Norton & Company, Inc.

Roosevelt, Eleanor. 1951, June 19. "The Seven People Who Shaped My Life." *LOOK*, pp. 54–56, 58.

Roosevelt, Eleanor. 1960. *You Learn by Living*. New York: HarperCollins Publishers.

Roosevelt, Eleanor. 1961. *The Autobiography of Eleanor Roosevelt*. New York: Harper Perennial.

3

Marriage, Motherhood, and Politics (1904–1911)

"I love you dearest," Eleanor Roosevelt wrote to Franklin, "and I hope that I shall always prove worthy of the love which you have given me. I have never known before what it was to be absolutely happy" (Lash 1971, 160).

She was nineteen when Franklin proposed; he was twenty-one. Their secret relationship had only been serious for a few months. In her letters, she had bolstered his confidence when he was not invited into Harvard's Porcellian Club. They had penned thoughts on poetry and literature, but they had spent little time together.

Reading her father's letters, she had constructed an image of Elliott Roosevelt only she would recognize. Did she really know Franklin or was she reading into his letters the man she wanted him to be?

Marriage to Franklin D. Roosevelt offered a sense of belonging and the stability of family. Eleanor was willing to make personal compromises to meet his expectations and please his mother. She was eager to know the love of being a wife and mother, but the self-confidence she had worked so hard to build would be challenged. "I know now," she wrote in her autobiography, "that it was years later before I understood what being in love or what loving really meant" (Roosevelt 1961, 41).

WAITING A YEAR

At Thanksgiving, Franklin shocked his mother with news of the engagement. Sara Delano Roosevelt felt the couple was too young for such an important decision. She also wasn't sure if any young woman was good enough for her son. Various Roosevelt relatives would convey to historians their belief that any woman married to Franklin would have been subjected to the same overpowering influence of his possessive mother.

Franklin's mother controlled his inheritance and gave the couple an ultimatum. She would agree to their marriage—if they waited a year. When Eleanor agreed to Sara's terms, she believed the purpose of waiting was to strengthen and deepen her relationship with Franklin. She did not expect his mother to actively try to separate them.

Because the engagement remained secret, there were no boundaries for the cluster of young women trying to capture Franklin's attention. Sara even took her son and his Harvard roommate on a six-week cruise to the Caribbean over the winter. She tried to use time and other young women to drive a wedge between the couple. When Franklin returned home still determined to marry Eleanor, his mother became unrelenting. She attempted to arrange a position for him as a secretary to the U.S. ambassador to Great Britain.

While he was away, Eleanor wrote to Franklin daily. She believed she had found the one person in the world who loved her as completely as her father had. She could confide in Franklin all her hopes, dreams, and vulnerabilities.

Eleanor continued her volunteer work and spent time with Bye in Washington, D.C. If anyone asked her about Franklin, she denied any romantic feelings for him and, in some cases, told tales about other young men she was interested in.

There was an air of intrigue and excitement in keeping their romance a secret. The downside was, it created a situation where friends and family did not believe they had heartfelt affection for each other. When the couple revealed their engagement on December 1, 1904, skepticism followed. Even Grandmother Hall questioned whether Eleanor was really in love with Franklin.

Eleanor Roosevelt was an intelligent young woman with a sizeable inheritance and established pedigree. Though her money lay in a trust, she had a specified annual allowance of $7,500, which is equivalent to approximately $218,000 in 2020 dollars (Official Inflation Data). She was educated, attractive, and active with a group of young women pioneering social reform. She had personal and familial connections to New York's wealthiest families, foreign diplomats and heads of state, artists, the U.S. Navy, and the highest levels of American politics.

Franklin Delano Roosevelt had moderate wealth, controlled by his mother ($5,000 annually; equivalent to approximately $145,000 a year

(Official Inflation Data)). His older half-brother had been a secretary at the American embassy in London and married one of the Astor heiresses. His links to New York society were fewer, but he had a battery of devoted Delano family connections. Franklin had graduated from Harvard, but wasn't considered exceptional in his studies or successful in law school. Several of his Harvard pals married wealthy women and dabbled with running for political office, though none had specific political ideals. Despite his mother's good opinion of him, Franklin also had a reputation as a heartbreaker. Most of Eleanor's relatives felt he wasn't good enough for her.

Though Eleanor Roosevelt would craft an image of herself as the shy wallflower who married a charismatic leader, the truth may be more complicated. At the time of their engagement, she was the one more active in community and social reform. She was the one who networked with Aunt Bye in Washington, D.C. She was the one staying at the White House and sitting in on presidential discussions regarding the establishment of a commission to investigate a canal through Panama. Whether or not Franklin was already contemplating involvement in politics, he married into the country's most prominent political family. Theodore Roosevelt had just been reelected to a second term as president. The betrothed couple sat in coveted seats, just behind the president and his wife, at the inaugural.

ELEANOR ROOSEVELT ROOSEVELT

Two weeks later, on March 17, 1905, the Roosevelt families gathered again. Uncle Theodore had offered to host Eleanor's wedding at the White House, as if she were his own daughter, but Eleanor chose to honor her Hall relatives by having the wedding in Cousin Susie Parish's home in New York City. A conciliatory move toward Franklin's mother, it enabled Sara Delano Roosevelt's participation in wedding planning and decisions.

Uncle Ted would stand in for her father and walk Eleanor on his arm down the aisle. The date for the ceremony accommodated his schedule. President Roosevelt officiated the New York City St. Patrick's Day Parade in the morning, then his security detail attempted to whisk him over to the Parish home on East 76th Street just off Central Park. Crowds on Madison and Fifth Avenues, however, delayed the president's arrival.

As Eleanor dressed, a telegram arrived from Mademoiselle Souvestre with a single word: "BONHEUR," happiness. Eleanor had planned to introduce her beloved teacher to her new husband during their honeymoon tour of Europe in the summer, but Souvestre was ill with cancer. She had survived to wish Eleanor well on her wedding day, but she would only live a few more days.

Despite the delays, frayed nerves, and some guests who missed the ceremony entirely, the March 18, 1905 *New York Times* hailed it as "one of the most notable weddings of the year." The interior of the Parish-Ludlow home had been transformed into a garden of ferns, palms, and pink roses. The Roosevelt coat of arms—three white feathers with crossed pink roses—was on ostentatious display. Each groomsman wore a tiepin designed by Franklin depicting the three feathers in diamonds.

The bridesmaids entered down a stairway in white silk gowns with silver roses embroidered on their sleeves. The young women represented both families: cousins Alice Roosevelt and Corinney Roosevelt Robinson, two of Franklin's Delano cousins, and Eleanor's friends Helen Cutting and Isabella Selmes. Each wore three silver-tipped white ostrich plumes in their hair and carried pink roses. The personification of the Roosevelt crest highlighted the family ancestry and showcased their status as longtime New Yorkers.

When Eleanor entered on Theodore Roosevelt's arm, she embodied not only her own hopes for happiness but also a confluence of wealth and status. Her white satin dress, with its train and high tulle neck, provided a canvas to showcase affluence. The society column reporters didn't just cover attendees, they also detailed which families were displaying treasure on the bride. Her mother's diamond crescent secured the Hall family's veil of handmade rose-point Brussels lace on Eleanor's head. The bride wore a diamond bowknot pin from the Delano family and a high collar of pearls with diamond bars gifted by Sara Delano Roosevelt.

The Oyster Bay Roosevelts offered status through their political power. The *New York Times* described the bride as the "daughter of the only brother of President Roosevelt" and the groom as a "cousin of the President" (Bloom 2017).

BALANCING MOTHER-IN-LAW AND HUSBAND

Eleanor now possessed what she had long desired—a romantic male companion with whom she could build a family of her own and a strong maternal figure to guide and teach her about life. She had spent years constructing these ideals in her mind. Now they were real people.

Like her father, her new husband was gregarious and enjoyed the company of other people. She encouraged his attending alumni events at Harvard, but seldom joined him. She didn't mind parties, if they included engaging conversation, but she never felt comfortable around the large consumption of alcohol. She gave Franklin the opportunity to go off and party with friends, but felt alone and somewhat abandoned when he did. She loved his easy flirtatious manner, but became jealous when his smiles were turned elsewhere.

She wanted to make him happy and believed subverting her own desires was the best way to accomplish that. If she acted the docile obliging wife, he would be the doting husband. Like her imagined prince, she expected him to know what she needed emotionally and physically. When he failed to read her mind, she felt hurt and distant.

Just as she had shared poetry and secrets with her father, she now shared those intimate moments with Franklin. But her husband was not a figment of her imagination. He also had a complicated relationship with his mother. As the only child of a very strong woman, Franklin avoided conflict. When disagreements arose between his wife and his mother, he refused to take sides.

When Eleanor married Franklin, there was only one riding horse in the stable at his family's Hyde Park estate. Franklin had trained his horse to do specific gaits along a specific path. Franklin and his mother could both ride the animal, but Eleanor found the mount unmanageable. Besides, she wanted to ride alongside her husband. Eleanor loved riding. The speed, motion, and sense of freedom that came from riding intertwined with memories of her father.

She asked if she could buy a saddle horse for herself to keep at "Springwood." Her mother-in-law adamantly opposed it, finding caring for a second horse an unnecessary expense. Eleanor hoped Franklin would support her, but he refused to take a stand either way. She felt a bit betrayed and chose to cease riding altogether. A passive aggressive act, it brought neither remedy nor resolution. Her husband did not run to her defense and her mother-in-law did not soften her position.

Sara Delano Roosevelt was a commanding figure and historians evaluating her relationship with Eleanor arrive at contradictory interpretations. Some note that Eleanor adamantly sought her mother-in-law's approval. She asked for Sara's assistance in choosing clothing and making wedding arrangements. She appreciated her mother-in-law's initial renting of an apartment with furnishings and servants, which enabled the young couple to move right into their new lodging while Franklin continued his studies at Columbia University law school.

Other historians see Sara's actions as domineering, controlling, and being reluctant to give up control of her son's life. Franklin's mother would continue to pay for "the children's" household expenses, including rent, until she died in 1941. (At that time, Eleanor and Franklin were in their late fifties.) As long as she supplied the money, Sara Delano Roosevelt had a voice in where the couple lived, what servants they employed, and many other aspects of their daily lives.

Both viewpoints hold some truth. There were times when Eleanor Roosevelt and her mother-in-law served as advocates for each other and became close companions. There were other times when they clashed and Eleanor felt her desires subverted by her mother-in-law's demands. While Eleanor Roosevelt typically portrayed herself in her memoirs and other writings as shy and needy as a young woman, at times, she could be just as stubborn and willful as her mother-in-law.

A HONEYMOON ABROAD

The newlywed couple postponed their three-month-long honeymoon tour of Europe until Franklin had finished his law classes in the spring. Eleanor stepped right into the task of making all of their travel arrangements. Employing the skills she had developed with Mademoiselle Souvestre, she booked ship passage, mapped out their travel, and secured lodgings. She readied their trunks and reached out to contacts abroad.

Eleanor suppressed her typical fear of the sea and was relieved when the Atlantic crossing remained calm and she avoided seasickness. Franklin loved ships and sailing; she wanted to appear a seaworthy companion.

Both Roosevelts had toured Europe with parents or other adults; now they shared their favorite places and discovered new treasures together. He showed her his favorite little bookstores in London and Paris. She introduced him to eating local specialties. He took her to explore the Black Forest in Germany, which he had loved as a boy. She led him through the narrow streets of Florence. The fantasy of her father merged with the romantic ideal of her new husband when she introduced Franklin to Venice and they toured the canals in a gondola.

There were also visits to friends and family. Some were connections of lasting consequence, like lunch with the family of Eleanor's College Settlement friend Jean Reid. Jean's father was the U.S. ambassador to Great Britain in London.

When a telegram arrived that Eleanor's good friend Isabella had married the Roosevelt family friend Bob Ferguson, Eleanor and Franklin detoured to spend time with the other couple at the Munro-Ferguson family estates in Scotland. Bob's older brother and his wife, Lord Ronald and Lady Helen Munro-Ferguson, were important political contacts. Lord Munro-Ferguson was a member of Parliament. He would serve as governor-general of Australia from 1914 to 1920 and later become secretary for Scotland (1922–1924). During World War I, Lady Munro-Ferguson founded and managed the Australian Red Cross.

Eleanor Roosevelt frequently told the story of having tea with Lady Munro-Ferguson. The older and politically savvy woman asked for an explanation of the difference between U.S. state governments and the American federal government. Eleanor claimed to nervously hesitate because she did not know the answer. She described herself as politically ignorant and ashamed of her lack of knowledge. In typical self-deprecating fashion, she told of Franklin appearing in the nick of time to deflect the question and save her.

It seems hard to imagine, however, that ER didn't have some understanding of the answer herself. She had spent two winters in Washington, D.C., with Aunt Bye interacting with political people. Her uncle had been the governor of New York and was currently the American president. Some historians wonder if she was choosing to appear subordinate to her husband or purposefully creating a relatable image of a woman who was naïve of politics but determined to inform herself.

As their honeymoon came to a close, word arrived that Franklin had failed two of his law classes and would have to retake them. His mother forwarded his law books so he could study on the ship coming home. During the crossing, Eleanor suffered from what she thought was seasickness; in fact, she was pregnant with their first child.

MOTHERHOOD

Eleanor and Franklin both longed for a large family. He had been an only child with an elderly father; he desired the raucous mayhem of other children. She relished the sense of security she found among the Delano and Roosevelt families. Both aspired to the ideal of Theodore Roosevelt's lively household bursting with children.

Eleanor, however, knew nothing of children or nurturing. She was trying to be a mother figure to her brother Hall. He stayed with the young couple in between school terms. But she had no model of what mothering a small child entailed.

While Franklin worked to earn his law degree, she spent her days and some evenings with Sara. They shopped, walked daily through Central Park, and planned for the baby's arrival.

Eleanor harbored fears concerning childbirth, but found herself unable to discuss her apprehensions with her husband or his mother. She was afraid of the pain, afraid that she wouldn't fulfill expectations, afraid of losing self-control. Fortunately, her friend Isabella was pregnant at the same time. Isabella confided to Eleanor that she took comfort in looking around and seeing all the people on the streets of New York; each one of them had come into the world through childbirth. There was no use in being afraid of a natural process.

On May 3, 1906, Anna Eleanor Roosevelt II was born without any complications. Isabella Selmes Ferguson became baby Anna's godmother. Eleanor had planned to raise the children herself, but Sara Delano Roosevelt and Cousin Susie were adamant—families of their standing hired nurses to care for their children.

The crying baby was overwhelming. Eleanor had no female relative to support and guide her. The easiest path was to give in and follow her mother-in-law's instructions. The baby nurse, Mrs. Springer, became a trusted ally. She would be called to swaddle each new Roosevelt infant. Other nurses, and then governesses, would take watch over the children, as they grew older. As long as they were small, there would always be someone between Eleanor and her children.

Motherhood did not come naturally to Eleanor Roosevelt. Like her own mother, Eleanor was twenty-one when her daughter was born. She was still trying to understand herself as a person. While Franklin would become the beloved playmate of his children, Eleanor would always be somewhat aloof, much as she felt her own mother had been toward her. She loved them and supported them, but she had a difficult time relating to babies and toddlers.

Just a year and a half after the first child, a son was born, easing Eleanor's need to provide an heir. James Roosevelt was named after Franklin's father. Franklin had passed his bar examination and secured a position in a law office. Their lives fell into a pattern. Summers began with a visit to Hyde Park and then several months at Campobello with Franklin's mother. In the fall, it was back to New York City, where Sara Delano Roosevelt was building her son and his wife a townhouse just off Central Park. Mother and son spent hours over the plans and supervising the construction, but Eleanor declined to be involved.

Eleanor remained a member of the National Consumers' League, though she was no longer active. She attempted to volunteer at the College Settlement, but her mother-in-law and Cousin Susie quickly chastised her. They feared she might bring home a disease from the slums and threaten the health of her own children. There was some truth in their concern. Exposure to small pox, tuberculosis, and typhoid fever was a threat in New York's tenement neighborhoods. Eleanor's efforts to help the poor became limited to donating money and serving on the boards of charitable organizations.

Each pregnancy seemed to reduce her interactions with the outside world. She was typically ill for six of the nine months and social propriety demanded she go into confinement for the last three to four months. Eleanor found herself increasingly limited to seeing relatives and a few female friends.

Within six months of James's birth, Eleanor again became pregnant.

NO PLACE OF HER OWN

Not only was Eleanor giving her body over to a third pregnancy, she was losing her physical privacy as well. Visiting Springwood or Campobello Island always entailed living under Sara Delano Roosevelt's roof. Eleanor and Franklin's early New York lodgings had been rented by Sara, but she had not lived with them. In 1908, the New York townhouse Sara had been building as a gift was completed. Eleanor had not participated in the design details. Now she moved into a six-story townhouse conjoined to a matching home for her mother-in-law.

The twin limestone-fronted townhouses—at 47 and 49 East 65th Street—were just a short two-block stroll from Central Park in a lovely upscale neighborhood with tree-lined streets. The young couple could not have afforded the location on their own. The dark wood shelves lining the library were reminiscent of Uncle Ted's library at Sagamore Hill. The wide windows on the second floor filled the rooms with light as they looked out onto the green branches of trees.

No matter how lovely the house was, the floor plan caused conflict. The two narrow street-front townhouses were strategically interconnected. The dining rooms of the two houses opened into each other, as did the drawing rooms, with the intent being to double the space and provide for entertaining. While the idea was sound, it also meant that half of the forty-foot-wide dining room resided in Sara Delano Roosevelt's house. She instantly had a say in who could be invited. No event could take place without her approval and/or participation.

Sliding doors had also been installed between the two houses at the children's floor, the servant's floor, and the floor with the master bedroom. As far as Eleanor was concerned, she had no privacy. Her mother-in-law could cross over into any part of her family's life at any time.

Rather than take a stance, Eleanor became resentful. She let Sara decorate both townhouses and hire the staff. When the family moved in, Eleanor sank into depression. It wasn't her home; nothing about it reflected her aesthetics or choices.

Franklin didn't understand Eleanor's side of the growing tension. He had always left household management to his mother. From his point of view, his mother had made choices when Eleanor would not. Besides, the living arrangement made it easy for Sara to look after the children or manage the household when he or Eleanor traveled.

As a young girl, Eleanor had never felt she had a home. She had expected that marriage would bring her the autonomy of a home of her own. The conjoined townhouses crushed that expectation. She relinquished her own personal power, allowing her mother-in-law to decide on menus for meals, hiring and managing of servants, and daily matters in general. She turned deeper into herself, suppressing her anger.

In November 1908, Theodore Roosevelt's handpicked successor, William Howard Taft, won the presidency. During the final days of his administration, Uncle Ted invited Eleanor and Franklin to visit the White House. Though nearing confinement for her third pregnancy, Eleanor eagerly accepted the invitation—she expected it would be her last opportunity to stay in the grand mansion.

Eleanor took in the history of the White House and the dramatic renovation of the presidential home that had taken place under Aunt Edith's supervision. Eleanor had watched Edith Roosevelt transform the position of First Lady into a combination of international hostess and White House manager. She even had initiated the hiring of a social secretary to help her run the nation's house as an integral part of the president's political office.

During their visit, Franklin was also absorbing the feel of the White House. He admired Cousin Theodore and his political success. He had already begun telling his young lawyer coworkers that he was planning his own political rise by following Theodore Roosevelt's path: state assembly, assistant secretary of the Navy, state governor, president. Eleanor knew her husband had no intention of staying with the law. He was an outgoing person who craved interaction with people. She saw him as perfectly suited for and in need of a political career.

TREASURED GAINS AND DEVASTATING LOSS

In the days leading up to the birth of their third child, Franklin was increasingly absent. Eleanor detailed in a diary how she dined at home with her mother-in-law, while Franklin stayed at the Knickerbocker Club or the Harvard Club until three or four in the morning. She knew these places. Her father had frequented the Knickerbocker Club. She would look back on this period and explain away her dark moods as her own petty jealousies and lack of self-confidence. If she ever thought of her own mother's distress waiting for her father to come home from late night romps, she never admitted it to anyone.

Eleanor gave birth to her second son, Franklin Delano Roosevelt Jr., a day after her fourth wedding anniversary. Weighing eleven pounds at birth, he was a big beautiful baby.

As expected, the family headed north to Campobello Island for the summer. When they arrived, however, Sara presented her son and daughter-in-law with a treasure: a vacation home of their own on the island.

The three-story "cottage" had belonged to a family friend who had passed away. While it neighbored Sara's summer home, the cottage was separate on its own piece of property. For the first time, Eleanor felt she had a home of her own. The house had been purchased completely furnished, down to the linens, but Eleanor could move the furniture where she wanted. She could invite whomever she pleased and make decisions on how to run the house. The cottage at Campobello offered freedom and autonomy.

Positioned on a picturesque bay with tranquil waters lapping along a wide beach, the wooden barn-shaped house had a rustic feel. There were eighteen bedrooms and six bathrooms, but there was no electricity, just kerosene lamps and candles. They had running water for bathing, but bottled drinking water had to be brought in.

Visitors arrived by boat. When the fog rolled in, the rugged island was closed off from the world. With a fire burning in the hearth, it was the perfect place to cozy up with a book or read to the children. Eleanor loved Campobello Island and now she had a piece of it for herself.

In the fall, the children contracted influenza. Anna and James soon recovered, but on October 25, Eleanor wrote to Isabella that "baby Franklin is not as fine as I would like" (Miller and McGinnis 2009, 19). Over the next week the baby continued to decline. The flu had either caused or aggravated congenital heart problems. Early on the morning of November 1, Sara Delano Roosevelt recorded in her diary: "The little angel ceased breathing at 7:45. . . . poor E[leanor]'s mother heart is well nigh broken. She so hoped and cannot believe her baby is gone from her" (Lash 1971, 235). Little Franklin Jr. died before he was eight months old. Sara marked her daughter-in-law's bravery and empathized with her grief.

If Eleanor had felt isolated before, now she felt entirely alone. She wore the full black of mourning and blamed herself for not being a more attentive mother. She could not express the depth of her sorrow even to her closest friend—Isabella faced her own crisis. Bob Ferguson was seriously ill with tuberculosis. Isabella and their two small children accompanied him to a sanatorium in upstate New York, where he received treatment. The two young women wrote to each other frequently to offer cheerful support, but Eleanor suffered with depression.

Within two months of Franklin Jr.'s death, Eleanor once more became pregnant. The combination of grief and pregnancy made 1910 a difficult year. Isabella reported that Franklin and Eleanor's fifth anniversary party was delightful, but afterward Eleanor "went all to pieces" (Miller and McGinnis 2009, 23). Eleanor traveled to Hyde Park the next day to spend baby Franklin's first birthday beside his small grave. She later confided to Isabella: "[N]o matter how little one's baby is, something of one's self dies with it. I think it leaves an empty place in one's heart which nothing can ever fill again" (Miller and McGinnis 2009, 41).

Was the fourth pregnancy a determined choice to replace the baby that had died? Eleanor and Franklin had married with the ideal of a large family, but motherhood proved more challenging than Eleanor had anticipated. Options for birth control were few in 1909 and there were social pressures on women to have children. Eleanor's own uncle had spoken out against Margaret Sanger and her attempts at disseminating birth control information. From his presidential bully pulpit, Theodore Roosevelt stated that white Protestant women who didn't have as many children as possible were traitors to their race. They were enabling immigrant races to outpopulate America's founding white Protestant race. Even if she had wished to space her children's births, Eleanor would have had few supporters among her immediate family and friends.

Their fourth child, Elliott Roosevelt, was born on September 23, 1910. Two weeks later, Franklin D. Roosevelt gained the nomination for state senator in New York.

WOMEN SUPPORTING WOMEN

While Eleanor spent most of the summer with the children at Campobello, Franklin sized up his prospects to run for the New York state assembly. When the incumbent Democrat decided to run again, Franklin was left hanging. Then it came to his attention that the state senate position for Dutchess County, where Hyde Park was located, was up for election. No Democrat had won the county for thirty years. If Franklin could flip the county, it would be an important win for the Democrats. Since the eager young Roosevelt could finance the campaign himself, the party leaders nominated him to run for the office.

Over the next few weeks while Eleanor recovered from giving birth to baby Elliott, Franklin traveled the county campaigning. In November, he won the state senate seat for a two-year term.

In November, Eleanor wrote to Isabella about looking for a house to rent in Albany, the New York state capital. For the first time, she would have a voice in where they lived. "I am looking forward to the winter there," she wrote. "It is all so quiet, no crowd, no rush, just stately houses overlooking a broad street with occasional passersby" (Miller and McGinnis 2009, 74). She hoped the slower pace would give her the opportunity to appreciate life.

Eleanor and Isabella had been bolstering each other through trying times. Eleanor faced the one-year anniversary of her baby's death as Bob Ferguson's illness worsened. The Fergusons had moved across the country to a remote area in New Mexico. They hoped the dry mountain air would improve Bob's tuberculosis. There the couple, their two children, and two domestic workers lived in semipermanent tent housing. The former debutante hauled her own water, but found solace in the peacefulness of their rustic life. Each day Isabella watched the wild horses travel through their canyon to evening pasture. In her letters she wished Eleanor similar moments of peace.

As Eleanor prepared to move her household from New York to Albany, she faced a dilemma. Women of her social status typically breastfed their babies for a few weeks at most. Then the children were handed over to a nurse and taught to use a bottle. There was, however, growing evidence among women's health advocates that breastfeeding for several months supported healthier babies.

Eleanor wondered if baby Franklin might have been more robust if he had been breastfed longer. She had no intention of breastfeeding the new baby for longer herself, so she hired a wet nurse. The woman spoke an Eastern European language Eleanor could not identify, and she did not understand English, but if the family was moving to Albany the wet nurse would need to come as well.

To negotiate her long-term hire, Eleanor navigated the tenement streets to locate the woman's dwelling. While her own life had changed over the past seven years, New York's slums had not. Poverty and crowding had worsened.

The desperately poor woman needed to work selling her breast milk in order to care for her own children. Relocating to Albany would necessitate the immigrant woman abandoning her own infant. Eleanor couldn't separate the woman from her child. She opened a bank account to help support the woman's baby and released the woman from her position.

Financially supporting one child wouldn't change the conditions of the New York slums, but it was the best action she could think of at the time. She reconnected with the Junior League and donated money to a charitable organization for impoverished Jewish children. Donations were the only way she felt able to help.

A POLITICAL WIFE IN ALBANY

Eleanor Roosevelt was fond of saying: "For ten years I was always just getting over having a baby or about to have one, and so my occupations were considerably restricted during this period" (Roosevelt 1961, 62). While frequently pregnant, less than six years into their marriage, she started playing an important role in her husband's political career.

The large brownstone house they rented in Albany was just two blocks from the capitol, and on Franklin's first day in office in January 1911, Eleanor oversaw the catering of an open house for over 250 people. Constituents filled the large covered porch and flowed through the house. While Franklin's mother came to assist, this was Eleanor's home and observers noted she managed the house with calm efficiency.

She quickly replaced her domestic staff with individuals of her own choice and supervised a household of three servants and three nurses, one for each child. As a young woman, she had mismanaged her financial allowance and sought assistance from Cousin Susie Parish's banker husband. He had taught her how to budget and manage her funds. Sara Delano Roosevelt was also an astute money manager. She may have added to Eleanor's knowledge on how to administer the family's finances.

There are varying accounts of who managed the Roosevelt finances, but most historians agree it was typically Eleanor, and not Franklin. Sara imprinted her sense of frugality on Eleanor. Franklin frequently overspent and turned to his mother for funds. In a time where men were regarded as the absolute heads of their households, Eleanor, like her mother-in-law and her Roosevelt aunts, was managing the household finances.

Despite having a newborn at home, Eleanor stepped naturally into the role of a political operative. Using Aunt Bye as a role model, Mrs. Franklin D. Roosevelt began making the rounds of political and journalistic connections. Rather than languish at home with the children, she networked. She also stepped into the thick of state politics.

On January 30, 1911, after only a month in Albany, Eleanor wrote to Isabella about her daily trips to sit in the gallery and listen to the discussions on the floor of the statehouse. She claimed it was thrilling to take in the "lively & diverting contest of tongues!" (Miller and McGinnis 2009, 33).

She used the experience to identify the speakers she thought were most effective and those who were not. She critiqued Franklin's public speaking and helped shape his speaking style. She suggested he speak more directly to the needs of his constituents and purposefully use specific facts. She also warned him against wording and gestures that made him appear pompous. Because he frequently wore glasses, Franklin had a tendency to tip his head back and look down his nose. Many people misread the gesture as haughtiness.

Eleanor Roosevelt understood isolation and loneliness. Reaching out to those who were new in town, she built relationships with assemblymen, senators, journalists, and their wives. Being identified with the most popular Republican family in the country while at the same time being married to a Democrat placed her in a unique position to build bridges between disparate sides.

Franklin's first political foray was to join a group of Democrats in opposing the powerful Tammany Hall political organization, which was entrenched in New York politics. At the time U.S. senators from New York were appointed, not elected. The Tammany Hall political bosses planned to select the senator of their choice rather than let the state-elected representatives decide who would fill the senatorial position.

Each night the group of men trying to overthrow the corruption of Tammany Hall met in the Roosevelts' library. ER frequently sat in on the meetings. In her letter to Isabella, she continued: "You have probably seen by the papers what excitement we have had here over the election of a US Senator. We talk & think of nothing else" (Miller and McGinnis 2009, 33). In August, Isabella wrote back: "We've had the pleasure of following Franklin's work this winter[—]that you can imagine—and like to think of the big share that's been yours" (Miller and McGinnis 2009, 34). Friends and family, who knew her best, regarded Eleanor Roosevelt as a political asset to her husband.

THE SPARK OF PROGRESSIVE REFORM

While the state government was in session, ER established a morning routine of engagement at the statehouse or making her rounds. She arrived home for afternoon tea with the children and spent time playing or reading with them until they went to bed.

Evenings were frequently spent in political socializing. Whether it was a small meeting, a reception, or a private dinner, politics filled most of their days. Occasionally, the Roosevelts hosted dinners for up to 100 people.

On Sundays, however, their cook had the night off and dining was casual. Neither Roosevelt was much of a cook, but Franklin boasted of being able to scramble eggs. Informal Sunday night dinners in the Roosevelt kitchen gradually became a gathering of friends and policy makers. Over eggs, cold meat, salad, and some kind of cold dessert, friendly discussions and policy debates became a weekly tradition.

As ER talked with men and women about how they perceived her husband, she discovered that many of the progressive Democrats considered Franklin D. Roosevelt dismissive and unsympathetic toward social reform. Frances Perkins, who was with the Consumers' League, found him to be disinterested in bills on labor reform. Two of New York's leading progressives— Assemblyman Alfred "Al" E. Smith (1873–1944) and State Senator Robert Wagner (1877–1953)—initially found FDR arrogant and self-promoting.

On March 25, 1911, with the legislature still locked in dispute over the choice of the U.S. senator, a fire broke out in one of the new ten-story factory buildings that were springing up in New York City's lower east side. Within eighteen minutes, the fire roared through the Triangle Shirtwaist Factory killing 146 workers—predominantly young immigrant women. Others were injured or killed in rescue attempts.

The next morning, images of young women laid out in rows of open coffins filled the newspapers. Family members walked a gauntlet of bodies trying to identify daughters, sisters, and wives. The innocent female faces sent a shockwave through the nation. The year before, the same faces had gone on strike for safer working conditions. Corrupt police had arrested the strikers, while business owners promised the public that working conditions were safe.

Both Eleanor and Franklin felt "horror" at the news. Since her first days volunteering at the College Settlement, the plight of impoverished women and child laborers had weighed on Eleanor. Purchasing clothing that bore the white label of approval from the Consumers' League and financially contributing to charitable groups no longer seemed adequate. Eleanor Roosevelt needed "to do something as an individual" (Roosevelt, March 25, 1961).

For ER and many others, the Triangle Shirtwaist Factory fire served as a tipping point. They would never forget the tragedy and the individual

THE TRIANGLE SHIRTWAIST FACTORY FIRE

The Triangle Waist Company was the largest manufacturer of women's shirtwaists, or blouses, in New York City. Over 500 workers, mostly young immigrant women, were employed cutting, sewing, and pressing cotton blouses on the top three floors of a ten-story building at Washington Place and Greene Street.

Minutes before the end of their workday, on March 25, 1911, a small fire ignited in a bin of scraps on the eighth floor. Within moments, tissue paper, cotton fabric, and machine oil stoked the fire into an inferno.

The owners testified in court that they feared employee theft. Therefore, workers were searched and required to leave through one elevator. Exits to stairwells were locked. Two additional elevators were initially inaccessible.

Emergency fire hoses did not work. Inward-opening doors delayed escape. A metal fire escape collapsed and twenty-four women fell to their deaths.

Trapped workers crowded at the ninth-floor windows, but fire department ladders and water hoses couldn't reach them. Individuals had a choice: die in the encroaching flames or leap to their deaths. Helpless onlookers watched young women and men die as their bodies smashed to the sidewalk.

Frances Perkins witnessed the "horrifying spectacle" and Assemblyman Al Smith visited each of his constituent families touched by the tragedy. Neither would ever forget the anguish they had seen in the faces of survivors.

Their work investigating the Triangle Fire would influence Eleanor Roosevelt and become the catalyst for safety regulations that protect us everyday: automatic sprinkle systems in high-rise buildings, adequate exit stairwells, unlocked doors during business hours, and more. The next time you push on a safety door that opens out, remember the 146 women and men of the Triangle Shirtwaist Factory fire.

Further Reading

Remembering the 1911 Triangle Factory Fire. 2018. Cornell University. http://trianglefire.ilr.cornell.edu/

Von Drehle, David. 2003. *Triangle: The Fire That Changed America*. New York: Atlantic Monthly Press.

faces of women who died merely trying to support themselves and their families.

The National Consumers' League and the Women's Trade Union League had been trying to improve working conditions for garment workers for over a decade. While conditions had improved to an extent, the tragic fire demonstrated that owners valued profits over workers' lives. Worker safety could not be left to employer magnanimity. True change could only come through laws. Following the tragic industrial fire, Franklin D. Roosevelt supported the fire and worker safety bills brought forward by Frances Perkins and the Factory Investigation Commission (FIC).

After FDR agreed to a compromise with Tammany Hall over the senatorial choice, many Democrats regarded him as disloyal to the party. Alliances and relationships needed rebuilding. Eleanor reached out to both Al Smith and Robert Wagner. Both men were leaders in the reform movement and also served on the FIC. They appreciated her sincere support for social reform and became her trusted allies.

Eleanor regarded her activities in Albany as a wife's obligation to support her husband. This was the model she had observed among her Roosevelt aunts. Women could not vote yet and Eleanor did not actively support women's suffrage. She could, however, advise and assist her husband, and have some influence on how he voted.

"Here in Albany," she wrote, "began for the first time a dual existence for me, which was to last all the rest of my life. Public service, whether my husband was in or out of office, was to be part of our daily life from now on" (Roosevelt 1961, 66). She discounted the public service she had participated in prior to her relationship with Franklin.

She also downplayed her political participation and importance. She painted a picture of herself as a timid mother bullied by her children's nurses and ignorant of politics. Some historians question why Eleanor Roosevelt devalued her own actions and influence. Why did she hide her participation behind a cloak of motherhood and wifely duty?

There is no doubt that the relationship between Eleanor and Franklin strengthened in Albany as she became involved in his political career. Politics united them as partners fighting for a shared goal. She was learning how to be adaptable, more self-reliant, and more self-confident. If she truly was as shy as she protested to be, she had tapped into her personal bravery and risen to a new level of engaging with other people. In Albany, she made a difference and acted with a sense of purpose.

As a young bride, Eleanor Roosevelt had believed that a husband's love could fill all of the empty spaces in her heart. She had had a girl's romantic ideal of love. A loving husband, loving children—her sense of self-worth had depended on these. As she began to play an important role in her husband's life and career, her self-confidence grew; yet, she seemed unwilling to admit that she too had a passion for politics and public service.

SOURCES

Bloom, Amy. 2017, January 31. "The Roosevelts' Wedding Announcement, Annotated." *New York Times*. https://www.nytimes.com/2017/01/31/fashion/eleanor-roosevelt-wedding-announcement.html?module=ConversationPieces&region=Body&action=click&pgtype=article

Cook, Blanche Wiesen. 1992. *Eleanor Roosevelt, Volume 1: 1884–1933*. New York: Viking Penguin.

Lash, Joseph P. 1971. *Eleanor and Franklin: The Story of Their Relationship Based on Eleanor Roosevelt's Private Papers*. New York: W.W. Norton & Company, Inc.

Letter from Theodore Roosevelt to Bessie Van Vorst. Theodore Roosevelt Papers. Library of Congress Manuscript Division. Theodore Roosevelt Digital Library. Dickinson State University. https://www.theo dorerooseveltcenter.org/Research/Digital-Library/Record?libID =o183324

Miller, Kristie, and Robert H. McGinnis, eds. 2009. *A Volume of Friendship: The Letters of Eleanor Roosevelt and Isabella Greenway 1904–1953*. Tucson: The Arizona Historical Society.

Official Inflation Data. 2020. "Inflation Calculator." Alioth Finance. https:// www.officialdata.org

Roosevelt, Eleanor. 1961. *The Autobiography of Eleanor Roosevelt*. New York: Harper Perennial.

Roosevelt, Eleanor. 1961, March 25. Speech made at the *Triangle Fire 50th Anniversary Commemoration, March 25, 1961*. http://trianglefire.ilr .cornell.edu/primary/audio/index

4

Becoming a Political Partner (1912–1918)

On the blizzardy night of January 29, 1912, Eleanor Roosevelt decided not to go and observe the Monday evening session of the New York senate. She wrote to her close friend Isabella Selmes Ferguson: "[H]ave had a lovely evening finishing such an amazing book 'Random Recollections of an old Political Reporter' quite an eye opener as to political methods & chances & of course that is all we talk of now!" Franklin faced reelection in November and Theodore Roosevelt was considering a run in the upcoming presidential election. "How do they feel out your way about Uncle Ted," Eleanor added, "& do you think any other Republican could carry the West against a democrat, say Harmon?" (Miller and McGinnis 2009, 39). Eleanor's letters reveal that rather than the naive political outsider she would later portray herself to be, she was someone who studied political strategy.

At twenty-seven years of age, Eleanor Roosevelt may have defined herself as a wife and mother, but her political instincts made her a vital asset to Franklin's career. She was also determined to play a more active role in helping other people. Being engaged outside of the home helped her focus on the future and not on her personal losses.

THE STATE SENATOR'S WIFE

Eleanor Roosevelt had settled into the life of a state senator's wife. Seasonally, she packed up the household of servants, three children, and multiple pets and moved. After the winter session in Albany, they trooped to Springwood in Hyde Park for a few months, then north to Campobello for the summer. In the fall, the route was completed in reverse.

She had become a statuesque woman dressed in the latest styles and confident in her position. Her brother Hall had graduated from Harvard, Phi Beta Kappa, with an advanced degree in engineering. She had fulfilled her promise to look after her charming and handsome little brother. Like their father, Hall Roosevelt tended to drink and party, but he seemed able to control his alcohol consumption. He was well respected and engaged to be married. Though Eleanor sometimes felt like more of a mother to him than a sister, she felt great pride in the man he'd become.

In the spring, Franklin took Hall to see the Panama Canal under final construction. Eleanor closed up the Albany house, settled the children at Hyde Park, and then traveled to New Orleans to meet up with her returning husband and brother. It was the first time she traveled west of Albany, New York; the first time she saw large expanses of the United States.

From Louisiana, Eleanor and Franklin headed west to visit the Fergusons at their remote canyon in New Mexico. Eleanor watched the vast expanses of Texas roll past the train window. She marveled at the austere beauty of New Mexico's desert landscape but was surprised at Isabella's rugged lifestyle. The Fergusons' home did not have access to electricity or running water. It was a revelation that well-made shoes could be a rare luxury. She promised herself that she would make a greater effort to send items to her friend that would help ease her daily burden.

As Eleanor and Franklin traveled home, they stopped in Baltimore, Maryland, to attend the Democratic National Convention. Running for reelection as state senator, Franklin had no real reason to attend the national gathering. He decided, however, to support Woodrow Wilson (1856–1924) as the Democratic nominee for president and hoped to introduce himself to the Wilson camp. FDR hoped to earn an appointed position in Washington if Wilson won the election.

It was Eleanor's first political convention and she soon tired of the political posturing, the cigar smoke, and the noise. She left for home. She felt obligated to join in her husband's support for Wilson, but she had her own thoughts on the election.

The Republican Party was divided, which she knew would help the Democrats. Uncle Ted had challenged his party to return to social reforms, but he lost the nomination for president to William Howard Taft. A large group of Republicans broke away and nominated Theodore Roosevelt to run as a third-party candidate with the "Bull Moose" or Progressive Party.

Many of the social activists Eleanor admired, Jane Addams and the women of the Settlement Movement, as well as family and friends supported Uncle Ted. The Progressive Party platform focused on women's suffrage, labor reform, and creating a national insurance program to assist accident victims, the elderly, and the unemployed.

Isabella and Bob were supporting Theodore Roosevelt. Eleanor confided to her friend: "I wish Franklin could be fighting now for Uncle Ted, for I feel he is in the Party of the Future" (Miller and McGinnis 2009, 61). When Theodore Roosevelt's campaign came to New York, Eleanor heard him speak. "Uncle Ted's progressive ideas," she confided to Isabella, "have fired so many of the young men to real work in this state that even if he doesn't win this time I feel a big work will have been accomplished" (Miller and McGinnis 2009, 61). As the campaign gathered momentum in November, she added, "I cannot help hoping he will win but if he doesn't this time he will four years from now" (Miller and McGinnis 2009, 62).

As a political wife, Eleanor stood by her husband and his endorsement of Woodrow Wilson. Her personal political beliefs were expressed only in confidence to her close friend. Women didn't have a vote and she still believed her husband's political thoughts superseded her own.

OFF TO WASHINGTON, D.C.

Franklin D. Roosevelt earned his seat back in the New York state senate with the help of a determined campaign manager, Louis Howe (1871–1936). Howe was a chain-smoking man of short stature who many said appeared as if he had slept in his clothes. He was a former newspaper reporter who knew how to sniff out undecided votes and spin situations to Franklin's benefit. Howe recognized that Franklin had the handsome athletic appearance and charming personality people wanted in a leader. He believed Franklin would be president some day and he was determined to help make it happen.

To Eleanor, the political operative was unkempt and low class. Howe's grizzled and scarred face gave him the appearance of a distasteful gnome. Eleanor's parochial childhood whispered in her ear: ugly people are evil, good people are beautiful. Leaning into social snobbishness, she found Howe distasteful.

Howe's constant attention to her husband seemed an invasion of family privacy. Sometimes, she questioned his motives. Yet, there was no denying that Howe had singlehandedly won Franklin D. Roosevelt a second term.

Woodrow Wilson had also won and Franklin secured an appointment as assistant secretary of the Navy, the same position Theodore Roosevelt had held before becoming governor of New York. Within months of his reelection, Franklin resigned his senate seat and Eleanor was packing up the family to move to Washington, D.C. Louis Howe came with them. He would be Franklin's personal assistant at the Navy Department.

In March 1913, the Roosevelts attended Woodrow Wilson's inauguration. Eleanor was less focused on the ceremonial pomp and more on the people. She wrote to Isabella: "The President has none of Uncle Ted's magnetism & really excites little enthusiasm in a crowd so if he becomes popular it will be entirely due to things done." With a dry sense of humor, she also noted that Mrs. Ellen Wilson seemed intelligent, "but was not overburdened with charm" (Miller and McGinnis 2009, 68–70).

Wilson had won the election by cobbling together a coalition of Democratic Party social reformers, Southern segregationists, and conservative Christian fundamentalists. Franklin's new boss, Secretary of Navy Josephus Daniels (1862–1948), a conservative segregationist from North Carolina, was appalled to see that the Roosevelts employed white domestic servants and caregivers for their children. Daniels believed only people of color should be engaged as servants. He adamantly suggested that Eleanor should replace her household staff. She stood her ground and refused to let go of the staff that she relied on and trusted. For the first time she realized that blatant racial prejudice existed—and that Washington was not Albany.

AUNT BYE'S INFLUENCE

Eleanor Roosevelt turned to Aunt Bye for insight pertaining to Washington and her new position as wife of the assistant secretary of the Navy. Despite near deafness and crippling arthritis, Anna "Bye" Roosevelt Cowles remained the wise advisor of the Roosevelt clan. She had been Uncle Ted's political confidante when he served as assistant secretary of the Navy and her husband had had a long career as a naval officer.

Her aunt's advice was simple: support Franklin in his new office and support the Navy. Both Bye and Uncle Ted conveyed to their niece that the families of young naval officers had a difficult time affording life in Washington. She would be in a unique position to advocate for them and network with them. She would be the role model for naval wives and families.

It was no time to be shy. Bye prompted Eleanor to make daily networking calls. The value of personal connections could not be underestimated.

Some Washington wives regarded making daily calls as an old-fashioned exercise and had given up the practice. Cousin Alice Roosevelt was now married to U.S. representative from Ohio, Republican Nicholas Longworth. She preferred to build her network of contacts by throwing notoriously scandalous parties. Eleanor held strongly to social conformity and deeply valued good manners and courteous behavior. She disapproved of Alice's flamboyant lifestyle. The distance between them grew.

Eleanor embraced Aunt Bye's advice. She summoned up her bravery, put on her white gloves, grabbed a stack of calling cards printed with "Mrs. Franklin D. Roosevelt," and had her driver take her from house to house. On Mondays she made a point of visiting the wives of Supreme Court justices, on Tuesdays she met with members of Congress, on Thursdays she met Wilson's Cabinet members, and on Fridays, various diplomats. Wednesday was her at-home day when she received visitors making their own calls. It was not unusual for ER to make sixty social calls in a week. She recalled: "My shyness was wearing off rapidly" (Roosevelt 1961, 72).

Eleanor wrote that Aunt Bye "had great executive ability, poise and judgment." Like Eleanor's father, the woman with lifelong physical disabilities could focus completely on a person and make them feel that what they had to say was of utmost importance. Aunt Bye "listened more than she talked, but what she said was worth listening to!" (Roosevelt 1961, 22). Bye inspired Eleanor. As she made her social calls, she listened, and quickly stood out among other callers.

As Aunt Bye predicted, Eleanor's calls resulted in invitations to dinners where deeper connections could be made and shared goals discussed. Writing in the 1970s, historian Joseph P. Lash viewed ER's role in Washington as merely "to make things easier and pleasanter for him [Franklin D. Roosevelt]" (Lash 1971, 258). But she was doing far more than making life easier; Eleanor Roosevelt built a network of influential people who would become vital to her husband's political career. The Roosevelts attended dinners with Washington's leading influencers and policy makers four to five nights a week. And at least one night a week, Eleanor Roosevelt hosted formal dinners for ten to forty guests.

Bye's home was always filled with interesting people of all ages and interests. Eleanor regarded her aunt's house, wherever it was, as "the meeting place for people from the four corners of the earth" (Roosevelt 1961, 22). Bye and her husband had retired to Connecticut, but they had kept their home in Washington, D.C.

In May 1913, Eleanor and Franklin rented Aunt Bye's Washington house, the former "Little White House." The address was already a frequent meeting place for senior foreign diplomats. ER stepped into her aunt's shoes, entertaining the British and French ambassadors who were close friends of her aunts and Uncle Ted. Eleanor did much more than make Franklin's life pleasant in Washington; she provided him with solid political clout. Historian Blanche Wiesen Cook says of Eleanor Roosevelt: "Old Washington embraced and welcomed her as one of their own; new Washington was enchanted" (Cook 1992, 203). Though Eleanor may have considered herself a quiet introvert, the young Roosevelt couple took Washington by storm.

Even on their "private" evenings, the Roosevelts engaged in political discussion. They continued their Albany practice of informal Sunday dinners with friends. Eleanor scrambled the eggs and "The Club" dined on simple cold fare. But even these "friends" were more highly positioned in the Wilson administration than Franklin. They included Assistant Secretary of the Treasury Charles Hamlin, Secretary of Interior Franklin K. Lane, and Lane's Stanford classmate Adolph Miller who served as his assistant but was an economist. Within the year, Miller would become one of the governors of the newly created Federal Reserve System. Caroline Astor Phillips, related to Eleanor by marriage and a dear friend from New York, came with her husband, William Phillips, a diplomat in the State Department who would later serve as FDR's ambassador to Italy. These powerful men and their wives gathered casually for dinner at the Roosevelts' house at least once a month. The friendships built over scrambled eggs provided the Roosevelts an education in economics and diplomacy.

MANAGING A BUSY HOUSEHOLD

Eleanor's daily life was a balancing act, but she had developed confidence in herself and honed her organizing skills. Each day had a regulated rhythm. The two oldest children had to be taken to school, menus had to be planned, her personal activities mapped out, shopping done, all with time for her to have afternoon tea with the children and read with them before she went out for the evening or hosted an event.

During their first six months in Washington, Aunt Bye recommended Lucy Mercer (1891–1948) as a social secretary to help Eleanor with correspondence. Mercer was socially well connected, but her parents had separated and she needed employment to support herself. She knew the city, and people found her gracious, pretty, and intelligent. Though Mercer was seven years her junior, Eleanor came to think of her as a dependable friend. The children loved her, and Mercer so easily fit in with Washington society that she could be called upon to make an even number at dinner parties. Within a short period of time, Lucy Mercer became part of the Roosevelt household.

Renting Aunt Bye's house was convenient and had political advantages, but the furnishings and the house itself all reflected the older woman. Eleanor was constantly reminded she was living in someone else's home.

Though the task of packing up to leave the city for the summer weighed heavily on Eleanor, the cottage at Campobello was the one place she felt at home. She loved the isolation and the independence it offered her. Days on the beach and hikes along rocky shorelines allowed her to recharge and reconnect with the children.

Franklin stayed in Washington longer than she had hoped, but she could invite whomever she pleased to the remote island. Her mother's youngest sister, Maude, became a frequent houseguest though she had divorced her husband and now had a new male companion. Maude's divorce scandalized Sara Delano Roosevelt, but Eleanor found her aunt's new companion delightful. She exercised her autonomy to invite David Gray to dinners and family picnics.

Several times during the summer, Franklin ventured to Campobello, but only for a short stay. His responsibilities with the Navy demanded more of his time. ER learned naval protocol for addressing officers and boarding ships so that her actions never placed officers or crew in uncomfortable situations.

On one occasion, Secretary of the Navy Daniels invited Eleanor and a group of women to watch a display of target practice from the battleship USS *Rhode Island*. In later years, when ER spoke of this incident, she told the story of a rough sea and a queasy stomach. Like all of the guests, the assistant secretary of the Navy's wife had a junior officer assigned to answer her questions. She recalled the lieutenant asking her if she would be interested in climbing up the mast for a better view? She claimed that without thinking, she said "Yes," just to get her mind off potentially being seasick.

The officer on the *Rhode Island* recounted the day quite differently. He witnessed Eleanor Roosevelt being very interested in all aspects of the ship. Ascending the ship's mast was no momentary diversion. Mrs. Roosevelt had to go downstairs, be fitted with men's clothing, and change into pants before attempting the risky maneuver of climbing the ship's mast. The officer and the sailors all saw one woman over all of the others, who went beyond her comfort zone to do something daring—to share part of their lives. None of the other guests gave it a thought, but Mrs. Roosevelt did what the sailors themselves had to do. To the officers and crew of the *Rhode Island*, Eleanor Roosevelt was not just an official's wife; she was a rare individual to be admired and remembered.

THE RUMBLINGS OF WAR

As 1914 began, Eleanor claimed that her life centered on her family and children. Yet, she had returned to her daily social calls—writing to Isabella on New Year's Day that she and Franklin "stood & shook hands with some 500 hundred [sic] people this afternoon at the [Secretary of the Navy] Daniels until Franklin began introducing me as Mr. Roosevelt!" (Miller and McGinnis 2009, 92). She was still an active public partner despite being three months pregnant and plagued by morning sickness.

In June, she happily retreated to Campobello for the last months of her pregnancy. She had planned on a quiet summer, but news of growing threats of war in Europe consumed the household. Eleanor wrote to Franklin that the children's nurses were gravely concerned for family members in Britain and France. On August 4, 1914, Germany invaded Belgium and World War I began. In Washington, D.C., Franklin D. Roosevelt prepared the U.S. Navy for possible participation in war.

A more personal side of the crisis swirled around Eleanor: the terrors of innocent civilians caught up in the aggression between countries. Her household staff had brothers and other relatives drawn into the fighting. Cousin Susie Parish, her husband, and Isabella's mother had been stranded at a health resort in Czechoslovakia as war swept across the continent. They struggled to get to London and to find transport back to New York. Extended family, like the Fergusons in Scotland, and debutante friends who volunteered as Red Cross nurses entered the conflict as well.

Isabella Ferguson had come east for a visit and for a few days the world was tranquil as the close friends walked the beaches of the "enchanted island." The two women took inspiration from each other that would help them through the coming challenges. Franklin arrived at Campobello just in time to retrieve a local doctor to deliver the baby. For the second time, they named a son Franklin Roosevelt, Jr. Eight-year-old daughter Anna now had three younger brothers: James (six), Elliott (three), and baby Franklin.

A few days before coming up to Campobello, Franklin had announced his intention to run in the Democratic primary for U.S. senator from New York. Eleanor did not participate in the campaign; she and the children stayed at Campobello past the late-September election and into October. There was time to recuperate and to teach the children to swim, ride, and fish. There was time to bond with the new baby and break with convention; she would breastfeed this baby herself. Franklin lost his campaign for U.S. senator.

MARCHING TOWARD WAR

The war in Europe consumed Washington. In her autobiography, Eleanor Roosevelt described the period 1915–1917 as "the battleground of opposing ideas." She wrote about her family "being torn by the differences between Theodore Roosevelt's philosophy and that of President Wilson and his Administration" (Roosevelt 1961, 81). Uncle Ted advocated for action and engagement in the European conflict. President Wilson strongly believed the United States had nothing to gain by entering the fight; he was determined not to be drawn into the war.

Franklin D. Roosevelt believed in the strategies supported by his revered cousin. He was attempting to build up the U.S. Navy in preparation for war but his efforts were hampered by the Wilson administration's policies. Josephus Daniels and other members of the Wilson cabinet held pacifist views. Eleanor found herself surrounded by discussions of military readiness while being drawn toward the arguments for peace.

With each passing day the price of conflict came closer to home. The children's governess had three brothers at the frontlines; one had already been wounded. Bob Ferguson's younger brother fought with the British troops at Gallipoli, a battlefront that would become synonymous with tragic loss of life on both sides.

As events moved the United States closer to involvement in the war, Eleanor and Isabella supported each other through the death of a close friend, Bob's worsening tuberculosis, and Franklin's emergency appendectomy. Isabella reached out to Eleanor: "your life has always been the most invigorating inspiration to mine" (Miller and McGinnis 2009, 113). Eleanor, in turn, regarded Isabella as someone who found joy in life no matter the tremendous burdens she bore. Each inspired the other toward a philosophy of resilience; even when the obstacles they faced seemed insurmountable, they could find a way to meet the challenge. If Isabella could build a home in the New Mexican wilderness and shoulder the responsibilities of her family while her husband's health continued to fail, Eleanor could not complain.

ANOTHER BABY

In November 1915, Eleanor wrote to Isabella that she and Franklin were consumed by "national Defense bills." Would the Congress appropriate the funds needed to prepare the military? On a personal note, she added "We're all very flourishing though as I'm expecting another baby in March, I fear I am not going to be of much use this winter" (Miller and McGinnis 2009, 126). Baby Franklin was not yet a year old when Eleanor became pregnant again. This would be her sixth child in ten years.

Far from being useless, Eleanor Roosevelt took advantage of changing social mores and remained publicly active rather than disappearing into confinement. In her eighth month of pregnancy, she hosted an official event for 225 naval and diplomatic leaders. She continued dining out most evenings and seemed confident as a thirty-one-year-old woman with her finger on the pulse of an edgy capital. Even Cousin Alice commented that Eleanor did her "job in Washington a little bit better than anyone else" (Miller and McGinnis 2009, 137).

Four days before the Roosevelts' eleventh wedding anniversary, Eleanor gave birth to John Aspinwell Roosevelt, a strong, healthy baby. By the end of June, Eleanor started preparations to move with the children from Hyde Park to Campobello for the summer. This time she would follow her own ideal and nurse the new baby for its first six months.

Franklin's visits to Campobello were few and short during the summer of 1916. Naval preparations and campaigning for Wilson's reelection kept him busy, but there seemed more to his absences. Aunt Corrine noted that Eleanor seemed well following John's birth, but she appeared fragile. Eleanor didn't confide in Isabella that she suspected a growing relationship between her husband and her social secretary Lucy Mercer.

Eleanor Roosevelt said little over the course of her life about her husband's extramarital affair, but it forever changed her marriage. Her father's infidelity had been the final cut that ripped her childhood apart. Yet, Eleanor held her mother's judgmental nature to blame for her father's affairs. How did Eleanor see her own role in her unraveling marriage?

The older Roosevelt sons held the opinion that their parents did not have a physically intimate relationship after John was born. Son Elliott would later write that his father was a virile sexual man, while his mother was prudish and aloof. Lucy Mercer was beautiful and sexually magnetic, like his father. He felt that when Eleanor denied Franklin her bed, no one should have been surprised that he turned to Mercer. In his book *An Untold Story; The Roosevelts of Hyde Park*, Elliot claimed that his mother regarded sex as a marital obligation and, after her sixth child she felt her obligation had been fulfilled. Elliott Roosevelt, however, was under eight years old during the troubled years of his parents' marriage. During his entire childhood, Franklin was the father who appeared for brief interludes and frolicked like one of the children. His mother was the day-to-day parent and disciplinarian.

Historian Blanche Wiesen Cook points out that children are notoriously unreliable documentarians of their parents' sexual lives. If Eleanor was an unwilling or reluctant sexual partner, it seems surprising how closely her children were conceived.

After six children in such a short amount of time, the physical consequences were a real consideration. Each of the Roosevelt children weighed ten pounds or more at birth. After her third child, Eleanor underwent surgery for hemorrhoids, which were most likely related to pregnancy.

If contraception was the issue, as son Elliott contends, it seems odd that Franklin wouldn't have introduced his wife to condoms. As assistant secretary of the Navy, he strongly advocated for the distribution of condoms among American sailors during World War I. Military men returning home from Europe displayed high rates of sexually transmitted disease. Condoms would protect these men and reduce the health threat posed by their returning to sexual relations with American partners. If Franklin took the lead in reproductive health for sailors, he should have been able to introduce the idea to his wife.

If Eleanor Roosevelt had no intention of returning to an intimate relationship with her husband, why didn't she display relief when his sexual attention strayed? Instead, she became suspicious and jealous. Her self-confidence and self-respect suffered. She lingered with the children at Hyde Park through Christmas that year, making short trips into New York or Washington. An outbreak of polio had spread through the northeast and Franklin felt it was unsafe for the children to return to the city.

A DECLARATION OF WAR

In early March 1917, Isabella slipped into Washington for a quick visit. The two women spent their time together where they held a shared interest—they sat in the visitors' gallery listening to the Congressional debates on whether or not the country should enter the war. They stayed engrossed in the discussion until two in the morning, but Congress achieved no consensus before the final session ended.

A month later, on April 2, 1917, Eleanor sat in the gallery as Woodrow Wilson asked a joint session of Congress to vote for a declaration of war against Germany. "I listened breathlessly," Eleanor wrote, "and returned home half-dazed by the sense of impending change" (Roosevelt 1961, 245). Entry into the war was a turning point in history. Daily life changed in Washington; social calls ceased altogether. All attention turned to the war effort.

The social reforms of the Progressive Movement were sidelined by the immediate needs of soldiers, refugees, and military conflict. Blockades stopped transportation of food across Europe. The government urged Americans to be frugal and consume less so more food aid could be sent to war-torn countries. In Belgium and northern France civilians starved.

Clothing fell into short supply as wool went unprocessed throughout Europe. Synthetic fibers had not yet been discovered. An international shortage of wool would have serious consequences as winter approached. President Wilson's second wife, First Lady Edith Wilson (1872–1961), grazed a flock of sheep on the White House lawn. She planned to shear the sheep for their wool. Across the United States, volunteers gathered and distributed wool to be knitted into clothing.

As men enlisted into the military, clerical jobs went unfilled. Banks, businesses, and government needed women in the workplace. The Navy Department accepted women into the rank of yeoman to fill clerical and secretarial positions. In the summer of 1917, Lucy Mercer applied and became a Naval Yeoman working directly for FDR. She continued to work for Eleanor three days a week.

Eleanor Roosevelt took the new frugality seriously. She examined the practices in her household and found ways to economize. She must have told others about her efforts, because the Food Administration identified the Roosevelts as demonstrating model practices for a larger household and a reporter from the *New York Times* interviewed her. Eleanor was proud of her actions to reduce food waste and consumption. She gave the reporter an honest interview, seemingly unaware of the differences between her household and most other American households.

With a note of irony, the article detailed how Mrs. Franklin D. Roosevelt did the shopping herself and then instructed her ten servants on how to economize: creating menu items with leftovers, using less laundry soap, and watching each other for waste. It was far from the everyman image that Franklin, as a politician, sought to portray. He dashed off a sarcastic letter to his wife: "[Y]our latest newspaper campaign is a corker and I am proud to be the husband of the Originator, Discoverer and Inventor of the New Household Economy for Millionaires!" (Lash 1971, 290). The incident didn't help the growing tension between them.

The mocking tone of the article had a lasting impact on Eleanor Roosevelt. She felt the reporter had purposefully twisted her words and intentions. It was a serious lesson. She wrote back to Franklin that she would be careful not to be "caught" again.

Historian Blanche Wiesen Cook notes that ER "never again referred publicly even to the existence of her household staff" (Cook 1992, 219). In her writings and interviews she would play down many of her personal attributes: family wealth, elite social status, personal connections, political knowledge, multilingualism, and feminist positions. Going forward, Eleanor Roosevelt paid extreme attention to shaping her public image.

She had already begun managing the appearance of her marriage. Despite a growing animosity between them, Eleanor continued to be the ultimate hostess and political partner. She casually recounted that British and French officials "found their way at times to our home" (Roosevelt 1961, 88). Actually, FDR worked closely with foreign envoys. Her fluency in French gave their home a convivial atmosphere for foreign diplomats.

Washington was at the center of the war effort and Eleanor hesitated to retreat to Campobello for the summer. She questioned if she should stay and fight for her marriage. Neither Franklin nor Eleanor, however, felt ready to directly confront the other. They argued over the necessity to take the children away from the sweltering summer heat of the capital. Ultimately, Eleanor did what was expected of her, she packed up the household and left for Campobello.

She wrote to Franklin of her loneliness and he wrote tales of work and overnight retreats with a list of friends on the Potomac River. Lucy's name was always among the friends and frequently paired with a bachelor pal of Franklin's, a shallow ruse at best. His mother might have believed Franklin's innocence, but Eleanor did not.

Her growing suspicion bred anger and self-doubt. Mercer was younger and prettier. She was carefree and at-ease at rollicking parties. Despite all of her own accomplishments, Eleanor Roosevelt's self-confidence eroded. Her fears of not being good enough and of abandonment fed the growing conflict. An affair between Franklin and Mercer was a double betrayal: betrayal by a husband and a trusted friend. Eleanor retreated into herself, she did not seek advice from her friends or reach out to family. She kept her humiliation a secret.

VOLUNTEERING

In the summer and fall of 1917, Eleanor was desperate to feel valuable. Cousin Ethel, Uncle Ted's younger daughter, had already been in Paris for several years, working as a nurse alongside her surgeon husband and treating soldiers wounded at the front. The male Roosevelt cousins were accepting military commissions and heading to Europe. Even her brother Hall was actively trying to join the newly established military aviation branch alongside Uncle Ted's youngest son, Quentin. Franklin attempted to get an assignment to Europe, but superiors allegedly told him he was too integral to the Navy Department in his administrative position.

Eleanor fantasized about leaving her domestic troubles behind and joining Ethel in Paris, but reality wouldn't let her leave her children. Instead, she committed herself to assisting the Comfort Committee of the Navy League in its relief efforts, which included knitting clothing items for soldiers. She filled every spare moment with knitting.

Beyond knitting items, ER became an organizer. She stockpiled wool to be distributed to knitters at the Roosevelts' Washington home. On Saturdays, they handed out free wool yarn to volunteers and collected completed items. Son Elliott recalled, "[S]he turned our house into a kind of warehouse" (Roosevelt and Brough 1973, 81).

As young men from across the country traveled to training camps and ports of deployment, most arrived on the east coast by train. Sailors and marines transferring between trains filled Washington's Union Station. Layovers could be long. The Navy Red Cross organized a canteen and Eleanor Roosevelt helped serve coffee, baked goods, jam sandwiches, and other light fare.

She described the makeshift shelter as a little tin-roofed shack with an old army kitchen. The canteen provided a place for the men to rest and find free refreshments. Volunteers also sold comfort items: tobacco products, candy bars, and postcards.

Postcards offered a quick way for military men to send a message home. ER and other Red Cross volunteers gathered up the postcards and conveyed them to the post office. The volunteers were also tasked with scanning the notes for security breaches that required censorship; concern about spies in the Capitol ran high. Information on where and when troops were to be

ELEANOR ROOSEVELT, A LIFELONG KNITTER

When did Eleanor Roosevelt knit? While watching children on the beach at Campobello, listening to debates in the U.S. House of Representatives and, thirty years later, during discussions at the United Nations. She was a lifelong knitter and her knitting bag accompanied her around the world.

Eleanor learned to knit as a child, but World War I prompted her to become an avid knitter. Allied forces were unprepared for the war's duration and cold winters. The American Red Cross (ARC) spearheaded knitting of wool socks, mufflers, gloves, sweaters, and headwear for soldiers, refugees, and the recovering wounded. The need only increased when the United States entered the war.

ER joined the national effort, and in her autobiography, she states: "I knitted incessantly." ARC patterns produced utilitarian items. Eleanor knitted similar practical pieces for friends and family. Keeping her hands busy and productive made knitting an active form of relaxation and a comfortable companion. During World War II, she led the national effort to again knit for soldiers and refugees.

Franklin D. Roosevelt's stamp-collecting hobby was frequently covered in popular media, but ER's knitting was regarded merely as a woman's task. Even she seldom mentioned her knitting; it was just part of her daily activity.

For a woman who regarded herself as shy, knitting in public provided an entry into discussions with strangers. Attention was drawn to the project and away from herself. Knitting also connected Eleanor with other women.

Within Eleanor Roosevelt's correspondences, historians have discovered patterns she shared. Through Ravelry, the international online knitting and crocheting community, you can access knitting patterns for "Mrs. Roosevelt's Mittens" and war designs by the American Red Cross.

Further Reading

Habit, Franklin. Winter 2009. "Stitches in Time: Mittens from Mrs. Roosevelt." Knitty. Issue 30. http://knitty.com/ISSUEwinter09/FEATwin09SIT.php
Ravelry. n.d. "American Red Cross." Accessed January 8, 2021. https://www.ravelry.com/designers/american-red-cross

---

deployed required redacting. It was not unusual for 500 postcards or more to be collected in a day. ER convinced the Red Cross that they needed a special unit of volunteers for this large and time-consuming job.

As well as food and rest, Eleanor Roosevelt and all the women at the canteen provided a friendly face and empathetic ear to young men headed far away from their families and home. How many of these young soldiers and sailors would remember a tall, kind woman who showed them motherly or sisterly concern?

She was interacting with a wide range of people she otherwise would not have encountered. She wrote to Isabella: "I see train load after train load go to ports of embarkation & it is a liberal education in the American soldier! My heart aches much of the time" (Miller and McGinnis 2009, 155–156). One afternoon, she encountered a woman she had met at Isabella's in New Mexico. Unintentionally, Eleanor Roosevelt cultivated a public image as an empathetic person, which would follow her and benefit her husband's political career.

Officially, Eleanor worked two to three shifts a week at the canteen, with the expectation of being home in time for tea with the children. Frequently, however, she left the house early in the morning and did not return until nine o'clock at night. Female friends remarked: "Eleanor works all day and half the night" (Miller and McGinnis 2009, 151).

Volunteering at the canteen gave her a sense of purpose during a difficult time in her life. Her managerial skills and willingness to take on any job that needed doing, from mopping the floor to balancing the cash box, quickly moved her into an overseeing position. Other volunteers noted Eleanor's capabilities with handling figures and she took on the general accounting for the canteen.

As work at the canteen provided her a greater sense of personal independence and purpose, Eleanor became less available to her family and husband. She stopped attending parties she considered frivolous. How could she engage in light entertainment after a day of watching young men go off to war? Some of her children regarded her absence as contributing to the growing distance between their parents. Franklin openly escorted Lucy Mercer to evening events while Eleanor volunteered.

GROWING CASUALTIES OF WAR

Eleanor Roosevelt and the Red Cross volunteers added sewing and the preparation of surgical bandages to their work. In the midst of it all, Eleanor moved the five children and the entire household out of Aunt Bye's Washington house and into a larger rented home. The children now ranged in age from eleven years old to almost two years old. With multiple nurses and a governess, a larger house was necessary.

Eleanor also appeared to be making her own preparations; she was reinforcing her relationship with Sara Delano Roosevelt. Personal letters to her mother-in-law became more frequent and effusive. "[H]ow lucky we are to have you and I wish we could always be together," she wrote to Sara. "Very few mothers I know mean as much to their daughters as you do to me" (Cook 1992, 227).

Some historians, including son Elliott, believe Eleanor considered divorce. In the event of such an action, it was imperative to have the sympathies of

ISABELLA SELMES FERGUSON AND THE WOMEN'S LAND ARMY

While Eleanor Roosevelt was volunteering with the American Red Cross, Isabella Ferguson and women in rural communities were maintaining the nation's food resources. Isabella had unique experience managing her family's ranch and organizing her neighbors during border hostilities with Mexico. With the onset of World War I, the governor of New Mexico enlisted her to head the state's branch of the Women's Land Army of America (WLAA).

So many men were serving in World War I, there were not enough agricultural workers to bring in the harvest. Ferguson organized and publicized New Mexico's need for women workers. She oversaw housing for the women and financing to run the state organization.

Harriet Stanton Blanche, daughter of suffragist Elizabeth Cady Stanton, directed the WLAA and many of the first enlistees were women from eastern colleges. The WLAA incorporated labor reforms into its structure: women worked eight-hour days and they were paid wages equal to men.

Isabella worked alongside the women of the WLAA in New Mexico, cutting hay and processing silage for livestock feed. They harvested corn and, according to her accounts, filled over a hundred railroad cars with apples. The WLAA kept food flowing into American cities.

Isabella's civic work established her among western politicians and government officials. She would become an important businesswoman and, as Isabella Greenway (the surname of her second husband), the first woman to represent Arizona in the U.S. House of Representatives in 1933.

Further Reading

Miller, Kristie, and Robert H. McGinnis, eds. 2009. *A Volume of Friendship: The Letters of Eleanor Roosevelt and Isabella Greenway 1904–1953*. Tucson: The Arizona Historical Society.

Spring, Kelly A. 2017. "Women's Land Army of World War I." National Women's History Museum. https://www.womenshistory.org/resources/general/womens-land-army-world-war-i

her mother-in-law. Other biographers point out that as Franklin became more engaged in the war effort, Eleanor had become more dependent on her mother-in-law to care for the children at Hyde Park. Even when Eleanor went to Campobello with the children, Sara's proximity as a neighbor meant the older woman could be depended on for assistance. They were both strong women and though they frequently did not agree, they were both invested in the five Roosevelt children.

After Alice Roosevelt Longworth spotted Franklin driving with Lucy Mercer in the countryside, she mischievously began inviting the pair to her parties. Alice seemed to revel in knowing the secret of Eleanor's humiliation and making it public. Throughout her life, Cousin Alice had bristled to hear her father aligned with Eleanor's good works. Highlighting Franklin's infidelity demeaned Cousin Eleanor; it might have also deflected attention from her own husband's affairs.

Through the spring of 1918, Franklin D. Roosevelt and Lucy Mercer became a common fixture on the Washington social scene. Eleanor's family members, many coworkers at the canteen, and most of the political class of Washington, D.C., knew of the affair. Franklin even enlisted their shared friends to facilitate his meetings with his mistress and made no attempt to protect Eleanor from the growing gossip.

In response to her personal strife, Eleanor Roosevelt focused outside of herself. The Red Cross asked her to visit "shell-shocked patients" at the naval veterans' ward at St. Elizabeth's Hospital. The patients were men who had returned from the war in Europe with what we now know as post-traumatic stress disorder (PTSD). Many had suffered extreme trauma during the hand-to-hand trench fighting, constant shelling, and toxic gas attacks commonplace in World War I.

Entering the special ward of the hospital, Eleanor faced an old fear. As the daughter and niece of men with substance use disorders, she knew the anxiety of living in a household with individuals whose behavior was unpredictable. She had an aversion to people who were unable to control their emotions or actions. The ward's metal security door slammed behind her and the head physician locked the door. The sound became etched into her memory; she felt as confined as the patients.

In 1918, a wing at St. Elizabeth's Hospital was one of the few federally funded psychiatric health facilities. It had always been underfunded and inadequately staffed. The number of veterans returning with serious PTSD and other psychiatric illnesses overwhelmed the facility. The sight of young men unattended in padded cells because of a lack of hospital staff haunted Eleanor. Young soldiers who trembled uncontrollably were chained to beds for their own protection. She felt deeply that these men who had fought on behalf of their country deserved better.

Eleanor Roosevelt overcame her apprehension and visited the patients in the psychiatric hospital one day a week. She had known depression after the death of her third child. She empathized with the young men who had survived night after night of bombing at Dunkirk trapped in underground cellars and powerless to protect themselves or others. Through personal interaction, she came to believe many of them could be helped with adequately funded treatment.

In her own life, Eleanor knew the therapeutic impact of purposeful work. At an orphanage and a home for the elderly, she had seen the positive results of occupational therapy. Individuals found solace in the making of useful items that could then be sold. Here, she saw men sitting with nothing to engage them but their own troubled thoughts.

At the time, veterans' affairs fell under the Department of the Interior. ER reached out to Secretary of Interior Franklin Lane who had eaten dinner so many times in her kitchen on Sunday nights. She believed conditions at the hospital should be investigated. Lane agreed to look into the matter, but Eleanor tenaciously implored him to personally visit the facility. When he finally did visit, Lane immediately initiated a congressional investigation. Congress appropriated more funding and turned St. Elizabeth's entire facility over to caring for veterans' mental health. It became a model for psychiatric hospitals across the country.

Eleanor Roosevelt wrote in her memoirs that she "begged" the Red Cross to fund the building of a recreation room at the hospital. Uncle Ted was so impressed by Eleanor's efforts on behalf of the veterans, he donated a third of his Nobel Peace Prize money to her efforts. Then she turned to the National Society of Colonial Dames of America to fund materials to start an occupational therapy program. The program became self-sustaining as the men sold what they produced.

She had developed a skill: recognizing a problem and knowing how to connect people and resources together to solve that problem. When a wounded soldier from Texas recovered his health, but didn't have the funds to return home, she reached out to the Daughters of the Confederacy to underwrite his ticket home. Her successes were rebuilding her self-confidence.

As the summer heat fell over Washington, D.C., Eleanor took the children to Hyde Park to stay with her mother-in-law. She returned to the city to work at the canteen and keep an eye on her husband.

In July, the reality of war struck the Roosevelt clan. Quentin Roosevelt, Theodore's youngest son, was killed when his plane was shot down over France. Franklin did not receive a commission, but he sailed to Europe to evaluate American ships, naval bases, and aviation fields.

During his absence, Eleanor stayed in Washington working at the canteen until one or two o'clock in the morning. She wrote frequently to Sara, checking on the children and deepening her connection with her mother-in-law. With her husband away, she had the chauffer teach her to drive. When she visited Hyde Park, she forced herself to get back in the water and swim. She was strengthening her resolve and challenging herself to face what she didn't think she could do. Her son Elliott believed she was preparing to be an independent and possibly divorced woman.

On September 12, 1918, Franklin was on a steamship headed back into New York harbor. On the voyage home, most of the passengers had become sick with the highly infectious H1N1 influenza, a deadly strain of flu that was sweeping across Europe and Britain. Numerous Americans returning home from the war had died on the ship and been buried at sea. Franklin sent a cable ahead for Eleanor to meet him at the dock with an ambulance. His flu had advanced into double pneumonia.

While Franklin was seriously ill, the family doctor determined that home was a safer place to convalesce. Their townhouse was rented, so they made him comfortable in his mother's master bedroom. As Eleanor unpacked her husband's luggage, she came across a neatly tied bundle of love letters from Lucy Mercer—explicit evidence of their ongoing affair.

Some accounts mark this as the moment Eleanor realized her husband's infidelity; others see it as the moment she finally held the legal proof of adultery in her hands and the grounds to file for divorce in the state of New York. Either way, the Roosevelt marriage became another casualty of the war.

THE CALCULATED PARTNERSHIP

There are only three people who truly know what happened behind closed doors: Eleanor, Franklin, and Sara Delano Roosevelt. None of them ever spoke openly of the diplomatic wrangling and emotional cost of the negotiations that took place.

Just over a week after Franklin's return, while he was still ill with pneumonia, Eleanor confronted him regarding his relationship with Lucy Mercer. She offered to give Franklin a divorce.

Elliot Roosevelt strongly believed his mother "preferred a divorce" (Roosevelt and Brough 1973, 92). She had been betrayed and publicly humiliated. Divorce was an active choice to move forward and reclaim her self-respect. Though still regarded as scandalous by some, divorce had become more common as women sought social and political autonomy. Eleanor's aunt Maude had divorced and found happiness in a second marriage. Eleanor was not quite thirty-four years old; she had her own finances and reputation; perhaps there could be another, happier future for her.

Elliott and historians close to the family agree that Franklin openly desired to start a new life with Lucy Mercer. But just as Sara Delano Roosevelt had weighed in on Eleanor and Franklin's marriage, she now employed her influence to stop what she saw as the destruction of the Delano and Roosevelt family names. She laid down a stern ultimatum: Franklin could choose that woman or he could choose his wife, children, family inheritance, and the financial backing to support his political career. If he chose Lucy Mercer, he would lose his father's Springwood estate and any claim to the Delano Roosevelt fortune.

There is no doubt that Franklin consulted his political advisor Louis Howe. Into the twenty-first century, divorce constituted political suicide. Howe assured Franklin that his political career would end if he divorced

Eleanor. Not only did he need his mother's financial backing, he also needed Eleanor's political connections and talents. Some historians also believe Howe influenced Eleanor's final decision to stay in the marriage. He may have advised her that her position as Franklin D. Roosevelt's wife would give her greater political power to pursue her own goals.

There were other forces at play as well. The very conservative Secretary of Navy Daniels would likely have fired Franklin from the Navy Department if he divorced. Other historians document that Franklin had established a lifestyle he could not financially support without assistance from his mother. Sara Delano Roosevelt paid for his memberships in all of the New York and Washington social clubs. She supported his hobby as a collector of stamps, books, art, and model ships. She was always available to write the check for his excessive expenditures.

In the end, Franklin D. Roosevelt chose his political career over Lucy Mercer. He deceptively told Mercer that Eleanor would not let him out of the marriage.

Publicly the Roosevelts appeared to stay together for the sake of their children; none of the children, however, believed this account. Within the family it was understood that an agreement had been struck between the three Roosevelts. Sara would continue to provide financial support for Franklin's political career and he would continue to be the family heir. Eleanor would maintain the appearance of a happy marriage and support her husband's political endeavors. And, Franklin would agree never to see Lucy Mercer again.

Eleanor Roosevelt confided to biographer Joseph P. Lash: "I can forgive, but I can't forget" (Lash 1971, 302). In the wake of such a scarring betrayal, she burned most of Franklin's love letters from their courtship days.

For Eleanor, there seemed to be only one person who would always be faithful to her—the memory of her father. His letters still spoke to her across the years. But she had found something that fed her soul, the same path that had originally opened to her as a young woman—working to help others. She had seen this model in Uncle Ted and she now shouldered this mantle for herself. In choosing to stay in her marriage, she also chose political power and the opportunity to bring about positive change for others.

SOURCES

Cook, Blanche Wiesen. 1992. *Eleanor Roosevelt, Volume 1: 1884–1933*. New York: Viking Penguin.

Lash, Joseph P. 1971. *Eleanor and Franklin: The Story of Their Relationship Based on Eleanor Roosevelt's Private Papers*. New York: W.W. Norton & Company, Inc.

Miller, Kristie, and Robert H. McGinnis, eds. 2009. *A Volume of Friendship: The Letters of Eleanor Roosevelt and Isabella Greenway 1904–1953*. Tucson: The Arizona Historical Society.

Roosevelt, Eleanor. 1961. *The Autobiography of Eleanor Roosevelt*. New York: Harper Perennial.

Roosevelt, Elliott, and James Brough. 1973. *An Untold Story: The Roosevelts of Hyde Park*. New York: G.P. Putnam's Sons.

5

New Friends, New Activism, and New Purpose (1919–1921)

"The bottom dropped out of my own particular world," Eleanor Roosevelt confided to biographer Joseph P. Lash. Coming face to face with the reality of Franklin's love for another woman marked the end of her romantic illusions. Despite the fact that they had six children together, her husband would rather be married to someone else. It was a crushing blow to her self-esteem and her fragile self-confidence. "I faced myself, my surroundings, my world honestly for the first time," Eleanor wrote. "I really grew up that year" (Lash 1971, 302).

Eleanor kept her anguish private; she did not write to Isabella for nearly a year. The two women were each struggling through personal challenges and chose not to burden each other. While she shared some personal thoughts with her mother-in-law, she felt she had no one she could confide in.

Gradually, her resentment turned toward Sara Delano Roosevelt. The matriarch held sway over Franklin and, frequently, over the grandchildren. Demanding that Franklin forswear Lucy Mercer did not erase the other woman from his heart. Eleanor questioned why she had made the bargain to stay in the marriage. Eventually, she would need to discover what she wanted as an individual and how she could accomplish her desires within their marital arrangement.

There was no specific moment when she transformed into a strong, independent woman. Change was a gradual and difficult process. The next few years were a roller coaster of depression and self-doubt countered with expansive new understandings of herself and her place in the world.

When Eleanor finally did write to Isabella on July 11, 1919, she alluded to her desperation. "This past year has rather got the better of me it has been so full of all kinds of things that I still have a breathless, hunted feeling about it though for the moment I am leading an idle if at times a somewhat trying life!" (Miller and McGinnis 2009, 160).

THE INFLUENZA PANDEMIC

The last few months of 1918 passed in a blur for Eleanor. With their emotional lines drawn, she and Franklin returned to Washington. Instead of having time to heal, they became immersed in a public health crisis. The H1N1 influenza that traveled back and forth on military transport ships between Europe and the United States ignited a deadly pandemic.

The first deaths had been documented in March 1918 at a military camp in Kansas. American troop transports heading to Europe in May delivered waves of the illness. The infectious virus swept across the European continent and Britain. By October, the influenza raged along the eastern coast of the United States.

When Franklin returned home from Europe, he suffered from flu that had advanced into pneumonia. Soon, all of the Roosevelt children and three of the servants fell ill with the virus.

Unlike most strains of influenza, the 1918 H1N1 virus was most dangerous to healthy adults between the ages of twenty and forty; men between twenty-five and thirty-five years of age were most likely to die. In October 1918 alone, as Eleanor nursed her family, 195,000 Americans perished. Cities were overwhelmed. Bodies were stacked in cold warehouses in Philadelphia because of a lack of people and resources to bury them.

In Washington, the Red Cross begged its volunteers to staff and provision soup stations to distribute food to people in need. Each day, the Roosevelts' cook made gallons of soup, and Eleanor risked going out into the ravaged city to deliver it.

In the midst of the pandemic, World War I ended. On November 11, 1918, an armistice was agreed upon, and hostilities were stopped. Washington and the nation erupted in happy relief, but the celebration was momentary. The pandemic raged on.

Schools and churches closed. Households, ports, and neighborhoods were quarantined. Cities passed ordinances banning public assembly and requiring individuals to wear face masks. Some localities threatened citizens with fines or arrest for noncompliance.

Men returning home from the war brought new waves of illness. The deadly virus was carried around the world to every continent. Records of the U.S. Center for Disease Control report that in less than a year, the influenza killed 675,000 people in the United States. More American soldiers died from the flu than in combat during the war. Many American families lost their primary wage earner and fell into poverty. Around the world, fifty million people died.

The Roosevelts benefited from their affluence; they could afford medical care. Their large house enabled Eleanor to quarantine the sickest family members in their own rooms. None of her family perished in the pandemic. She witnessed how a lack of access to medical care impacted poor families and households of color; they were more likely to lose family members than the affluent. Long-term side effects among survivors, however, crossed economic classes. Franklin's vulnerability to respiratory illnesses for the rest of his life was most likely connected to his battle with the deadly flu.

During the dark days of nursing and ever-looming death, Eleanor considered her life and her situation. She blamed her mother for being cold and judgmental toward her father. Perhaps if her mother had been more forgiving, her father might have survived.

As health returned to their family and the nation, Franklin extended an olive branch. Perhaps if they could each try to be more of what the other desired and expected in a partner, they could revive their relationship. He devoted more time to the children and family. She joined him at social events and tried to be more lighthearted and fun. There were still tense moments and occasional harsh words, but both made an attempt to rekindle trust and respect.

DIPLOMATIC ASSET

In January 1919, despite Franklin's recent recovery from pneumonia, the Navy Department deployed him to Europe. As military forces withdrew from the continent, they needed his executive management skills to identify American property worth shipping back to the United States and resources that should be sold.

A two-month separation could have doomed the Roosevelts' tenuous marriage. Sara Delano Roosevelt pushed for Franklin to take Eleanor. Travel might bring them together. While it was typically against policy for lower-level government officials to take spouses on foreign assignments, especially into a recent war zone, Franklin was able to get a special dispensation for Eleanor to travel with him to France.

On this voyage across the Atlantic, Eleanor felt at ease. She had become a confident sailor and swimmer. Though other passengers recorded a rough crossing, she engaged daily in on-deck activities. She actively reached out to other passengers, making a profound impression on investor and philanthropist Bernard Baruch (1870–1965). The successful Wall

Street speculator and economic adviser to President Wilson was journeying to the peace negotiations. Seasickness kept him in his stateroom during much of the crossing, but he sent roses to Eleanor when they arrived in port. It was the beginning of a lifelong friendship that would challenge her superficial preconceptions about Jewish people.

The ship also transported the Chinese and Mexican delegations to the peace talks in France. All of these high-ranking diplomats spoke French, the diplomatic language of the time. ER eagerly conversed with them and hosted a tea in their honor during the crossing, proving to be a political asset not just for Franklin but also for the American government.

While the Roosevelts were crossing the Atlantic, word came that on January 6, 1919, after a short period of ill health, Uncle Ted had died in his sleep from a pulmonary embolism. Theodore Roosevelt's death at sixty years of age shocked not just America but the world. For the diplomats on board, Eleanor Roosevelt was a connection to the world's most famous international diplomat. She wrote little of her feelings regarding Theodore's passing. He was one of her few connections to the father she cherished. As the Roosevelts traveled through Europe, they encountered multiple tributes to Eleanor's charismatic uncle.

THE AFTERMATH OF WORLD WAR I

The Europe that greeted them had been transformed by war. All of France appeared to be in mourning. "Every other woman," Eleanor wrote in her diary, "wears a crepe veil to her knees" (Lash 1971, 316). Approximately 1,400,000 French soldiers had died; more than half of the French military had been killed or wounded.

Disabling injuries and disfigurement impacted thousands. In Paris, ER visited hospitals with First Lady Wilson, finding her heroic in the face of the gruesome injuries they saw there. Edith Wilson stopped and gazed into each disfigured face requiring reconstruction and interacted with the person behind the injury. Eleanor steeled herself to do the same. She held one thought in her mind—she could walk away from the horror; these people would live with their disfigurement every day for the rest of their lives; for them, the war would never be healed.

Traveling from Paris to Boulogne with Franklin and his entourage, the landscape became brutally alien. The tranquil green countryside that she loved had been trampled and torn open. Miles of deep trenches created muddy gouges in the earth.

Here and there a wooden marker with a name scrawled across it rose precariously from a small pile of rocks. Each marker stood like a tombstone for a quaint village or romantic town that had been obliterated from the map.

Civilization seemed to have turned on itself with cities reduced to a skeleton of bombed rubble. Cathedrals appeared purposefully destroyed, forests reduced to stands of bare stumps.

"I do not think one can quite realize without seeing," Eleanor wrote. "Bourlon Wood[,] with its few bare sticks to mark what once had been[,] gave one an even more ghostly feeling than the shelled & ruined towns." The destruction haunted them as they drove across the countryside. "The sea of mud on every side also must be seen to be fully realized & what the men who fought there lived through is inconceivable" (Miller and McGinnis 2009, 161).

Witnessing the devastation caused by World War I influenced Eleanor Roosevelt for the rest of her life. The war created over five million orphans. If this was what winning the war looked like—destroyed landscapes, shattered lives, and overwhelming emptiness—then surely future leaders would prefer peaceful diplomacy to warfare.

There were moments of shared loss that brought Eleanor and Franklin together, but there were also late nights alone for Eleanor as Franklin socialized with military and foreign leaders. Mistrust lingered in her heart. Rather than sulk, however, she spoke up for her hurt feelings and voiced her complaints. Still, depression seeped in along with moments of blaming herself for not being as pretty or as vivacious as Lucy Mercer.

As they headed to the port to catch their ship home, word came that the peace talks had resulted in a charter for a League of Nations. A reporter supplied the Roosevelts with a copy of the document. "What hopes we had that this League would really prove the instrument for the prevention of future wars," Eleanor wrote, ". . . and how eagerly we read it through!" (Roosevelt 1961, 101).

Eleanor and Franklin sailed back to the United States on the same ship as President and First Lady Wilson. There was a feeling of a positive outcome from a horrible war. Eleanor took the sense of a new beginning to heart and applied it toward her own life.

Upon returning home, she attempted to sweep clean her past feelings of inadequacy. She replaced her entire household staff. The cook and housemaid may have helped economize during the war, but they also had known about and potentially enabled Franklin's affair with Mercer. Governesses who had bullied her or pushed their own agendas for how the children should be educated were let go. Eleanor Roosevelt's new staff would be loyal to her.

THE RED SUMMER OF 1919

As soldiers returned to reclaim employment, they pushed aside African Americans who had stepped in to fill open positions during the war. ER made the choice, in the face of political opposition, to hire an all–African American staff. This was exactly the opposite of the position she had taken when she first arrived in Washington, D.C. This time, however, she was actively choosing to support employment of a racial group otherwise being denied employment.

While Eleanor's action appeared liberal-minded, she continued to be an elite, upper-class New Yorker who didn't quite trust African Americans. Her intentions were admirable, but she still harbored stereotypical opinions toward people of color.

When race riots flared up during the Red Summer of 1919, Eleanor showed concern for Franklin's safety in the city but never inquired about the safety of her African American servants. White sailors roamed the capital's African American neighborhoods allegedly searching for an individual who had insulted an officer's wife. They dragged innocent Black men out of their homes to beat and lynch them. Women and children were injured. When the police did nothing to stop the violence, the African American community protected themselves, and the situation escalated. Eventually the military was brought in to stop the violence.

Across the country African American soldiers returning from Europe spoke out for equal access to public spaces: parks, beaches, and businesses. They demanded equal access to job opportunities. As W. E. B. Du Bois wrote in his May 1919 essay "Returning Soldiers," African American soldiers had saved democracy in France, and "we will save it in the United States of America, or know the reason why."

The segregationist policies of the Wilson administration, however, did not align with equal benefits of democracy for all citizens. Nor did the government provide protection when Ku Klux Klan members marched through African American neighborhoods to intimidate and oppress.

Poor immigrant populations also felt left out of the American dream. Worker organizations, including labor unions, had members who felt so disenfranchised that they embraced communist philosophies and anarchist activities.

Wilson's attorney general, A. Mitchell Palmer (1872–1936), regarded all labor unions as hotbeds of anarchist terrorist activity. He and his protégée J. Edgar Hoover (1895–1972) used informants and spies to infiltrate unions and labor-supporting groups. Palmer considered anyone opposed to President Wilson as a threat. Union members were routinely intimidated and beaten. Animosity toward the attorney general mounted, and on the night of June 2, 1919, a bomb exploded at the front door of Palmer's home.

Attorney General Palmer lived across the street from the Roosevelts in Washington. Eleanor and Franklin returned home from an evening out to find a swarm of police officers, the front windows of their home shattered, and bits of blood and bone from the bomber on their doorstep.

Eleanor supported the National Consumers' League and female workers, but here was a tangible threat of violence on her family's doorstep. Supporting labor reforms no longer seemed a straightforward proposition.

THE STATUE OF "GRIEF"

While Americans rejoiced that the war was over and the pandemic was subsiding, Eleanor seemed stuck in a cycle of despair. Franklin would flirt with other women and stay out late. On one occasion he danced with Lucy Mercer at an event while Eleanor watched. Each time her self-confidence started to return, it would be dashed by an incident that made her feel like the awkward child who had never been good enough.

During this turbulent period, Eleanor discovered the unique memorial for the wife of a Washington insider, Henry Adams (1838–1918). Adams was a distinguished historian descended from two American presidents: political icons John Adams and John Quincy Adams. Eleanor admired Adams's ancestry but appreciated him as a kindly older gentleman who had befriended her.

His wife had died the year before Eleanor was born. Marian "Clover" Hooper Adams had been an independent woman, a celebrated Washington hostess, and a professional photographer during the Civil War. At age forty-two, she committed suicide by drinking potassium cyanide, one of the chemicals used in developing photographs.

Her father's death had weighed on her, and she battled depression. Some Washington insiders, however, felt her despondency grew out of Adams's suppression of her career. Others speculated she had committed suicide after discovering her husband's romantic involvement with another woman. Clover's story spoke to Eleanor Roosevelt; she felt a connection to this woman and her anguish. However, one major difference between them was that Eleanor had five young children.

A larger-than-life bronze sculpture marked Clover Adams's grave at Rock Creek Cemetery. Eleanor frequently went out of her way to spend time in contemplation before the statue. The seated bronze figure draped in a cloak, its face somewhat shrouded, was a mirror for her turbulent thoughts. Depending on her emotional state, its serene face with eyes closed could be silent in sorrow or lost in thought. Genderless and inherently calm, the bronze figure was an open well absorbing Eleanor's sorrow and anger. Each of Eleanor's visits to the grave filled a specific moment's need and ultimately provided a sense of peace.

All of Franklin's traits that had drawn Eleanor to him—his charming flirtatiousness, carefree nature, and gregarious personality—were now the traits that brought her pain. She was coming to realize that he had not changed; it was her perception of him and her expectations that had changed. Though they both thrived in politics, the way they approached life was different. To stay in the marriage, she had to determine what she wanted from her life, not what he or anyone else expected of her.

QUESTIONING HER ROLE AS A MOTHER

As Eleanor sought direction, the women's suffrage movement captured her interest for the first time. As a Roosevelt, she had followed the lead of her aunts Bye and Corinne, who didn't believe that women needed the right to vote. The men in their lives had always included them in political discussions. Even as president, Theodore Roosevelt had considered his sisters and wife as important political advisers.

In the spring of 1919, an amendment to the Constitution was being seriously proposed, which would give women the right to vote in all elections. Once approved in Congress, on June 4, the Nineteenth Amendment went to the states for ratification. Female anti-suffrage groups, opposed to the amendment, approached Eleanor Roosevelt, but she did not support their efforts. Before his death, Uncle Ted had come out in support of women's suffrage, and she had begun leaning in that direction as well. Her turbulent personal life, however, kept her from engaging in the battle to ratify the Nineteenth Amendment.

On the twenty-fifth anniversary of her father's death, Eleanor's grandmother Mary Hall died. Through the lens of her own situation, Eleanor saw a warning in the legacy of the woman who had raised her. She believed Grandmother Hall had forfeited her own opportunities for personal fulfillment as a painter by concentrating her life on her children. She also believed Mary Hall's single-minded behavior had made her children overly dependent, rather than benefiting them. Eleanor laid the blame for her Hall uncles' alcoholism on the indulgence of her grandmother.

The only aspect of her life Eleanor believed she could control was her children; she became fiercely strict. When school grades dropped, she increased study hours. She demanded the children be held accountable for their behavior and actions, but without support from Franklin, the children came to resent her punitive measures. As tensions flared between Eleanor and Franklin, the children increasingly viewed "Granny's" home as a sanctuary. Especially over the summer, the older children chose to stay at Hyde Park with their grandmother.

Eleanor became indignant when her mother-in-law replaced broken or lost toys or other items. She felt that Sara purposefully spoiled the children and actively gave them things she had forbidden. Pointing to the parenting mistakes she attributed to Mary Hall, she gave herself an excuse for her unsentimental mothering style. Like her own mother, Eleanor seemed to have difficulty relating to young children. It didn't help that during her children's early years she had been engulfed in marital strife. She excused her own aloofness and claimed it helped strengthen the children's character. She also gave herself permission to look beyond motherhood for a life purpose.

Eleanor spent her thirty-fifth birthday alone. The children were at Hyde Park and Franklin was away. She wrote to Isabella about her work winding up the Navy Red Cross activities and advocating for the establishment of women's restrooms at a Navy Department facility. She desperately yearned to see her close friend. "I need your help & advice in so many ways," she wrote on October 26, 1919, "for I never want anyone as I want you" (Miller and McGinnis 2007, 169). But she chose not to put the cause of her strife on paper.

A TURNING POINT

Two days later, Eleanor Roosevelt's life came to another turning point— one of those moments that have a profound impact on the future without being obvious. As she was the wife of a government official and also possessed foreign language skills, the International Congress for Women Workers asked ER to volunteer as a translator for foreign delegates.

The female activists' goals aligned with those that ER had supported with the National Consumers' League: an eight-hour workday and laws regarding maternity benefits. In addition, there were issues and viewpoints that were new to her. The Negro Women Laborers of the United States presented a petition signed by two million African American women seeking assistance in forming a union. Eleanor also met female labor leaders, like Rose Schneiderman of the Cap Makers' Union, who were laborers themselves.

These women impressed Eleanor Roosevelt. These weren't wealthy women acting philanthropically; they were women workers speaking with fervor and determination toward their own needs and goals. Following the conference, ER invited the American leadership to lunch at her home. Schneiderman and Leonora O'Reilly of the Women's Trade Union League, leaders from the International Ladies' Garment Workers' Union, telephone operators' union, teacher unions, and Federal Employees Union represented a new world of activism to Eleanor; in them, she saw a new network of future friends and colleagues.

How she would be involved in this new world was still unknown to her. At the end of the year, Eleanor wrote in her diary: "I do not think I have ever felt so strangely as in the past year, perhaps it is that I have never noticed little things before but all my self-confidence is gone and I am on edge" (Lash 1971, 324). She was still trying to find her way, find herself, and find a purpose; change would come in small steps.

Historian Blanche Wiesen Cook believes Eleanor's repeated pilgrimages to the Clover Adams memorial helped her find answers within herself. The tranquil site provided a place for meditation and private thought.

Eleanor knew other women who had reinvented their lives. Aunt Bye had been labeled a spinster, even by family members, but had redirected her future by marrying at age forty-two and having a child. Marie Souvestre had built an entire school in Britain after losing a partner and a career in France. Recently widowed, Aunt Corinne had left the quiet of her Connecticut farm to become a highly regarded public speaker, adding a female Roosevelt voice to politics. Likewise, Eleanor reshaped the personal philosophy that would evolve and guide the rest of her life: You can't depend on others to secure your personal happiness. You can't live your life for others. You must live your life for yourself; only then can you give portions of that life to others.

AN UNEXPECTED CAMPAIGN

Louis Howe and his family joined the Roosevelts at Hyde Park for Christmas dinner, just as they had for Thanksgiving. Both Eleanor and her mother-in-law grudgingly accepted Howe, finding his wife Grace and their two children pleasant enough. But neither woman understood why Franklin included his employee and the employee's dependents in Roosevelt family gatherings.

Franklin's devotion was a reciprocation of Howe's loyalty. Despite a low salary at the Navy Department that left his family nearly evicted from their home, Howe had remained Franklin's acquisitions dealmaker throughout the war. Inclusion at the Roosevelt table enabled Howe's family to celebrate the holidays in a manner they otherwise wouldn't have been able to afford. Franklin also wanted Howe near because they were planning his next political step.

During the war, Franklin had been behind a desk and out of the public eye. 1920 was a presidential election year. President Wilson had become desperately unpopular and his health was deteriorating. Political opportunity was in the air.

Bolstered by a visit to Isabella, Eleanor chose not to accompany Franklin to the Democratic Party Convention in California. She took the children to Campobello Island for the summer. When a telegram arrived congratulating her and the family on Franklin's nomination to the Democratic Party ticket as vice president, it stunned Eleanor. Considering the personal conflict of the last several years, it is not surprising she "felt detached and objective, as though [she] were looking at someone else's life" (Roosevelt 1961, 107). She had to wonder if their scarred personal life would become public. How much of her growing independence would she have to sacrifice?

Franklin D. Roosevelt's addition to the Democratic ticket with midwestern candidate James M. Cox had been a last-minute compromise. Eleanor had no voice in Franklin's decision to run for vice president and she sought to play no role in the campaign.

Franklin resigned from the Navy Department and Eleanor moved the household back to New York. By fall, Franklin was campaigning by train across the country. He left Louis Howe in Washington, however, to finalize work at the Navy Department. Without Howe's guiding force on the campaign trail, Franklin veered off message during his stump speeches. In the Pacific Northwest, he promoted himself as having written the Constitution for Haiti while it was under naval military control. He spoke in support of a mob in Washington State that had lynched striking lumber workers. Swept up into the racist stance of a crowd, he called Italian immigrants un-American. Republican opposition, including the Oyster Bay Roosevelts, was quick to pick up on his dubious statements.

Franklin's candidacy for vice president on the Democratic ticket had familial consequences for Eleanor. While Aunt Bye had been quick to offer congratulations, Uncle Theodore's children saw Franklin's political use of the Roosevelt name as usurping their father's legacy. Ted Jr. had his own political career and his older sister, Alice Roosevelt Longworth, was adamant that her brother was the Roosevelt most worthy of higher office. Eleanor found Alice's animosity particularly hurtful. A long-lasting division tore through the Roosevelt family.

ON THE CAMPAIGN TRAIL WITH LOUIS HOWE

On August 18, 1920, the Nineteenth Amendment to the U.S. Constitution was ratified and the right to vote could no longer be denied "on account of sex"; women across the nation would be casting votes in the presidential election. As FDR set out on his final four weeks of campaigning, he implored Eleanor to join him. Louis Howe had convinced Franklin that they needed Eleanor as part of the campaign.

Though reluctant to join the all-male campaign team, Eleanor took on the role of documenting the trip through notes and a daily diary. She compiled press coverage. As the private train car traveled across the country toward Colorado, Franklin gave two to twenty speeches a day. Eleanor had to be seen listening to the speech with rapt attention at each stop. She soon realized she was a prop—the visibly devoted and supportive wife. Both

Cox and the Republican presidential candidate Warren G. Harding had divorce in their backgrounds. Franklin D. Roosevelt was determined to appear as a solid family man.

Even at the end of day, Franklin had no time for her. He frequently played cards and drank late into the night with the reporters following the campaign. She spent more and more time alone in her cabin, growing impatient and indignant.

Writing in her autobiography, Eleanor Roosevelt would have us believe this trip taught her to be more understanding of how men networked and that she was completely new to the world of politics. But she had read books on political strategy seven years earlier when Franklin served as state senator. She had observed from the gallery in the New York State House and critiqued the politicians' speeches. She had already played a role in shaping FDR's speaking style.

We don't know how she truly felt about the xenophobic sentiments that Franklin occasionally inserted into his speeches to connect with specific constituencies. We do know that such statements were fewer when she and Howe were with the campaign. Even if she "encouraged him to be more a statesman and less a careless politician," as biographer Cook suggests, Eleanor Roosevelt never admitted her influence or openly criticized her husband's statements (Cook 1992, 282).

After a short time, Louis Howe began seeking ER out, discussing Franklin's speeches with her, and invoking her opinions. He introduced her to the male reporters. Once she knew the journalists, she appreciated their witty humor and lack of pretense. She respected them and many would go on to be her good friends. The reporters enjoyed her company; they found her warm, genuine, and intelligent. They helped her to interpret the flirtatious women in the crowds as ridiculous rather than threatening. For the rest of her life, she would seek out the company of reporters.

Apart from the campaign reporters, Eleanor Roosevelt began establishing a deep relationship with Louis Howe. Through the years, Eleanor had regarded Howe as Franklin's employee. At times she had been envious of the time Franklin spent with Howe and their intellectual intimacy. Now it was Franklin who became a bit jealous. At the end of the campaign trip, the train passed near Buffalo, New York. Eleanor had never seen Niagara Falls. Howe took her on a day trip, while the campaign went on to its final stops. Franklin's belittling sentiments echo through the words of his son Elliott: "like a honeymooning bride, [Eleanor] insisted on being taken to Niagara Falls" (Roosevelt and Brough 1973, 126).

While the sights and sounds of the falls were magnificent, Eleanor found that exploring the natural wonder with Howe made the experience all the more memorable. They shared an appreciation for nature and he happily provided his knowledge of the area. Howe also brought his viewpoint as a watercolor artist to their observations, and they discovered they both loved. the theater. Howe wrote, acted, and occasionally directed in small regional productions.

Howe respected her political views and admired her resilience. More than anyone else, he knew all of the fractures in Eleanor and Franklin's relationship. He understood why she went through periods of depression and anger. In Howe, Eleanor had found a new and trusting friend who could be honest with her about the importance of her role as a devoted wife for Franklin's political career. He also explained that as her husband climbed the political ladder, she would gain her own power to apply toward her own priorities and goals.

ELECTION RESULTS

As the race for president intensified, Eleanor's aunt Corinne and cousin Alice actively campaigned for the Republican candidate Warren G. Harding. All the Oyster Bay Roosevelt women supported the Republican candidate because he embraced the reform platform put forth by the newly formed League of Women Voters. Privately, however, they all considered Harding a scoundrel. Later, when allegations of corruption surfaced, they would not hesitate to denounce the man they had once supported.

On the day of the election, two women who had not sought the vote headed out to their local polling place. Eleanor Roosevelt and Sara Delano Roosevelt cast their first votes as emancipated women for Franklin as vice president.

The economic and human cost of World War I had pushed Americans toward isolationism and away from trusting a League of Nations. Many of the newly emancipated women used their vote to support peace through isolation and Republican promises of social reform. The Republicans crushed the Democratic ticket of Cox and Roosevelt. Finally, Eleanor felt she was going home to New York and a quiet life.

THE LEAGUE OF WOMEN VOTERS

Franklin D. Roosevelt returned to law and private business, but Eleanor struck out to rediscover herself. She took cooking lessons from one of her former cooks and joined the Women's City Club to reconnect with other New Yorkers interested in social reform.

Within days, the New York branch of the League of Women Voters (LWV) recruited her to join their board. As the wife of a well-known

Democrat, Eleanor would help bring bipartisan balance. Chair Narcissa Cox Vanderlip (1880–1966) had also volunteered for the American Red Cross during the war. She knew Eleanor to be a hard worker and believed she could contribute unique knowledge about national politics and policy.

One of the new friends Eleanor made at the LWV was Esther Lape, a college professor, social scientist, health policy researcher, and one of the organization's founders. Lape's questioning mind and persevering energy inspired Eleanor.

With support from Lape, Vanderlip enticed ER to become the director of the LWV's national legislation committee. The committee worked to

---

LEAGUE OF WOMEN VOTERS

In February 1920, suffragist Carrie Chapman Catt transitioned the National American Woman Suffrage Association into the League of Women Voters (LWV). The Nineteenth Amendment was on the verge of ratification. If women were going to make informed choices about issues and candidates in the 1920 presidential election, they needed quality information independent of political bias or party-system propaganda.

Catt structured the LWV as a reflection of American democracy. Local branches were constituents of states, and state groups were members of the national League. At each level, female leaders were elected and members voted on topics for political action.

Prior to the 1920 election, the LWV submitted a platform of issues to both the major political parties: abolishing child labor, greater funding for education and public health, stabilization of home and food prices, employment for women, and independent citizenship for women.

When many eligible women declined to vote in the election, the LWV analyzed their failure. Scientific data revealed women (and men) only voted when they understood an issue and felt the outcome held personal consequences. The LWV needed to communicate better.

They explained to voters how child labor created a cycle of poverty. They provided evidence that federal programs could help mothers and reduce infant mortality. They demonstrated how stripping away a woman's U.S. citizenship when she married a noncitizen consequentially took away her right to vote and, in some states, to own property or initiate lawsuits, including divorce.

The LWV gave Eleanor Roosevelt a political voice and she would always be the organization's ally. The relationships Eleanor built with the women of the LWV influenced the rest of her life.

Further Reading

Perry, Elisabeth Israels. 1995. *Women in Action: Rebels and Reformers 1920–1980*. Washington, D.C.: League of Women Voters Education Fund.

identify issues in national legislation that were of interest to the LWV and created reports that could be understood by members with varying levels of experience. Vanderlip realized ER possessed an analytical mind combined with an innate teaching ability. To be successful in its mission, the LWV needed individuals like Roosevelt.

Eleanor had long been an observer of the New York statehouse and the U.S. Congress. Though she would write in her autobiography that she felt unqualified for the job, there were few women more qualified. To enhance her capabilities and professionalism, she enrolled at a business school and took daily courses in typewriting and shorthand.

Roosevelt partnered with lawyer Elizabeth Read, an independent woman with her own law practice. Initially, she felt "humble and inadequate" to work with the brilliant lawyer, but she wrote: "I liked her at once and she gave me a sense of confidence" (Roosevelt 1961, 112).

Their committee of two met one morning a week at Read's office. Read would highlight proposed or pending bills mentioned in the *Congressional Record*, which addressed topics of concern to the LWV. During their office hours, the two women discussed the specific legislative bills, then Eleanor would return home to break down the information and write her report.

Twelve years older than Eleanor, Read provided a calm grounding force and became a vital mentor, introducing her to feminist ideals and international issues. A deep trust and friendship developed between the two women. Read became Eleanor's lifelong personal attorney and financial advisor.

The older woman was also Esther Lape's life partner. In Lape and Read, Eleanor found role models: independent, confident women determined to make a positive difference in the world. Representing a new kind of modern woman, they had careers, financial autonomy, and their own outspoken political voice. As social feminists, they empowered women to take action and secure social change.

At home, Eleanor and Franklin grew more distant. Frequently, Franklin stayed out late, at what Eleanor referred to as his "men's dinners," networking with business connections to expand his clientele. Rather than stay home alone, she reached out to her new friends. In her autobiography, she wrote: "I remember many pleasant evenings spent with Elizabeth and Esther in their little apartment. Their standards of work and their interests played a great part in what might be called the 'intensive education of Eleanor Roosevelt' during the next few years" (Roosevelt 1961, 112–113).

THE EDUCATION OF ELEANOR ROOSEVELT

Beyond law and legislation, Eleanor Roosevelt was also learning about philosophy, publishing, and herself. "[M]y friends are responsible for much that I have become," she wrote, "and without them there are many things which would have remained closed books to me" (Roosevelt 1961, xiv). Elizabeth Read and Esther Lape introduced her to a network of creative thinkers and social activists living in Greenwich Village. Evenings included reading French poetry aloud and discussing political strategy and policy. Lape and Read published a political journal called *City, State and Nation*. ER joined Lape, Read, Vanderlip, and Helen Rogers Reid on the editorial committee.

Eleanor had known Helen's husband Ogden Reid since her teens. He was the brother of her friend Jean Reid, who had worked with her at the College Settlement. On their honeymoon, Eleanor and Franklin had visited Jean and Ogden's parents in London. Their father, Whitlaw Reid, had been the U.S. ambassador to Britain during Theodore Roosevelt's administration. Ogden Reid inherited the *New York Herald* from his father and within a few years would combine it with the *Tribune*. Knowing the publisher of a major newspaper would prove beneficial.

Eleanor's evenings in Greenwich Village provided the same dynamic feeling she had experienced at Allenswood. She felt freedom expressing her opinions among other women.

The Village had attracted not only Bohemian artists and poets but also a community of female social activists. The women embraced a Bohemian lifestyle. They were unconventional and dedicated to a life integrated with nature, art, music, and nourishment of the spirit. While gentrification in 1920 pushed out the artists, the ladies tended to be professionals who had bought their own buildings.

Around the corner from Lape and Read lived two other lesbian couples who would become close friends with Eleanor. Marion Dickerman and Nancy Cook eventually became her business partners, while Polly Porter's partner Molly Dewson became ER's political right hand. This community of women played an integral role in transforming Eleanor's understanding of political strategy, social justice, and her place in the world.

Eleanor was not naive to intimate relationships between other women. One of the most influential people in her young life, Allenswood headmistress Mademoiselle Marie Souvestre, had intense personal relationships with other female teachers at the school. Nor was Eleanor judgmental about these women's homosexual partnerships. In Lape and Read, she saw two people thoroughly devoted to each other; two souls who complimented each other and helped make the other greater than they would have been alone.

While Eleanor felt an intellectual and emotional connection with these women, elements of government saw them as a menace. Conservative groups regarded anyone who urged women to vote as provoking change and therefore destroying American families. Attorney General Palmer and J. Edgar Hoover, who would soon go on to serve as director of the Federal Bureau of Investigations (FBI), regarded the LWV as a threat to American democracy. Hoover began compiling information on the LWV and its activities.

THE VISION AND INFLUENCE OF CARRIE CHAPMAN CATT

In January 1921, Eleanor Roosevelt attended her first state LWV conference. She rose above her shyness about speaking in public and explained to the gathered women how the national legislative committee would function and provide analysis of proposed New York state and national legislation.

She also had her first opportunity to be inspired by the LWV's founder, Carrie Chapman Catt (1859–1947). The newly elected Republican governor of New York, Nathan L. Miller, had been invited to speak at the LWV's Albany conference. The organization had actively campaigned against the Republican incumbent for U.S. senator because of his adamant stance against female emancipation. This irritated the New York Republican Party. Governor Miller came before the gathered women and berated them. He stated flatly that he saw "no proper place for a league of women voters." The women needed to understand that political voice could only be expressed within the existing party system, which was controlled by men. Governor Miller rebuked the women, stating: "[Y]ou cannot be nonpartisan and seek to exert political power" (Harvey 1998, 190). He believed that to do so was to be a menace to democracy.

Catt stood up and responded to the governor's paternalistic remarks. She reminded all of the women that the reason they were being regarded with suspicion was because they did have power. They had achieved emancipation. They could use their vote toward the policies and leaders they supported, regardless of party.

Catt inspired and emboldened Eleanor toward her own independence.

BECOMING A POLITICAL ACTIVIST

The political parties in New York started devising legislation to limit female participation within the parties. The LWV enlisted Roosevelt and Lape to draft a bill requiring political parties to act with equal participation of women and men at all levels. The pair then secured bipartisan sponsorship for the bill at the state legislature. In committee, the male senators amended the bill to exclude female input in the governorship and statewide offices. The LWV could no longer support their own legislation. Roosevelt and Lape countered and wrote the LWV's opposition to the bill. No longer a political bystander, Eleanor Roosevelt was in the political game.

Eleanor wrote her first published articles for the *League of Women Voters News Bulletin* and began rising as a political star. Still nursing the wounds of his first political loss, Franklin struggled to find relevance outside of politics. Legal work bored him and he began partying to intoxication. When he became drunkenly brash at the wedding celebration for Aunt Bye's son and his new wife, family whispers hinted that poor Eleanor had a husband who was following in her father's footsteps.

Eleanor had little patience for recreational use of alcohol; this time, however, she empathized with Franklin's political disappointment and loss of purpose. She knew her husband was a talented politician and she began enlisting his assistance in drafting legislation. Franklin and Louis Howe were intrigued by the women's efforts. During many evenings in the Roosevelt townhouse, Eleanor, Lape, and Howe worked on practical political tactics while Read and Franklin considered the legal ramifications.

Franklin and Howe derogatorily referred to the lesbian activists as "she-males," but they respected their intellectual capabilities and organizational skills. Franklin realized what Governor Miller did not—that these women took their responsibility as voters very seriously. A politician who disregarded them did so at his or her own peril.

In April, Eleanor attended the LWV's national conference in Cleveland. The conference committee offered lectures on child welfare issues, such as child labor, food safety, and high rates of maternal and infant mortality. Efforts on these fronts had stumbled in the 1920 election. Now the LWV was building its campaign to unite female constituents in both political parties to urge the passage of the Sheppard-Towner Maternity Act. The legislation would establish the first federally funded social welfare program. Federal funding would match state programs for clinics providing prenatal care, educational resources on nutrition and hygiene, midwife training, and home-visit nurses.

The LWV galvanized its state and local branches to pass this bipartisan public health legislation. The Sheppard-Towner Maternity Act would show the political parties the commitment that women voters had toward improving their communities. In the thick of it, Eleanor wrote home to report on the speakers; through politics, Eleanor and Franklin renewed a personal bond.

The pivotal moment of the conference, for Eleanor, came while listening to Carrie Chapman Catt speak out against President Harding's action to abandon the League of Nations. Catt put aside her prepared speech.

The April 13, 1921 *New York Times* reported that Catt spoke directly to the audience of women. "The people in this room tonight could put an end to war," she said. "Everybody wants it and everyone does nothing." Her passionate words brought the women to their feet. She asked them to pledge themselves "to put war out of the world." Perhaps men were born to instinctively engage in war, but she saw hope in the women before her. "It seems to be God is giving a call to the women of the world to come forward . . . to say: 'No, you shall no longer kill your fellow men.'"

The words in the air, the feeling in the room in that moment—Eleanor Roosevelt could never forget them. She had believed in Uncle Ted's call for a "League of Peace" and supported Wilson's League of Nations. Catt's words inspired her to see world peace as a life mission. She had witnessed the destruction caused by World War I across Europe. She had comforted those with damaged bodies and disfigured faces. The war had brought so much pain and left the world less stable. The quest for world peace owned a piece of her heart for the rest of her life.

FRANKLIN IS STRICKEN WITH POLIO

In June, Eleanor and the children headed to Campobello. Most of the year she had been engrossed in political work, but now she was determined to enjoy the summer. She invited a string of guests to join her and the children.

When Franklin finally arrived at Campobello in August, he brought an entourage. His political career was spiraling downward. He held despondency at bay by treating his work guests to several days of manic fishing trips and activities. When they left, his general fatigue quickly deteriorated into a fever and severe illness.

At the remote island retreat, Eleanor was the only nurse available. Louis Howe searched out the local doctor. Franklin became delirious. He lost the use of his limbs.

Eleanor attended to all of his physical needs, including catheters and enemas when necessary. She bathed him and, with Howe's help, moved him frequently to prevent bedsores. Franklin was vulnerable to her in a way he had never been before. His fears, his sorrows, were all laid bare. The hours they spent together as illness stole his physical strength bound them to each other in another, deeper way.

After three weeks, a specialist gave devastating news. He had diagnosed Franklin with infantile paralysis, or polio, a seriously debilitating and incurable disease. Eleanor focused her attention on her husband's survival and recovery. Once again, forces beyond her control swallowed up the life she had been building for herself.

SOURCES

Center for Disease Control and Prevention. 2019, March 20. "1918 Pandemic (H1N1 Virus)." https://www.cdc.gov/flu/pandemic-resources /1918-pandemic-h1n1.html

Cook, Blanche Wiesen. 1992. *Eleanor Roosevelt, Volume 1: 1884–1933.* New York: Viking Penguin.

Harvey, Anna L. 1998. *Votes Without Leverage: Women in American Electoral Politics, 1920–1970.* Cambridge, UK: Cambridge University Press.

Lash, Joseph P. 1971. *Eleanor and Franklin: The Story of Their Relationship Based on Eleanor Roosevelt's Private Papers.* New York: W.W. Norton & Company, Inc.

Miller, Kristie, and Robert H. McGinnis, eds. 2009. *A Volume of Friendship: The Letters of Eleanor Roosevelt and Isabella Greenway 1904– 1953.* Tucson: The Arizona Historical Society.

Roosevelt, Eleanor. 1961. *The Autobiography of Eleanor Roosevelt.* New York: Harper Perennial.

Roosevelt, Elliott, and James Brough. 1973. *An Untold Story: The Roosevelts of Hyde Park.* New York: G.P. Putnam's Sons.

6

Developing a Political Voice (1922–1928)

The private train car waited on the track. It would be uncoupled and changed to another train line in Boston. They needed to travel from Maine all the way back to New York without changing cars.

Franklin lay on a stretcher, barely able to raise his head. With no way to carry the stretcher into the private car, all Eleanor could do was watch as the knot of men raised the stretcher over their heads and tried to slide Franklin in through the train's small window.

"I have always had a bad tendency to shut up like a clam," Eleanor confided in her autobiography, "particularly when things are going badly" (Roosevelt 1961, 119). She had just begun to find her independence. Now with Franklin completely dependent on her, the victim of paralysis, voicing her personal complaints was unthinkable. Like a clam she isolated herself, silencing her frustrations and fears.

MAKING HER MOTHER'S MISTAKES

Just as her mother had done when faced with complex family problems, Eleanor Roosevelt chose not to confide in her older children. She put on a reassuring smile, claimed everything was fine, and closed them out. She attempted to protect them from the seriousness of their father's illness.

In their early teens, Anna and James could see that their father was unable to walk or even sit up on his own. Even ten-year-old Elliott sensed something was terribly wrong. Why didn't their mother trust them? Why was she keeping them away from their father? They felt marginalized. Mistrust and resentment settled in, and it would taint their relationships with their mother for the rest of their lives.

Eleanor stifled her own questions. What if Franklin never walked again? Would she be trapped in a relationship as a nurse? What future was there for a man crippled by polio? She didn't reach out to friends or family for help. With Louis Howe, she set about keeping the severity of Franklin's illness out of the newspapers. Even the suggestion of polio might destroy the possibility of a political career.

Out west, Isabella found out about Franklin through her mother. She wrote to Eleanor extolling her "superb courage & determination" (Miller and McGinnis 2009, 184). She offered support, but also confided some of her own apprehensions about caring for an invalid husband. If Eleanor needed an empathetic ear, Isabella was willing to listen. But the clamshell of self-protection stayed clamped tight; Eleanor remained silent.

THE CHALLENGE OF POLIO

After weeks in the hospital Franklin came home, but with a dire prognosis. At thirty-nine years of age, he had little chance of ever walking again. His relationship with Eleanor was beyond physical and emotional romance; they were bound together by crisis, survival, and a shared desire to make a difference in the world. Eleanor could have resigned Franklin to the care of his overbearing mother, but she chose to stay at his side and fight for his recovery and future.

Franklin regained use of his hands and arms; he resolved to stay positive and cheerful. Eleanor and Howe maintained the facade of hopefulness no matter how challenging reality became. There were excruciating efforts to stretch Franklin's atrophying leg ligaments and horrible disappointment when his paralysis failed to improve. By February, his shriveled legs were fitted with painful metal braces.

Their household now included a private medical nurse and Howe, who had moved in to help Franklin. The responsibility of maintaining an image of normalcy fell completely to Eleanor.

Only occasionally did her protective shell crack. One afternoon, while reading to the younger boys, she began to sob uncontrollably. For a household built on her steady foundation, it was a moment of anxiety. The children had seldom seen their mother show such emotion. Frightened and confused, they fled the room.

Louis Howe attempted to console her, but failed. For hours, Eleanor sobbed until there were no more tears to cry. Did she think of Isabella and her similar challenges? If she felt she couldn't face another day, she knew that Franklin had no choice. Finally, she found her bravery and applied cold compresses to her reddened face. She picked up the burden she felt she could not shoulder and continued on.

Increasingly, conflict flared with Franklin's mother. Sara Delano Roosevelt barged into their side of the townhouse at any time. She could see her son was not improving. Sara believed Franklin needed to accept his invalid condition and live out his days in tranquility at Hyde Park.

Franklin's doctors disagreed. They prescribed returning to as active a life as possible. Franklin thrived on challenge. Without engagement, he would wither. Building his upper-body strength, training himself to turn over in bed on his own, these efforts would help him live with his condition rather than be a victim. Eleanor sided with the doctors.

The battle between the two women came in small skirmishes. Eleanor and Howe would bring political and business visitors to see Franklin. His mother would argue they were overtiring him. Eleanor would push Franklin to care for his own urinary needs; Sara would insist he needed the nurse's assistance.

When all else failed, Sara enlisted the children in her maneuvers. She convinced fifteen-year-old Anna that she had been sidelined into a small bedroom so Eleanor could give special treatment to Howe. She insinuated to the children that their mother did not want their father to improve.

One afternoon, Sara stormed through the conjoining doors bullying her daughter-in-law for the last time. Eleanor refused to let her mother-in-law sweep Franklin off to Hyde Park and deny him a future. Standing firm for her husband, Eleanor finally stood up for herself. Sara marched back to her side of the twin townhouses. Eleanor seized the moment, and according to son Elliott, moved a large cabinet in front of the conjoining door to keep grandmother out.

RETURNING TO ACTIVISM

While Eleanor was consumed with Franklin's recovery, the League of Women Voters (LWV) scored its first legislative success. Female voters swept candidates into office committed to passing the Sheppard-Towner Maternity Act. The women's vote had been energized and directed to create the first federally funded social program in the nation's history.

The American Medical Association vocally opposed the act, labeling its programs as "socialism" and a government takeover of health care. Once implemented, however, education and preventive care dramatically increased infant survival. The landmark success of the Sheppard-Towner Maternity Act philosophically influenced both Eleanor and Franklin D. Roosevelt. Precedent had been established that federal social programs could deliver positive outcomes.

While Eleanor continued to be a member of the LWV and remained invested in their goals, Louis Howe began directing her toward party politics. Progressive elements were becoming more influential, and Howe was determined to keep the Roosevelt name on the minds of voters and party bosses. He encouraged Eleanor to get involved in the Women's Division of the Democratic Party. He also felt involvement in a cause beyond her husband's recovery could be vital to her personal well-being.

The Roosevelt name held political prestige and the Women's Division welcomed ER with open arms. Since her teens, she had been drawn to labor issues and problems relating to working conditions for women. Among the Democratic women, Marion Dickerman held similar interests. An English professor with an aristocratic New York upbringing, Dickerman had a serious nature and a determination to improve the lives of women workers. Eleanor and Dickerman quickly became friends.

Dickerman reintroduced Roosevelt to the Women's Trade Union League (WTUL). This time Eleanor didn't just have lunch with labor activists Rose Schneiderman and Maud O'Farrell Swartz; she joined the WTUL as a member and led the fundraising effort to secure ownership of their headquarters building.

One evening a week Roosevelt volunteered at the WTUL, reading to illiterate female workers. She wanted to understand the lives of these women. She wanted to hear from them, directly, on how they would benefit from unionization.

Eleanor respected the WTUL because it enabled working women to represent themselves. These women wanted education, health care, and a better life for their children, just as she did. It was impossible to maintain her inherited racist views of Jewish people when she had so much respect for Rose Schneiderman. She couldn't continue to think of the Irish as an ignorant working class when she admired the leadership skills of Maud O'Farrell Swartz.

Eleanor invited the two WTUL leaders to Sunday dinner at the Roosevelts' 65th Street home. The Sunday dinner tradition of scrambled eggs and cold food served casually in the kitchen provided an informal way for Eleanor to bring people in to talk with Franklin. Schneiderman's bold, straightforward personality and O'Farrell Swartz's insight intrigued Franklin. Sunday dinners with the WTUL leaders gave both the Roosevelts a thorough grounding in matters related to labor issues and unions.

THE DEMOCRATIC WOMEN'S DIVISION

In the summer of 1922, Marion Dickerman's life partner Nancy Cook approached Eleanor Roosevelt to speak at a fundraising luncheon for the Women's Division of the Democratic State Committee. She felt having a

Roosevelt as a featured speaker would attract the upper crust of New York's society and their pocketbooks.

While Eleanor described herself as having been intimidated to speak before the gathering of a hundred influential women, including her mother-in-law Sara Delano Roosevelt, the words she spoke to the group were inspiring and motivating. The resoundingly successful event brought in thousands of dollars in donations, and the Women's Division invited ER to chair their Finance Committee.

Eleanor's autobiography and numerous books resound with her protestations of being an introvert and afraid to speak in public. Yet, time and again, she faced that fear. When she was nervous, her voice tended to get higher. She actively worked on her vocal tone and honed it into a lower, more confident speaking voice. Louis Howe encouraged her memorization of prepared speeches and groomed her to be a more natural public speaker. She claimed his succinct advice was: "Have something you want to say, say it, and sit down" (Roosevelt 1961, 124). Subconsciously, Eleanor also knew the political speakers she had found motivating: the New York politician Al Smith and her uncle Ted. While she may have continued to be nervous before a crowd, public speaking gradually became second nature to her. Her only limitation continued to be living up to her own expectations.

Nancy Cook was completely won over by Eleanor Roosevelt. Marion Dickerman remembered that ER strode confidently into the luncheon, asked for Cook, then walked over and handed the assistant chair of the women's committee a small bouquet of violets. Some historians claim violets are a literary symbol of female affection, but violets also represented modesty and Dutchess County, the home of Hyde Park, was the violet capital of the flower industry at the time. A nosegay of violets would have been a considerate, modest, and branding gesture by Eleanor.

Roosevelt, Cook, and Dickerman became fast friends. They worked together, traveled together, and nurtured each other. Roosevelt had connections to men in political power and her new friends had political ideas looking to be heard. Dickerman was an educator and Eleanor envisioned herself following in Mademoiselle Souvestre's footsteps as a teacher. Cook could organize and build things—from furniture to campaigns. Dickerman and Cook were inspiring and deeply committed to each other. Being a third wheel to their partnership felt motivating, emotionally fulfilling, and safe. Similar to her relationship with Esther Lape and Elizabeth Read, Eleanor could enjoy the affection of these women while regarding herself as an outsider to their romantic partnerships.

The more ER worked within the Women's Division of the Democratic State Committee, the more she valued partisan politics and the right to vote. "I became a much more ardent citizen and feminist than anyone about me in the intermediate years would have dreamed possible. I had learned

NANCY COOK AND MARION DICKERMAN

Nancy Cook and Marion Dickerman were life partners; they were also intimate friends of Eleanor Roosevelt. Playfully, Eleanor and Dickerman bought matching baggy men's breeches that fastened at the knee—knickerbockers. The practical knickers were a rebellious female fashion statement. Sara Delano Roosevelt was not amused.

Nancy "Nan" Cook (1884–1962) was only two months older than Eleanor. Energetic and confident, she was a skilled potter, woodworker, photographer, and jewelry maker—trades typically thought of as masculine. Eleanor described Nan as "an attractive woman who could do almost anything with her hands." She had large expressive eyes and rakish curls bobbed in the 1920s style of female independence.

Marion Dickerman (1890–1983) was younger, but her calm manner moderated Cook and bolstered Eleanor. The tall brunette was an eloquent public speaker and education innovator. She taught English and American History and became a college dean.

Cook and Dickerman initially met at Syracuse University and became a couple when they were both teaching at a New York high school. With the onset of World War I, they traveled to England and volunteered for the Red Cross at Endell Street Hospital, a medical facility administered and staffed by women. Cook employed her woodworking talents to craft artificial limbs for war victims.

Immediately upon returning to the United States, Dickerman ran as a Republican candidate for the New York State Assembly and Cook managed the campaign. Dickerman was the first woman to run for state office in New York. She didn't win, but she garnered enough votes to shut out the anti-suffrage conservative. The two women were Progressive activists and became ardent Democrats.

Cook and Dickerman remained a devoted couple for forty-nine years. In her later years, Marion Dickerman helped found Mystic Seaport, the Museum of America and the Sea.

that if you wanted to institute any kind of reform you could get far more attention if you had a vote than if you lacked one" (Roosevelt 1961, 103).

"MISSY" LEHAND

Eleanor Roosevelt still had two sons under ten and a husband struggling to walk with crutches, but her days were frequently filled with activities away from home. One concession made this possible. Following the election of 1920, Eleanor hired a young female secretary to wrap up campaign correspondence. Marguerite "Missy" LeHand (1896–1944) had worked for Franklin's campaign manager. She was efficient and hard-working, though childhood rheumatic fever had left her somewhat physically frail. According to her biographer, medical records reveal LeHand's cardiac condition made childbirth a potentially life-threatening proposition. In a time of unreliable birth control, this made sexual activity even more risky.

Eleanor may have regarded Missy as less likely to have an affair with her husband. The young woman became Franklin's personal secretary, managing his office at the Fidelity and Deposit Company. LeHand had a cheerful, fun-loving nature that buoyed Franklin's spirits and they shared a playful enjoyment of jokes. Because of her own health issues, she also empathized with the change in his physical ability. She was a tall brunette with a deep voice and blue eyes reminiscent of Lucy Mercer. However, she was not quite as beautiful and came from a working-class family. She presented less of a threat to the appearance of a solid Roosevelt marriage and her presence allowed Eleanor to pursue her own interests.

CAMPAIGNING FOR AL SMITH

In the summer of 1922, the Roosevelts urged progressive Democrat Al Smith to run for governor of New York. The incumbent Republican governor, Nathan Miller, had opposed the Sheppard-Towner Maternity Act and refused to sanction New York State's participation in the healthcare program. He provoked the LWV by saying that if they didn't like his positions, they could vote him out. The ladies leapt to the challenge.

The Women's Division of the state's Democratic Party ramped up their outreach and Eleanor Roosevelt became a visible canvasser across Dutchess County. She even did media interviews. On August 6, 1922, the *New York Times* quoted her reaching across party lines to women like her Oyster Bay cousins: "It is impossible to be both a Republican and a progressive under the leadership of Governor Miller." Women like Esther Lape and Marion Dickerman had once been Progressive Theodore-Roosevelt Republicans, now they were aligned with the Democrats.

When the election came, the women's vote tossed Miller out and ushered Al Smith into the governorship. The women had demonstrated they were a powerful constituency.

COMPARTMENTALIZING PUBLIC AND PRIVATE LIFE

While Eleanor Roosevelt was actively campaigning for Smith, Franklin was building up his strength at Hyde Park. Each day, he would attempt to walk the quarter-mile driveway on his crutches. He no longer had a private nurse; a male chauffer/valet helped him physically maneuver through his day.

When Eleanor wrote to Isabella in September, she mentioned nothing of her political activities or her new group of female friends. She spoke of children and casually mentioned Franklin's slow progress. She clammed up and gave the appearance that all was well.

Within a few weeks, Isabella telegrammed that her husband had died suddenly in her arms with their children at his side. Bob Ferguson had been like an older brother to Eleanor. Everyone had prayed his tuberculosis would improve, but after thirteen years of deteriorating health his kidneys failed. The shell protecting Eleanor's emotions cracked. "If only I could feel free to fly out to you," she wrote immediately upon hearing of Bob's death. "It's the one thing I long to do" (Miller and McGinnis 2009, 190). But Eleanor didn't go; she convinced herself she would just be in the family's way.

Off and on, Isabella had reached out to her friend for emotional support, but since Franklin's illness, Eleanor's responses had been thin or remiss. "[T]he waters seem to have closed over my head," Isabella wrote, "while you seem forever capable of striding ahead always in the pace that circumstances call for—my admiration knows no limit" (Miller and McGinnis 2009, 190).

To the casual observer Eleanor Roosevelt did seem to stride through life, but in reality, her life was diverging into different paths. Her two oldest children, Anna and James, had gone off to Europe with their grandmother; they were growing distant. The three younger boys played tricks on Eleanor's new female friends. Franklin was in Florida on a houseboat for months at a time. He believed swimming in the warm saltwater was therapeutic. Missy LeHand was his primary companion and acted as hostess to the string of male buddies who joined him for fishing, drinking, and game playing. Whether or not the young woman had also become his mistress, Eleanor didn't really want to know.

After more than a year of treatments and doctors, Franklin's medical expenses were stretching their finances thin. His Florida trips were a financial drain. Prohibition made alcohol pricey and staffing the houseboat was expensive. During his rehabilitation, Franklin had also invested in a variety of risky schemes. Speculating in foreign currency and slot machines paid well, but he had lost large sums on failed investments. He was allegedly managing the household finances, but when Eleanor received bills that had gone unpaid, she became impatient.

Every year, Eleanor arranged an event for Franklin's birthday. On birthdays, anniversaries, Thanksgiving, and Christmas, the Roosevelts meshed their children with their two independent worlds. Publicly, they appeared as a large stable American family, but resentments and barbed words lay just under the surface.

The following year, when Isabella came east and stayed with Eleanor, she confided to John Greenway, the man who would soon become her second husband, that there was a "weight of tragedy" in the Roosevelt home. At times she found the dissonance overwhelming. Yet she remained confident that Eleanor would continue on "triumphantly" (Miller and McGinnis 2009, 192).

THE AMERICAN PEACE PRIZE

While Eleanor Roosevelt and many progressive Democrats continued to support participation in the League of Nations, American politics had turned against global engagement. A new approach was needed to reengage the American public in the value of international diplomacy.

Edward W. Bok (1863–1930) made a fortune as the editor and publisher of the magazine *Ladies' Home Journal*. A committed peace advocate, Bok proposed a competition to produce a practical plan for U.S. participation in stabilizing international relations, while limiting U.S. involvement in future European wars. Any American could submit an idea for consideration. The winner would receive $50,000, plus an additional $50,000 when the U.S. Senate ratified the plan or a public referendum approved it.

Esther Lape had written numerous articles for the *Journal* in support of peace efforts. Bok chose Lape to facilitate and design the parameters of the competition and to assemble an organizational team. Lape reached out to two women she knew shared her commitment to peace: Narcissa Vanderlip, a Republican, and Eleanor Roosevelt. ER would help devise the prize policy, secure a team of judges, and act as the competition publicist. Finally, she felt engaged in a serious endeavor with long-range ramifications.

Even before ER's October 1923 article in the *Ladies' Home Journal* formally announced the competition, submissions started coming in. The prize money engaged Americans. Suddenly, everyone cared deeply about the role the United States should play in an international community.

Ten individuals, mostly men, were chosen to serve on the Policy Committee with Lape and Roosevelt. The Policy Committee laid out the procedures for submission and consideration, but the three women implemented the procedures.

During this busy time Eleanor was working on behalf of the Democratic Party in state elections while also supporting the LWV's campaign to pass the Cable Act restoring full American citizenship to women married to noncitizens. She promised Lape her full attention once the elections ended.

By the November deadline, over 22,000 plans had been submitted for the American Peace Prize. Everyone, from professional male diplomats to rural housewives, had contributed ideas. Lape, Roosevelt, and Vanderlip vetted each submission and passed serious plans on to the jury.

The three women went to great lengths composing a bipartisan group of seven jurists to review the submissions, mostly men of high academic or political standing. Jury Chair Elihu Root, a former Republican secretary of state, had been awarded the Nobel Peace Prize for his international diplomacy. When the *New York Times* published the list of jurists, isolationists protested that too many supported the League of Nations. Controversy began to swirl around the competition.

The committee planned a national referendum to engage the public. The ladies organized a network of ninety-seven national entities, ranging from labor and academic organizations to religious groups. The winning plan would be dispersed through these organizations. In addition, over 4,000 newspapers agreed to carry the text of the plan and the official ballot. The *New York Times* estimated forty to fifty million Americans would have the opportunity to voice their opinion through the referendum process.

In January 1924, they revealed the winning plan. The name of the winner was withheld to avoid media and voter bias. The plan proposed U.S. participation in the World Court and a cooperative relationship with the League of Nations.

Anti-League politicians cried foul. Allegations were made that the entire process had been an attempt to circumvent elected officials and legitimate government policy. Isolationist senators denounced the "Bok Peace Prize" as "un-American." Within days, the same senators demanded public hearings before the Senate Committee on Propaganda.

TESTIFYING BEFORE THE SENATE

Lape was called to testify and Eleanor Roosevelt sat at her side. The senators alleged the competition had been manipulated to support U.S. participation in the League of Nations. They demanded to know: Who had made the decisions? How was the Policy Committee chosen? Who selected the jurists? Lape's answer caught all of the men by surprise. She explained that she, Eleanor Roosevelt, and Narcissa Vanderlip had asked individuals to serve on the Policy Committee. They had implemented the management of the competition and they had determined the jury members.

Senators from both sides of the political aisle were aghast. Women had managed the entire American Peace Prize competition! The controversy deepened and attacks came from all sides. What authority allowed these women to participate in men's business?

Lape's testimony defused any pretense of impropriety, but all three women were marked as participants in "un-American" activities. J. Edgar Hoover initiated an "Eleanor Roosevelt" file to track her anti-government actions.

The Senate investigation ended suddenly when former president Woodrow Wilson died. Washington moved on to its next headline.

Eleanor Roosevelt's participation in the Peace Prize became a defining moment in her life. She had developed her ability to form a complex organizational structure. She also had successfully executed her first national campaign. She had become adept at networking and building coalitions.

The experience of managing the competition provided ER with a blueprint for the rest of her career in activism. The most complicated, utopian enterprise began with an idea. Idealistic ventures could be achieved working one small step at a time.

THE INFLUENCE OF THE AMERICAN PEACE PRIZE

Roosevelt, Lape, and Vanderlip believed in the value of the winning peace plan and they initiated small steps toward its goals. Vanderlip integrated support for the World Court into the LWV platform. Lape published *Ways to Peace*, a book detailing twenty of the top peace plans submitted. With Elizabeth Read, Lape also founded the American Foundation for Studies in Government (a public institution that promoted U.S. participation in the World Court and other Progressive policies).

Eleanor Roosevelt took the Foundation's ideals on the road, speaking to women's clubs and civic groups. "Now when many of the nations of the world are at peace and we still remember vividly the horrors of 1914–1919 . . . now is the time to act." She warned: "[We] all know that the next war will be a war in which people not armies will suffer." Then she looked her female audiences in the eye. If war came again, loved ones would be lost and women would suffer the double horror of "knowing that they lifted no finger when they might have worked hard" (Lash 1971, 384–385).

Roosevelt portrayed her involvement in the American Peace Prize as that of a casual assistant, but she, Esther Lape, and the LWV would continue quietly influencing public opinion toward the goals of the chosen peace plan. They would keep alive the ideal of U.S. participation in the World Court and a League of Nations.

FEMALE DEMOCRATIC PARTY BOSS

Throughout the previous summer and fall, ER had given public addresses on behalf of the LWV and the Women's Division and to promote the American Peace Prize. Isabella Ferguson (now Greenway) observed that Eleanor was "deep in politics, speech-making all over the state." She honestly felt her friend would "end in Congress" (Miller and McGinnis 2009, 196). It wasn't a fantastical idea—Eleanor's cousin Corinney Robinson was considering running for elected office. While Franklin was in Florida for more than half the year rebuilding his strength and conducting informal political meetings on his houseboat, Eleanor Roosevelt was taking political centerstage.

She joined the Board of Directors for the Women's City Club of New York and took a bold technological leap: she gave a public address on "Women in Politics" over broadcast radio. Radio offered a new medium, a new way to reach a larger audience, and New York City was the capital of broadcasting. Eleanor had been reading aloud to her children since they were born. Talking into the microphone as if she was speaking to one other person gave her a very personal informal style; people felt she was speaking directly to them. Broadcast radio and Eleanor Roosevelt came into political prominence at the same time.

THE BIRTH OF BROADCAST RADIO

In 1924, broadcast radio was a novelty. Most programming was created locally and transmitted short distances to small audiences. Government records estimate that less than 5 percent of Americans, fewer than 1.2 million households, owned radios. The presidential election, however, was about to give birth to must-hear radio, forever transforming politics.

In early June, radio newscasters hauled their equipment into a presidential convention for the first time. The Radio Corporation of America (RCA) owned radio stations and manufactured radios. Their *Radiola* advertisement read: "Hear the actual nomination of a president. It used to be all for the delegates' wives and the 'big' folks of politics. Now it's for everybody."

Over the three well-organized days of the Republican Party National Convention in Cleveland, Ohio, microphones picked up and broadcast the music bands, cheering crowds, and scheduled political speeches. Reporters adhered to strict rules, avoiding "disturbances" and broadcasting only civil discourse. Then they packed up and headed to the Democratic National Convention in New York City, home of the nation's two largest radio stations.

Over fifteen days, the Democratic Convention became hot, contentious, and chaotic. Factions struggled to settle on a nominee through 103 roll call votes. One afternoon, a young reporter was in the glass-sided press box when a brawl broke out. Instinctively, he narrated a play-by-play account of chairs scattered and signs broken over delegates' heads.

Listeners clustered around radios to hear the live, raw, and unpredictable coverage. People rushed to buy radios. RCA estimated that 5 million homes heard Calvin Coolidge's inaugural speech six months later.

Eleanor Roosevelt understood that political success now required mastering broadcast technique. Radio had become the media of the moment.

Further Reading

Sterling, Christopher H., and John Michael Kittross. 2009. *Stay Tuned: A History of American Broadcasting.* Mahwah, NJ: Lawrence Erlbaum Associates.

Eleanor Roosevelt's position as an influencer transformed her. As a young woman, her name and social position had enabled newspaper reporters to use her image—her fashion sense, hairstyle, and presence at balls and luncheons—to influence other young women. When she volunteered at the Settlement House, American Red Cross, and other social service organizations, her actions unintentionally influenced individuals who came in direct contact with her. Now, ER purposefully crafted her own words to inspire women (and men) to embrace their political power and take a stand on progressive reform issues. She stepped fully into the public realm and used technological innovations—radio and the mimeograph machine (an early copying machine that made self-publishing inexpensive)—to reach a wide audience of strangers. She controlled her message and shaped her influence.

Historian Blanche Wiesen Cook identifies four bastions of female political power in New York state in the 1920s: The League of Women Voters, the Women's Trade Union League, the Women's Division of the New York State Democratic Party, and the Women's City Club. Eleanor Roosevelt served in the leadership of or interacted with the leaders of all these organizations. Newspaper columns and editorials, as well as magazines, profiled and discussed her positions. Speaking throughout the state, she delivered blunt critiques of current officials, candidates, and policies. She described Republicans as having "moral blindness" and claimed their behavior in office was due to them being either "stupid or dishonest public servants" (Cook 1992, 352). Her words were highly quotable. Despite her later accounts describing this period as one where she worked on keeping her husband's name in the public arena, she was in fact the Roosevelt that reporters sought out for statements.

At the New York Democratic State Convention of 1924, the women's committee learned they would not be allowed to nominate their own female delegates; the male party bosses would choose delegates for them. The *New York Times* reporter covering the convention recounted in his April 15, 1924 article, "Women Are in Revolt," that Eleanor Roosevelt rose to address the party leadership. "The whole point in women's suffrage," she said, "is that the Government needs the point of view of all its citizens and the women have a point of view."

The women met with Governor Al Smith and he took their side. Party leaders allowed the women to name their delegates and the female coalition supported Smith's reelection for governor.

The National Democratic Party reached out to ER and the women's committee, courting their opinions on social issues for the party platform. They appointed Roosevelt chair of the women's platform committee. For three months, she led a team of female experts from a range of states gathering data to identify social issues most important to American women.

They arrived at the Democratic National Convention in New York with a list of priorities: the establishment of a federal department of education, equal pay for women, worker rights, elimination of child labor, and support for a League of Nations.

A large faction of the male party bosses wanted the female crusaders to go back to their kitchens. They had no intention of including the women in decision-making or embracing their progressive policies.

When the all-male committee met to draw up the party platform, the women waited outside to be invited in to give their report. Minutes stretched to hours. The men locked the door and left the women waiting in the hall overnight and into the next morning. Roosevelt and her female compatriots were never allowed to present their data. The reality was clear: most male politicians did not take women seriously. When it came to women in politics, ER said, "They stood outside the door of all important meetings and waited" (Roosevelt 1961, 125).

But whether the male power structure liked it or not, change was happening. Progressive ideals and activists like Eleanor Roosevelt had attracted new members to the Democratic Party. Once devoted to Theodore-Roosevelt Republicanism, Isabella was at the convention with her husband John Greenway. Like Bob Ferguson, Greenway had fought in Theodore Roosevelt's Rough Riders, but now he served as a delegate from Arizona to the Democratic National Convention.

Franklin D. Roosevelt came onto the stage to deliver the speech nominating Al Smith as the Democratic presidential candidate. He had practiced for weeks to develop a method of "walking" using a crutch and leaning on the arm of their sixteen-year-old son, James. It was Franklin's first public political appearance since contracting polio nearly three years earlier.

Smith did not win the nomination, but Franklin made a triumphant return. His locomotion remained precarious, but his resolution captivated the crowd in Madison Square Garden. His strong resilient voice carried across the nation over the radio. The Roosevelts emerged from the chaotic Democratic National Convention as dominant figures of the Democratic Party.

FAMILY VS. POLITICS

Eleanor Roosevelt hit the campaign trail for Al Smith's reelection as governor of New York, despite his Republican opponent being her cousin Colonel Theodore Roosevelt, Uncle Ted's eldest son. The younger Theodore earned the rank of colonel fighting in World War I. Like his father and Franklin, he served as assistant secretary of the Navy and used the position to springboard his political career.

Colonel Roosevelt worked under the Harding administration. As the campaign began, revelations of corruption and bribery within the Interior Department came to light regarding the leasing of government oil reserves. Newspapers labeled the bribery incident the "Teapot Dome" scandal, after one of the oil fields involved.

ER, Cook, Dickerman, and an upstate member of the women's committee, Elinor Morgenthau (1892–1949), campaigned across the state for Al Smith. They followed the colonel in a car with a large three-dimensional teapot built on the roof. Steam billowed out of the teapot, attracting crowds. They didn't have to say the words "Teapot Dome"; the visual made the connection.

There was no evidence implicating Colonel Roosevelt in the scandal, but it was a strong campaign ploy against him. Cousin Corinney, successfully campaigning herself for the Connecticut House of Representatives, and Aunt Bye understood it was just politics. The rest of the Oyster Bay Roosevelts were outraged and severed all ties with their Hyde Park relatives; Cousin Alice couldn't forgive the attack on her half-brother.

Republican Calvin Coolidge easily gained election as president, but Democrat Al Smith routed Colonel Theodore Roosevelt. ER and her network of women had capitalized on the colonel's lack of local experience and highlighted Democratic priorities that resonated across the state: minimum wage laws and a forty-eight-hour workweek for women. Their targeted campaigning helped Smith retain the governorship. Eleanor would later admit that the spouting teapot was a rough stunt, but her candidate had won.

VAL-KILL COTTAGE AND INDUSTRIES

Participating in Smith's winning gubernatorial campaign energized Eleanor Roosevelt and her friends to transform dreams into realities; 1925 became a time of grand ideas.

During a picnic the previous summer, Eleanor, Cook, and Dickerman had expressed how they would miss the hillsides around Hyde Park after Franklin's mother closed up Springwood for the winter season. As the women traversed the state, Hyde Park served as an intermediary location between rural communities and the city.

Franklin had gazed across the small hillside overlooking Fall Kill Creek and suggested building a "cottage," which the three women could use all year round. Franklin owned the property adjacent to his father's estate and happily leased the site to the three women. While they campaigned for Smith, he had overseen the design and construction of a Dutch Colonial style house. Though Franklin referred to it as a shack in the woods, the "Stone Cottage" had an elegant high-ceilinged living room and four bedrooms.

He had built a rustic swimming pool for his use as well. Two miles from the main house and on the point of land where the stream entered the pond, "Val-Kill" felt tranquil and private. A noisy log bridge over the creek announced visitors several minutes before their arrival.

The Stone Cottage became Cook and Dickerman's residence. Eleanor preferred living there as well. She only stayed at the big house when Franklin came to stay. The three ladies decorated their cottage. Eleanor embroidered monograms on linens with their combined first initials: "EMN." The ladies received numerous gifts of glassware, silver, and porcelain with their monogram.

While campaigning, the women had observed poverty throughout rural New York, driven by the unproductive nature of farming during the winter. Younger generations felt forced to relocate to the city. Light industry could supplement rural income without changing the splendor of the rural environment. Nancy Cook had dreamed of building Early-American-style furniture. If local people could be trained to make furniture, they might earn additional income and preserve their farming communities. The Val-Kill Furniture Factory became a social and economic experiment. Eleanor Roosevelt provided the investment and acted as the primary sales person. Cook designed the furniture, managed operations, and oversaw the handmade production. They built furniture workshops adjacent to the Stone Cottage.

WOMEN'S DEMOCRATIC NEWS

In March 1925, Eleanor helped realize another dream: the first *Women's Democratic News* became available to subscribers. The monthly publication contained political articles, analysis of proposed and pending legislation, news reports, and pieces written by influential Democrats. ER wrote and edited articles, while also being treasurer and selling advertising. Partners in the venture included Cook and Dickerman, along with Caroline O'Day, the new chair of the Women's Division, and Elinor Morgenthau.

Louis Howe, an experienced newspaperman, provided practical assistance in publication layout and crafting headlines. Using a mimeograph machine, the women produced the publication themselves.

Through the *Women's Democratic News*, ER and her companions shaped the Women's Division's political focus and agenda. They established a bureau of female speakers who discussed with constituents how legislative policy impacted their daily lives. They also worked to increase voter registration and used radio to publicize their activities.

While Eleanor participated in a variety of fulfilling political ventures, she shared little of these successes with her longtime friend, Isabella

Greenway. Both women were steeped in politics. John Greenway ran for governor of Arizona and Isabella was happy with a new husband, a new baby, and two children in college; she was openly recreating herself. Eleanor, however, confided nothing of her own changing self-image or her friendship with Cook and Dickerman.

It came as a shock when Isabella's husband died following routine gallbladder surgery. They had only been married two years. "Dearest, I want to put my arms around you & hold you tight," Eleanor wrote. "I know how hard, how unreal much of life must seem . . . but if it helps at all to know that there are people who love you & need you & think of you very constantly just remember that you mean more to me than I could ever tell you & in ways that you don't even know" (Miller and McGinnis 2009, 203–204). This time Isabella remained silent. It was Eleanor's turn to write frequent and uplifting letters.

SEPARATE LIVES

Eleanor Roosevelt's life continued branching away from her husband and her children. Franklin had discovered the naturally heated mineral springs of a rundown resort in Warm Springs, Georgia. Other polio patients had experienced some recovery after physical therapy treatments in its warm waters. He became determined to purchase the decrepit facility and transform it into a treatment center. Eleanor, Howe, and his financial advisors opposed the investment. It would take the majority of his inheritance.

Despite Franklin going through years of hydrotherapy in Florida, the benefits had been temporary. Eleanor realized Franklin would never walk again. Though she believed his financial investment was imprudent, she also understood that the facility at Warm Springs represented hope. Rebuilding the resort gave her husband a sense of control over his life and a vision for the future. While she never visited for more than a few days at a time, ultimately, Eleanor passively supported her husband's purchase of Warm Springs.

Whether due to financial, political, or interpersonal conflicts, tensions in the Roosevelt household remained high. In June 1926, the couple's twenty-year-old daughter Anna escaped the stress of her family's home by marrying Curtis Dall, a stockbroker nine years her senior, and quickly became pregnant. While other mothers might have focused on helping their newlywed daughter, Eleanor Roosevelt dove deeper into political activities. Her experiences with women laborers confirmed her belief that unionization was the key to women achieving equal pay. In December, she and Marion Dickerman joined 300 WTUL members on the picket line to support striking women paper-box makers.

At forty-two years of age and knowing she would soon be a grandmother, Roosevelt walked the picket line. Her behavior scandalized her mother-in-law, especially when ER and Dickerman were arrested with the protesting workers.

THE TODHUNTER SCHOOL

Marie Souvestre envisioned her students returning to their communities and transforming the world into a more just and equitable place. Eleanor Roosevelt felt the influence of her beloved teacher as she participated in social justice feminism. Improving the lives of women workers, she believed, would eventually improve the lives of all workers.

Marion Dickerman and Nan Cook knew how deeply Eleanor valued her years at Allenswood. Dickerman had become an assistant principal at a private girls' preparatory high school. When the Todhunter School went up for sale, Dickerman and Cook suggested that this was Eleanor's opportunity to recreate the educational experience she had so admired. She might also pursue her dream of teaching.

ER and Dickerman purchased the school, expanding their Val-Kill partnership. Dickerman became the principal and Roosevelt taught American history, English, American literature, and analysis of current events. ER delighted in taking her students out into the world. They observed courtrooms in action and visited tenement housing. "All this made the government of the city something real and alive, rather than just words in a textbook" (Roosevelt 1961, 146).

The year 1926 was bringing dreams into fruition. The Val-Kill factory was producing furniture pieces: bed frames, nightstands, chests of drawers, and tables. ER negotiated contracts with Vassar College and a popular department store. She sold the handcrafted furniture to Franklin for the buildings at Warm Springs and bought numerous items herself to give to family and friends. For once, Eleanor felt she was directing her life and embracing her dreams.

AN OUTSPOKEN POLITICAL VOICE

During the summer of 1927, voices of fear and intolerance grew louder against immigrants, African Americans, and workers seeking to unionize. Through the *Women's Democratic News*, Roosevelt published Carrie Chapman Catt's criticism of the Daughters of the American Revolution for denouncing the League of Women Voters, the Women's Christian Temperance Union, and the National Association for the Advancement of Colored People (NAACP) as anti-American. The LWV sent "attack kits" to state leadership with procedures and specific wording to counter accusations that it had engaged in subversive activity.

Roosevelt warned her readers that the true anti-American threats were oppressive injustice and poverty imposed by leaders who suppressed public criticism. She maintained: "Courage, justice and fair play do not breed revolutions" (Cook 1992, 244).

Roosevelt wrote editorials questioning U.S. military intervention in Nicaragua. She hosted 400 women at Hyde Park to initiate a national campaign advocating peace and U.S. participation in the Kellogg-Briand Pact. The United States signed the agreement for diplomatically resolving disputes between nations, but without enforcement provisions the Pact was ineffective.

As another presidential election approached, ER strategically wrote an article for the April 1928 issue of *Redbook* magazine; it was titled "Women Must Learn to Play the Game as Men Do." She boldly stated that women "have no actual influence or say at all in the consequential councils of their parties." She cited how neither the Republican nor the Democratic parties included women in discussions on selecting candidates or on their platform committees; female influence was "frozen out."

From her own experience, she continued, only New York governor Al Smith gave women a voice, "believing they had something to contribute" (Roosevelt 1928). (It was a strategic advancement of the candidate she planned to support for president.)

ER directly rejected the idea of a separate women's party. Women's issues were no different from men's issues; they concerned family, community, nation, and participation in a global community. Women needed to be equal participants in the current party structure.

She put it simply to her female readers: if they were going to truly play a role in national and state politics, they needed to network and build coalitions. "[P]olitics cannot be played from the clouds," she wrote. "[W]omen must learn to play the game as men do . . . [They must] learn diplomacy, subordinate their likes and dislikes of the moment and choose leaders to act for them and to whom they will be loyal. They can keep their ideals; but they must face facts and deal with them practically" (Roosevelt 1928). Far from being on the political sidelines, Eleanor Roosevelt took the lead, ready to stand toe-to-toe with the men.

The article grabbed the attention of voters and the media. Stories on Eleanor Roosevelt appeared in magazines and newspapers. She was compared to her tenacious presidential uncle. With headlines like "A Woman Speaks Her Political Mind" in the *New York Times Magazine*, she heightened the status of the Women's Division of the Democratic Party and helped secure equal office space and staffing.

She had met Mary "Molly" Williams Dewson at the Women's City Club. Dewson had a degree in social work and had played a decisive role in Massachusetts becoming the first state to establish a minimum wage law. She and her life partner, Mary G. "Polly" Porter, had relocated to New York's Greenwich Village and Dewson had become president of the New York Consumers' League (1925–1931). Dewson was ten years older than Roosevelt and highly experienced in organization and management. However, she had less political experience. Dewson became Eleanor's political protégé and right hand.

At the New York State Democratic Convention, Eleanor Roosevelt took center stage and gave the speech seconding the nomination of Al Smith for president at the upcoming national convention.

AL SMITH FOR PRESIDENT AND FRANKLIN FOR GOVERNOR

If Al Smith was running for president, the Democrats needed a strong progressive candidate to take his place as governor. Smith wanted someone to continue his social reforms and secure the Democratic vote in New York.

At the state convention, Smith and the Democratic National Committee Chair approached Eleanor Roosevelt to ask Franklin to run for governor of New York. Franklin was purposefully thousands of miles away at Warm Springs, keeping a low profile.

Multiple times, Eleanor said "No," her husband's health had not recovered sufficiently for him to run for office. Franklin echoed her response over the phone. Finally, at the insistence of Smith and with Eleanor's eventual urging, Franklin agreed to accept the Democratic Party nomination for governor.

Everyone believed the campaign would be a straight party ticket election. Franklin could only win the governorship if Smith carried the state for president. ER was in a position of specific political power; she was committed to Smith's election and she led an organized group of women.

Belle Linder Moskowitz (1877–1933), Al Smith's speechwriter, publicist, and adviser, became the director of publicity for the National Democratic Party. She asked ER to act as director of the women's section of the Democratic National Campaign Committee, organizing the women's effort for the presidential election. ER and former governor of Wyoming, Nellie Tayloe Ross, became codirectors. Ross would travel the country while Roosevelt managed the national headquarters.

From her vast network of contacts, Eleanor Roosevelt pulled in an effective staff of women, interweaving social reform activists and female organizers with established male politicians. The Smith campaign empowered a group of talented women with experience and recognition. Many went on to become personal assistants to future elected and appointed officials. Malvina "Tommy" Thompson (1893–1953) became Eleanor's personal secretary. Numerous others entered ER's pool of influence. She would remember their skills and specific expertise, referring them for positions for decades to come.

ER campaigned and strategized side by side with Belle Moskowitz. The older Jewish woman was a progressive influencer and had managed Al Smith's reform programs in New York City. Labor activist Frances Perkins served Governor Smith as the chair of the State Industrial Board. She described Moskowitz as "an able, high-minded woman of energy and shrewdness" (Perkins 1946, 50). Roosevelt and the Women's Division answered directly to Moskowitz.

ER activated her political network, including Isabella Greenway in the west. She wrote to Isabella about information to be gathered and how "in every state a group of women" would be needed "to help in organizing work" (Miller and McGinnis 2009, 207). Isabella traversed Arizona, speaking in seventeen cities in twenty-seven days. "[T]he women are organized 100% thruout [sic] the State," she wrote (Miller and McGinnis 2009, 212). She forwarded Eleanor a copy of her speech "written primarily with the object of drawing back into the fold our anti-[c]atholic democrats and our prohibitionist women" (Miller and McGinnis 2009, 209). These were the two major hurdles facing Smith's election: his religion and his stance on alcohol.

Eleanor Roosevelt took to the radio waves and to the podium campaigning for Smith. She did what the men were unwilling to do; she challenged Democratic women's groups who were opposed to Smith's anti-prohibition position. ER had supported prohibition; she knew the tragedy of a father trapped in substance use. However, she had also come to understand how illegal alcohol bred corruption. Her position had evolved. In editorials, she squared off against those who would support the Eighteenth Amendment over all other rights and responsibilities.

Roosevelt, Dewson, the speaker's bureau, and Francis Perkins—all hit the campaign trail for Smith. Perkins wrote in her memoir how she and Eleanor came face to face with the "depths of prejudice" against the idea of a Catholic president; "too many people were frightened . . . that the Church of Rome might take control of the United States" (Perkins 1946, 46).

Ultimately, prejudice against Smith, his stance on alcohol, and his lack of experience in rural and international issues presented obstacles too overwhelming to overcome. Republican candidate Herbert Hoover had national and international experience. Economic prosperity soared for the upper classes and Hoover promised more of the same. While Smith lost, the efforts of ER's women positively impacted down-ticket candidates. All of the Democratic candidates won in Arizona and Franklin D. Roosevelt slipped in as governor of New York.

A NEW ROLE

When reporters pressed Eleanor Roosevelt about her husband's election as governor, her words were terse: "I don't care. What difference can it make to me?" (Cook 1992, 379). The truth was it made a big difference. With Franklin as governor, her own political ambitions would have to change. She resigned her official party positions and stepped down as editor of the *Women's Democratic News*. Voicing her opinions would have to be tempered by the reality of her husband's office.

She had invested her entire effort into Smith's election and lost. It was a blow to the life she had been building for herself. If Smith had won, she would have possibly found a career in his administration, like Belle Moskowitz. Instead, Eleanor was the First Lady of New York—a role historically defined as social hostess and supportive wife.

As they headed to the governor's mansion, Eleanor advised her husband on the people she had interacted with during the campaign. Al Smith suggested Belle Moskowitz act as Franklin's secretary; she had experience and would be a significant resource. Eleanor had worked closely with Moskowitz; many people regarded them as friends.

Eleanor adamantly advised Franklin not to hire Moskowitz. She warned that the accomplished woman would manipulate him as she had Smith. Moskowitz would be governor, not Franklin. At the same time, Eleanor invited Frances Perkins out to Hyde Park so the labor reformer could quietly speak with Franklin undisturbed. (See Primary Documents: *Frances Perkins' Letter to Eleanor Roosevelt, Dec. 17, 1928*.)

Eleanor didn't suggest Perkins as the first female to head the New York State Department of Labor; she provided Perkins the opportunity to make her own case to Franklin D. Roosevelt.

Eleanor Roosevelt had become an astute political manager. She knew all of the players and their talents. She separated friendship from practicality. Her initial ambitions had been curtailed, but she would find a new path. She would connect women of vision to the rooms of power. Perkins was right; Eleanor Roosevelt was going to make "a new kind of contribution" to the nation (Perkins to ER, Dec. 17, 1928).

SOURCES

Anderson, Elaine M. 2004. "Eleanor and The Bok Peace Prize." *Historical Perspectives: Santa Clara University Undergraduate Journal of History*, Series II: 9:7. http://scholarcommons.scu.edu/historical-per spectives/vol9/iss1/7

Cook, Blanche Wiesen. 1992. *Eleanor Roosevelt, Volume 1: 1884–1933*. New York: Viking Penguin.

Lash, Joseph P. 1971. *Eleanor and Franklin: The Story of Their Relationship Based on Eleanor Roosevelt's Private Papers.* New York: W.W. Norton & Company, Inc.

Miller, Kristie, and Robert H. McGinnis, eds. 2009. *A Volume of Friendship: The Letters of Eleanor Roosevelt and Isabella Greenway 1904–1953.* Tucson: The Arizona Historical Society.

Perkins, Frances. 1946. *The Roosevelt I Knew.* New York: Viking Press.

Roosevelt, Eleanor. 1928, April. "Women Must Learn to Play the Game as Men Do." *Redbook* magazine, pp. 78–79, 141–142. https://www2.gwu.edu/~erpapers/documents/articles/womenmustlearn.cfm

Roosevelt, Eleanor. 1961. *The Autobiography of Eleanor Roosevelt.* New York: Harper Perennial.

Smith, Kathryn. 2016. *The Gatekeeper: Missy LeHand, FDR, and the Untold Story of the Partnership That Defined a Presidency.* New York: Simon & Schuster, Inc.

7

Transforming the Role of First Lady
(1929–1933)

Eleanor Roosevelt sat silently. She wrote, "The turmoil in my heart and mind was rather great" (Roosevelt 1961, 163). Traces of a former life spilled across her desk: a stack of student essays unread and ungraded, the first draft of an editorial on the vital role of education in a democracy, and an invitation to speak at a luncheon, which she now felt obligated to decline.

The house was quiet. Following New York's gubernatorial election, Franklin and his entourage retreated to Warm Springs to rest, rejuvenate his health, and plan the transition into the governorship. Eleanor was left with the wifely task of moving the household from New York City into the Executive Mansion in Albany.

The life she had built as a political activist, teacher, and businesswoman was slipping through her fingers. Franklin did not insist she abandon her interests, but it was assumed that as First Lady of New York, Eleanor would preside over the social responsibilities of the capitol: receptions, dinner parties, gatherings of state dignitaries and other important guests. A storm of expectations rushed toward her. The unpaid job of First Lady directly threatened her self-identity.

There were two lists before her: obligation and desire. Marie Souvestre's portrait sat in a place of honor on her desk. The wise mentor looked back at her. When faced with difficult choices, where do you begin? "The first thing to do is to sit down and become immovable," Roosevelt later told an interviewer. "Get possession of yourself! Let the world go by altogether until you have decided for yourself just exactly what you want" (Woloch 2017, 21).

A TEACHER FIRST

Eleanor Roosevelt wanted to teach. It gave her purpose and confidence. It didn't matter that she was the First Lady of New York. Engaging her students at the Todhunter School challenged her intellect and gave her influence over a new generation of women. She would not give it up.

As she prepared her lessons in history and current events, she analyzed issues and fleshed out her own political ideology. Questions on the final exam for her current events class probed the intersection between the individual and society: list the ways in which the government touches your everyday life; why is there a struggle between labor and management; argue for and against women participating in governmental politics and holding elected office. She pushed her wealthy upper-class students to compare their own rights to the treatment of others. She asked them to explain in detail the methods Southern states used to exclude African Americans from voting. She was empowering her female students to think for themselves and to support their positions with facts.

A governor's wife working outside of the home was unprecedented in New York. Eyebrows were raised among the social establishment. The *New York Times* ran an article detailing the varied employments of the State's new First Lady. She had resigned her club and political party positions but held on to her professional occupations. She could manage the finances and orders for the furniture factory from a distance, but teaching in the city required strategic planning and a weekly commute between Albany and New York City.

Her own children were no longer at home. Anna was married and the two older boys, James and Elliott, were at Harvard. Franklin Jr. and John were fourteen and twelve, but they were away at Groton boarding school. Eleanor lived in the family's 65th Street house in the city and taught Monday through Wednesday afternoon. Wednesday, she caught the afternoon train to Albany. Thursday through Sunday afternoon she fulfilled her role as New York's First Lady. Sunday, she returned to the city to start the week over again. It was a modern woman's answer to fulfilling her wifely duty while maintaining her own career. She was becoming a role model for the growing class of female professionals and small business owners.

Her personal experience in the classroom also inspired her advocacy for increased wages for teachers and pay equity for female educators. She became an early promoter of integrating students of diverse racial and socioeconomic backgrounds. Her ideals, however, were ahead of her practices. She advocated for public schools, but the Roosevelt children all attended exclusive private schools with predominately white students. Even Todhunter School remained an expensive private academy where the inclusion of a few Jewish students was considered liberal-minded.

On Wednesdays, at noon, Eleanor Roosevelt dashed to the train station, her leather satchel weighed down with papers to be graded and lessons to be planned. The train became an extension of her office: a place to finish schoolwork and read personal letters. A lone figure, without a security detail, the First Lady of New York hurried to the train platform and never seemed to realize the train conductor often held the Albany train for her.

THE ROLE OF NEW YORK'S FIRST LADY

Eleanor Roosevelt confided to her closest friends that her political activism would cease on January 1, 1929, when her husband was sworn in as governor. She felt it wasn't fair to him if statements she made were mistaken as official positions. During FDR's governorship, her role would be to facilitate the smooth operation of the Executive Mansion. While she may not have enjoyed her new social role, nearly everyone agreed that Mrs. Roosevelt proved herself to be an adept organizer and a delightful hostess.

Most formal dinners and receptions were scheduled in the later part of the week, when the First Lady was in residence. Sunday afternoons, she left detailed instructions regarding guests who might be arriving in her absence, dinner menus, and seating arrangements for events in the coming week.

In Eleanor's absence, Missy LeHand acted as hostess for happy hours and less formal dinners for Franklin's male advisers. Eleanor had little tolerance for cocktail parties and poker. Prohibition was still the law of the land and she remained judgmental of hard alcohol use. Alcoholism threatened Eleanor's brother, Hall. He had inherited their father's predisposition for chemical dependency.

Cousin Alice Roosevelt Longworth remained furious that Franklin had—in her opinion—usurped Theodore Roosevelt's political legacy by winning the New York governorship. But the Roosevelt women were linked by a common bond. Eleanor, Alice, Corinney, and Ethel shared the sorrow of watching brothers, sons, and nephews struggle with alcohol. Eleanor willingly relinquished hosting Franklin's hard-drinking evenings.

Missy LeHand had her own bedroom in the Executive Mansion. Living with the family, FDR's personal secretary easily stepped in as hostess.

The Roosevelts' unconventional living arrangements also included Louis Howe. Franklin's political advisor continued to live in the Roosevelts' 65th Street home in the city. Weekday evenings, he and Eleanor discussed politics, occasionally attended the theater, and continued to deepen their friendship. Howe had become a trusted adviser to Eleanor as well as Franklin. He moderated their conflicts and acted as a personal bridge between them. Each weekend, Howe traveled to Albany to meet with Franklin and then returned to the city with Eleanor on the Sunday evening train.

As Eleanor Roosevelt settled into the Executive Mansion, she expanded her position as a facilitator. The rambling three-story brick mansion, with its soaring ceilings, had the warmth of a drafty museum. Eleanor gave the mansion a beating heart. She instituted a four o'clock afternoon tea in the family sitting room.

From the sprawling corridors and distant rooms, people of varying power levels and social circles came together in community. Tea and chocolate cake brought everyone together on an equal footing. A visiting foreign ambassador might chat with a young Roosevelt home from school, an African American housemaid might voice labor concerns to the State's industrial commissioner, and a seamstress from the Women's Union Trade League visiting the First Lady might have momentary access to the busy governor.

Franklin's physical mobility limitations made it difficult for him to roam among New York's people. At afternoon tea, Eleanor provided her husband an opportunity to interact with a broad range of people and to encounter their point of view directly. Afternoon tea was casual. Franklin was not obligated to engage, but he might hear a perspective his advisers couldn't offer. If the governor was interested in hearing more, he could reach out to that person directly. Frances Perkins had accurately predicted Eleanor Roosevelt's unprecedented role in connecting the governor with people and issues typically overlooked by those in power.

Initially, the new First Lady baffled journalists. Some referred to her appearance as plain or dowdy. Lorena Hickok (1893–1968), one of the few female reporters assigned by a major news outlet to cover New York politics, initially took little note of the governor's wife. To Hickok, Eleanor Roosevelt appeared awkward and lacking any fashion sensibility .

However, the capitol's reporters soon came to appreciate Mrs. Roosevelt's straightforward personality and intelligence. She, in turn, regarded them as partners in communicating to the people of New York.

ACTIVIST BEHIND THE SCENES

The women close to Eleanor Roosevelt understood that their friend and colleague was in a delicate situation as New York's First Lady. The general public wasn't ready for a husband-and-wife partnership in the governor's mansion. In 1929, motion pictures had only recently thrilled moviegoers with sound. Popular American culture depicted two kinds of women: controlling seductresses, who were eventually punished for their independence, and innocent ingénues. The hit movie of the year—*The Broadway Melody*—spelled it out clearly: beauty was more valuable than talent and women should aspire to marriage. A career was a poor substitute for a woman's preferred role: supporting her husband.

Franklin D. Roosevelt was also unlikely to take direct advice from his wife. He trusted and appreciated Eleanor's insight and truthfulness, but he had grown up with a controlling mother and resented being ordered.

On the other hand, he respected strong intelligent women. Sarah Delano Roosevelt had long been the head of the family and managed much of the family's finances. Eleanor's aunt "Bye" Roosevelt Cowles had been an early political mentor. Franklin depended on the political instincts of his wife and her business partners, Nan Cook and Marion Dickerman. Eleanor's longtime friend Isabella Greenway had demonstrated to Franklin that women could be effective community leaders and business owners. Over the last eight years, Eleanor had introduced her husband to a circle of intelligent, innovative women.

Now Eleanor had to maintain a fragile balance. Biographer and friend Joseph P. Lash wrote that ER realized that her ability to sway Franklin "depended on how well she buried her tracks and how persuasively she disavowed that she had any influence" (Lash 1971, 434).

ER had facilitated Frances Perkins' meeting with Franklin, but he decided to appoint her as the first woman New York Industrial Commissioner. Now Eleanor provided Molly Dewson with the opportunity to meet with Franklin at Warm Springs. While Eleanor was hundreds of miles away in New York, Dewson spoke directly to the new governor about the talented women who had worked on Democratic campaigns and deserved positions in his administration. Dewson would later write in her unpublished memoirs that she purposefully did not mention Eleanor Roosevelt's influence as she worked to bring more women into appointed civil service positions. She understood her friend's precarious position. Any appearance of Eleanor's influence over the governor might result in his freezing out the Women's Division. A wife perceived as interfering risked public backlash.

Eleanor Roosevelt laid a path of activism behind the scenes. While the masthead for the *Women's Democratic News* listed Caroline O'Day as the editor, ER continued to write anonymous editorials and edit articles. Her hand guided the publication, but her name was seldom credited.

She continued to share office space with Cook at the New York Democratic Women's Division and Malvina "Tommy" Thompson stayed on as her part-time private secretary. ER also continued to work with Esther Lape and Elizabeth Read on public policy issues at the American Foundation.

Publicly, Eleanor Roosevelt appeared to have settled into teaching, managing the furniture factory, and acting as New York's social hostess. Molly Dewson, however, knew otherwise.

Early in FDR's governorship, the New York State Assembly passed a bill limiting the total daily hours women could work in retail shops. Business leaders protested and FDR answered their concerns by holding a public hearing on the legislation. Dewson arrived to testify at the hearing and was shocked to find that she and a few representatives from the LWV were the only advocates supporting the bill. Labor and union leaders had not been notified of the hearing. The room was packed with merchants and industry lobbyists opposing the reforms.

Dewson left the hearing dispirited and angry. She arrived at the Executive Mansion to have tea with ER at four o'clock and complained heartily about the injustice of the hearing. The two women feared the labor reform bill would languish, unsigned. When Franklin rolled into the sitting room for tea and cake, Eleanor confronted him directly. "What are you going to do about the bill?" There was an awkward silence. "Sign it, of course," Franklin responded with a smile and held out his cup for tea (Lash 1971, 438).

A NEW FRIEND AND CONFIDANT

As First Lady of New York, Eleanor Roosevelt was entitled to a personal driver, but she enjoyed driving and refused the special treatment. Franklin regarded it as a security issue and demanded she accept a bodyguard.

He personally chose Earl Miller (1897–1973), a state police trooper assigned to the governor's security detail. Franklin had first met the former naval officer in Europe during World War I. Miller had provided security for Franklin when the latter was assistant secretary of the Navy and they shared an inclination toward athletics. Miller taught judo and boxing at the New York State Police Academy.

Eleanor Roosevelt was twelve years older than Miller, but the bond between them was immediate. He, too, had been orphaned as a child. While she had felt homeless, he had literally lived on the streets. While she was contemplative, he was outgoing and playful. He loved to tinker on the piano while Eleanor and others sang along. His gregarious personality reminded her of the best aspects of her father.

Eleanor and Miller also shared a love of the outdoors, horses, and riding. He gave her a chestnut mare named "Dot." It was an acknowledgment of the personal mount she had desired twenty-four years earlier but had been denied. Riding now became part of her daily exercise routine. Miller also reignited her interest in tennis and guided her to achieve a long-deferred personal goal: learning to dive.

Earl Miller deferentially referred to Eleanor Roosevelt as "the Lady" and demanded that others treat her with respect. Where her husband and even her own sons tended to tease and ridicule her, Miller was supportive and consciously bolstered her self-confidence. His admiration was honest and his loyalty unyielding.

FDR'S INVESTIGATIVE EYES AND LEGS

In July 1929, Franklin D. Roosevelt proposed a boat cruise up the Hudson River and along the Erie Canal. The trip with Eleanor and their three youngest sons appeared to be a vacation, but it was actually a strategic effort to raise Franklin's profile in the rural regions of the state and to collect information on state facilities.

The 1920s was a decade of financial boom, but there were hints of economic fragility. Governor Roosevelt wanted to see how state hospitals, prisons, and cities were really holding up. He enlisted Eleanor to act as his undercover civil investigator.

Franklin typically walked assisted by one of his sons and a cane. He did not use a wheelchair in public situations and his mobility was therefore limited. The Roosevelts came up with a strategy. The governor's yacht would arrive in a town or city. Local officials, reporters, and a car would meet them at the dock. Following the enthusiastic welcome, FDR would casually suggest he meet with the officials and state facility managers, and while they talked, perhaps the First Lady could look around the facility.

Eleanor acted as Franklin's investigative eyes and legs. She walked the hospital wards noting if beds were pushed too close together in order to increase patient numbers beyond restrictions. In the prisons, she peered into cooking pots to see if the men were being fed the food the warden claimed was being provided.

With Earl Miller at her side, looking unquestionably official in his full-dress New York State Police uniform, all doors were opened for New York's First Lady. ER would write that Franklin taught her what to look for during her inspections, but she had investigated working conditions for shop girls as a young woman. Her delving into conditions at the Navy's psychiatric hospital led to improvements in U.S. mental health care. Franklin had inspected Navy facilities during the war and Miller also had a keen eye and a background in public inspections. Between the three of them, they uncovered graft and discrepancies in state services.

Before the summer was over, President Herbert Hoover allowed the Sheppard-Towner Maternity Act to expire. ER's compatriots at the LWV were disheartened. New York continued to fund programs supporting mothers and infants, but without matching funds from the federal government many other states dropped their efforts.

A MAJOR TURNING POINT

On October 11, 1929, Eleanor Roosevelt turned forty-five years old. She felt she had survived the passionate emotions of young womanhood and was discovering her true self. She wrote in an article for *Vogue* magazine that at forty-five, she was engaged in the world beyond her home, working to establish a life that interested and fulfilled her.

That same month, she gave the keynote address at the eighth annual Exposition of Women's Arts and Industries. She challenged industrialist Henry Ford's statements that women were incapable of accomplishing precision manufacturing work and belonged in the home. She pronounced his views ridiculously antiquated and narrow-minded. Women were working in ever-increasing numbers, but she feared growing economic issues would unequally impact women. If job opportunities declined, women would be the first to be pushed out of the workplace.

Days later, on October 24, the stock market began to tumble. Stock prices gyrated for five days until the market had lost 23 percent of its value. Looking back, historians and economists would mark this as the beginning of the Great Depression, but for the people living through it, the turning point did not seem immediately apparent.

Initially, neither Roosevelt registered concern about the stock market's fall, even though both of their fortunes were invested there. The week of the crash, Eleanor was working with Esther Lape and The American Foundation trying to influence congressmen and senators to ratify World Court protocols and bring the United States into the international body. She prodded Isabella Greenway to use her personal relationships to lobby Arizona's two senators.

Isabella had been widowed for a second time, leaving her one of the wealthiest women in Arizona. She held controlling stock in copper mines, owned several ranches, and was known throughout the state. There were hopeful whispers that she might run for governor. Eleanor asked her friend about it directly, but Isabella felt that even Democratic women in Arizona wouldn't rally behind a widow with a four-year-old child.

Throughout November, the stock market continued to collapse, dropping to 40 percent of its former value. The unemployment rate, however, appeared to remain low at 3 percent of workers. The crisis seemed confined to the financial sector. Franklin D. Roosevelt himself was still bidding on bargains at an art auction.

Frances Perkins understood, however, that "one could never count the unemployed—one could only count the employed" (Perkins 1946, 95). Counting people who are not doing something is tenuous; it doesn't tell you why they are not participating in an activity. Her labor statistics showed that the number of people employed was dropping quickly.

Eleanor Roosevelt's trust fund provided her annual income. She used her invested inheritance to support the Orthopedic Hospital, invest in Val-Kill Industries, and pay off the mortgage of the WTUL's headquarters. Suddenly her trust fund lost half of its value. Though it scandalized her mother-in-law, Eleanor Roosevelt realized earning an income was necessary if she wanted to continue the work that gave her purpose.

When the editor at *Vogue* magazine read her article on turning forty-five years old, he was thrilled with the piece, but Eleanor quickly responded that he had not provided information on payment. Other magazines paid her. She asked for the usual compensation.

THE ECONOMIC CRISIS DEEPENS

Throughout 1930, the impact of the stock market crash rippled through the economy. The Hoover administration followed a hands-off philosophy, letting financial institutions fend for themselves. Interest rates climbed, and small banks couldn't borrow funds to stay open. Nearly 10,000 banks failed and families across the nation lost their savings.

In an attempt to protect American companies and farmers, Hoover imposed tariffs on foreign products. But tariffs only succeeded in increasing international trade conflicts. The economy contracted and millions of people lost their jobs.

The ripples directly impacted the Roosevelts. Medical bills for Franklin and two of their sons forced them to take financial help from Franklin's mother. Daughter Anna's husband was a financial speculator; the stock market's continued decline forced him into bankruptcy. The couple lost their home and their marriage suffered. They and their two young children moved into Eleanor and Franklin's New York house. Sales decreased for Val-Kill furniture, requiring Eleanor to personally increase her financial support to keep the craftspeople employed.

As the economy weakened, people clamored for government help. ER sent a message of support from the governor's mansion to striking members of the International Ladies' Garment Workers' Union. She openly lobbied with the WTUL in support of legislation for a five-day workweek. Limitations on hours and workdays would not only create healthier working conditions, but also help to spread the work out and keep more individuals employed. The declining economy emboldened labor, minorities, and women.

Franklin D. Roosevelt was up for reelection as governor in November 1930. The Women's Division of the New York Democratic Party felt his male advisers were taking it for granted that he would win an easy victory. The women strategized a campaign. ER and her team—Molly Dewson, Nancy Cook, and Caroline O'Day—mapped out a plan to canvass rural areas of the state, which leaned Republican. They created written materials and organized meetings to directly communicate how FDR's governorship had benefited rural communities and would continue to work for them. ER rallied labor-union voters with editorials in the *Women's Democratic News*, encouraging workers to vocally support all Democratic candidates.

In the early weeks of October, while Franklin was at Warm Springs, Frances Perkins came to Eleanor Roosevelt with a confidential offer. She believed the state commission, which had modernized the New York Public Employment Service to help the unemployed find jobs, could be used to investigate the practicalities of an old-age pension plan—a social safety net for those unable to earn an income. Eleanor recognized the vision in Perkins' plan, which included individuals with physical disabilities. If the plan was expanded nationally, it could financially protect the elderly, widows, and those unable to work—the people who were increasingly falling into severe poverty. Eleanor sent the plan to Franklin with a note extolling how this could be the idea that would propel the Democrats ahead of Hoover in the 1932 presidential election.

Bolstered by the Women's Division's activism, Franklin D. Roosevelt easily won reelection as New York Governor.

In the following weeks, Eleanor was interviewed in the *New York Times Magazine*, not for being New York's First Lady, but for being a successful business owner. In the face of a declining economy, she had continued to invest in Val-Kill Furniture. With Nan Cook's designs and oversight, the furniture operation had grown in employees and products. The *Times* highlighted Val-Kill Furniture as one of the few factories "in the country initiated, built, managed and owned entirely by women" (Cook 1992, 419–420). What the article didn't spell out was the purpose of the factory: keeping people gainfully employed in rural communities.

Across the country, Isabella Greenway similarly underwrote a furniture workshop staffed by disabled veterans. To keep the workshop operating, Greenway opened the Arizona Inn in Tucson. She filled the Inn with the handmade furniture. She was also helping found one of the country's first small commercial commuter airlines.

The two former debutantes regarded each other as entrepreneurial role models in the effort to create sustainable communities.

A NEW WOMEN'S NETWORK

Eleanor Roosevelt had grown up at the outer fringe of a network of aunts, cousins, and debutante friends. Aunt Bye had been her greatest champion and first political role model.

During the 1920s, however, the two strong women had grown apart. The elderly aunt disapproved of Nancy Cook and Marion Dickerman. Bye felt their influence inspired Eleanor to be too openly political. She worried Eleanor's new outspokenness had tarnished her charm.

Aunt Bye was from a different age; she had lived through the Civil War and been ten years old when President Abraham Lincoln was assassinated. Crippled by arthritis, Bye spent her last few years confined to her home. When she died in the summer of 1931, only one living family member remained to connect Eleanor with her father, his youngest sister Corinne Roosevelt Robinson. While Aunt Corinne and her daughter Corinney Robinson Alsop remained close to Eleanor, politics separated her from the other Oyster Bay relatives.

Rather than the traditional circle of women connected by blood and marriage, Eleanor Roosevelt built a network of female friends and activists bound together by shared philosophy. Though not close personal friends, ER and Frances Perkins were loyal cohorts working toward social justice. The memory of young female workers losing their lives in the Triangle Shirtwaist Factory fire and families left without a primary wage earner after the flu pandemic bound them in a sisterhood of social reform.

Eleanor Roosevelt publicly claimed: "I did not want my husband to be president" (Roosevelt 1961, 160). Yet, by the fall of 1931, she and her network of female activists were considering the viability of Franklin D. Roosevelt as a presidential candidate. The Democratic National Convention was eight months away when Eleanor reached out to Isabella Greenway to secure her vote, as a party delegate from Arizona, for Franklin.

The economy continued to sink into depression. The Republican majority in the Senate offered no response to the crisis. The public blamed President Hoover and his party abandoned him.

While all of Eleanor Roosevelt's biographers agree that Franklin D. Roosevelt did not directly consult with his wife before running for the presidency, she had already identified Hoover as a weak incumbent. The presidency had been Louis Howe's goal for Franklin since 1912. Franklin and Howe were following the path to the White House laid out by Theodore Roosevelt. Once Franklin became New York Governor, there was no question his goal was the presidency.

Eleanor asked Isabella to meet with her new friend Molly Dewson, who headed to California to weigh the support for a Franklin D. Roosevelt nomination. Eleanor was strengthening her network of female connections for the presidential campaign and the administration ahead.

A BUMPY TRIP TO THE DEMOCRATIC CONVENTION

Early in 1932, Eleanor Roosevelt wrote to Isabella Greenway to share news of her son Elliott's marriage. He seemed too young to be married, though she admitted he was twenty-one. The heart of her letter, however, returned to the Democratic Convention. Would Greenway coalesce the Arizona delegates as a block to vote for Franklin?

In her speech to the New York League of Women Voters, ER pointedly said that charity in a time of emergency was not enough. Resolving the realities of why people ended up in serious economic need required new thinking and new solutions. Franklin had instituted Perkins' unemployment relief program in New York. ER signaled to fellow reformers that a Roosevelt presidency would ensure sweeping change.

At the June convention in Chicago, New York's former governor, Al Smith, was Franklin D. Roosevelt's main opponent. Isabella Greenway gave the first speech seconding Franklin's nomination as the Democratic Party's candidate for president. After the first roll call vote Franklin held the greatest number of delegates, but not enough to win the nomination. Smith had been Franklin's political mentor; now he labeled the younger man an ungrateful usurper. Smith refused to concede his delegates.

Two more ballots resulted in deadlock. Franklin needed nearly a hundred more votes to reach the required majority.

The Roosevelts were listening to the convention on the radio 800 miles away at Hyde Park. Greenway, Dewson, Cook, O'Day, and Dickerman were delegates on the convention floor in Chicago. The key to the deadlock required moving the California delegation's support from Texan Speaker of the House John Nance Gardner (1868–1967) to Franklin.

While Isabella Greenway negotiated with the Californians, Louis Howe got on the phone to make a deal with Congressman Gardner. Joseph Kennedy (1888–1969), the father of future president John F. Kennedy, supported Franklin and had connections to William Randolph Hearst (1863–1951), the most influential American newspaper publisher. Hearst opposed Al Smith's internationalism and held great sway over California politics.

Kennedy connected Franklin to Hearst. The two men spoke over the phone. If Franklin D. Roosevelt would promise to abandon the League of Nations and the World Court, Hearst would throw his support behind his nomination.

Franklin sealed the bargain. John Nance Gardner was offered the vice presidency. Whether by Greenway's persuasion or Hearst's power, the California delegation moved into Franklin's column. Other Gardner supporters followed and Franklin D. Roosevelt won the nomination.

At Hyde Park, the barn had become a makeshift pressroom with journalists following the political wrangling through the night. When the final convention vote came over the wire, most reporters dashed off to file their stories, but two remained behind hoping to rustle up some coffee. They found Eleanor Roosevelt alone on the side patio. Without any hint of emotion, she invited them in for breakfast. Associated Press (AP) reporter

Lorena Hickok later wrote that she turned to her male colleague and said, "That woman is unhappy about something" (Cook 1992, 452).

Biographers have speculated widely about Eleanor Roosevelt's self-professed lack of enthusiasm for her husband's run for the presidency. Many of Franklin D. Roosevelt's biographers claim she couldn't bear the loss of her privacy or the burden of being the First Lady. But Eleanor had been a public persona for most of her adult life. She had found a way to balance official duties with her own personal goals. She had been actively helping Franklin secure the nomination for over eight months.

Marion Dickerman claimed Eleanor sent a note to Nan Cook on the convention floor saying she wanted a divorce and was running away with Earl Miller. Dickerman said Cook passed the note to Louis Howe, who destroyed it and cautioned the two women to keep the secret.

Eleanor and Miller were close; they may even have had an affair. Her son James later confided in his book *My Parents* that Earl Miller provided his mother with self-respect and emotional support, which her husband and sons failed to give her. With Miller, Eleanor felt comfortable enough to be silly and to laugh. Photographs reveal a physical closeness: her hand rests unconsciously on his knee while his arm casually drapes around her waist. James Roosevelt felt that biographers who left Earl Miller out of his mother's story failed to portray her personal warmth and humanity.

Eleanor was unhappy to discover that Franklin had removed Miller from the security team assigned to accompany them on the campaign trail. At the same time, she was also arranging the details for Miller's wedding to someone else. For the rest of his life, Earl Miller revealed little about his personal relationship with Eleanor Roosevelt. None of their numerous personal letters survive, and Miller denied any notion of their running away together.

When Franklin D. Roosevelt struck his deal with William Randolph Hearst, he rejected years of Eleanor's work on international peace. He abandoned their shared belief in the League of Nations and the World Court. This betrayal was cutting. As historian Blanche Wiesen Cook writes, Eleanor Roosevelt "never accepted without a struggle FDR's willingness to sacrifice principles for pragmatism" (Cook 1992, 453).

In the moment when Eleanor was questioning her husband's motives toward the presidency, Franklin instituted a new tradition: he would accept the Democratic Party nomination for president in person. Rather than wait at Hyde Park for the Party to officially contact him and then start organizing a campaign, Franklin set out for Chicago to speak directly to the gathered delegates. The Roosevelt family and their entourage piled into a private airplane and took a very turbulent seven-hour flight from Albany, New York, to Chicago.

As Eleanor sat listening to Franklin delivering his acceptance speech about a "New Deal" for the American people, what did she think?

"Ours must be a party of liberal thought," FDR told the cheering Convention crowd, "of planned action, of enlightened international outlook, and the greatest good to the greatest number of our citizens" (June 2, 1932).

"Enlightened international outlook" was blatantly open to interpretation. Would Franklin keep his promises to the people or to Hearst? How deep did the betrayal have to be before she followed through with a divorce? Was she unhappy about becoming First Lady of the country or concerned that Franklin would not be the reformer she hoped he could be?

RELUCTANT CAMPAIGNER

Despite personal reservations about her husband as a candidate, Eleanor Roosevelt believed the Democratic Party offered the best solutions for ending the economic crisis gripping the nation. Over the past two-and-a-half years, the stock market had continued to collapse, losing 89 percent of

In 1932, presidential candidate Franklin D. Roosevelt (left) campaigns with daughter, Anna (center), and Eleanor (right) from the back of a convertible car. The Roosevelts purposefully maximized the power of images. Seated in a car surrounded by a crowd, FDR's paralysis was not apparent to most voters. (Franklin D. Roosevelt Library)

its value. A growing number of homeless individuals and families were living in encampments at the edges of towns, referred to as "Hoovervilles."

Behind the scenes, ER coordinated Franklin's campaign aimed at female voters. In New York, the Women's Division typically increased Democratic votes by ten to twenty percentage points. They hoped to accomplish the same results across the country.

Initially, Eleanor avoided the cross-country campaign train. Her daughter Anna and at least one of her sons traveled with their father. Eleanor extended her speaking tour to the southern and western states, advocating for Democratic candidates and the Party platform.

In late September, she met up with the campaign in Arizona at Isabella Greenway's sprawling new ranch. Her friend threw an authentic western barbeque to introduce FDR and his entourage of U.S. senators to the political class of Arizona and New Mexico. It was a private event; the press was not invited.

Lorena Hickok was one of the campaign correspondents sidelined in the small town of Williams, Arizona. Anna Roosevelt Dall had invited a junior reporter to the event as her guest. The established journalists were furious. Why was a junior reporter getting unfettered access to the gathering of political bigwigs?

When Eleanor Roosevelt arrived at the Williams train station, the keen-eyed Hickok spotted her. She had interviewed the governor's wife several times and the two women shared a love of dogs. Eleanor Roosevelt cherished her Scottish terrier "Meggie" and Hickok's closest companion was her German shepherd "Prinz."

Hickok made her complaint to Mrs. Roosevelt, who agreed that if there was going to be a press representative at the event, it should be one of the senior correspondents. Eleanor invited Lorena Hickok to come along as her personal guest.

Traveling through the vast high-plateau pine forest of the immense ranch, the AP reporter began to realize there was more to New York's First Lady than she had originally realized. Eleanor Roosevelt provided the nexus for this gathering. She wasn't just an observer of her husband's political climbing; she was the ladder. While the newspapers clambered for information on the male politicians, it was the two women—Eleanor Roosevelt and Isabella Greenway—who were making the event happen.

Hickok suggested to her editor that a reporter be assigned to cover Mrs. Roosevelt. Another female reporter received the assignment, but she quit after a few days. Hickok continued filing her campaign stories and began covering Eleanor Roosevelt as well.

Without Earl Miller, Eleanor was alone on the campaign train. She hadn't been assigned a specific job and Anna was romantically distracted by reporter John Boettiger (1900–1950). Though both were married, their flirtation rapidly became an affair and a campaign liability. Eleanor needed a friend she could confide in.

When Franklin spoke out directly against the League of Nations and the World Court, Eleanor's discontent deepened. She refused to speak to him for days. On a train full of people, she felt isolated and alone. Lorena Hickok was the only one who seemed to notice.

A NEW CONFIDANT

Lorena Alice Hickok was an independent woman with a sharp sense of humor and an astute political mind. Born into a poor working-class household, she had financially supported herself from the age of fourteen. She had worked her way up from being a dishwasher to being one of the top investigative journalists in the country.

Originally, she viewed Eleanor Roosevelt as a gracious political wife quietly knitting in her husband's shadow. Now she realized the knitting hands were functionally engaged while the strategist's mind planned. Eleanor was intelligent, funny, and in need of a friend. Stuck on a train traveling long days across the country, the two women gravitated toward each other.

As the November election neared, Franklin D. Roosevelt's momentum was cresting and the presidency seemed in hand. When Missy LeHand's mother died in late October, Eleanor offered to leave the campaign to help the grieving younger woman make funeral arrangements. Hickok, now covering Eleanor full time, opted to accompany her back to New York.

The two women shared a drawing room on a train as they traveled east overnight. Nearly ten years separated them in age, but the heiress and the working-class reporter both knew personal sorrow and disappointment. As children, both had lost a mother. Both eased low self-esteem by serving others.

They shared personal confidences late into the night. Hickok revealed that her father had raped and disowned her as a teen. Eleanor was stricken by Hickok's experience. The two women consoled and counseled each other, establishing a special friendship and intimacy.

A week later, Franklin D. Roosevelt was elected the thirty-second president of the United States. He carried forty-two of the forty-eight states, winning 57 percent of the popular vote. Democrats took control of the Senate and the House of Representatives with a wide majority. The Women's Division had contributed greatly to the landslide victory. Even lifelong Republicans, like Aunt Corinne, crossed party lines to vote for social reforms.

As soon as FDR's win became apparent, the Secret Service arrived at the Roosevelts' home on 65th Street. "Life began to change immediately" (Roosevelt 1961, 163). Aunt Edith Roosevelt had spent eight years consumed

LORENA HICKOK AND THE LETTERS

Lorena Hickok was at the height of her journalistic career when she fell in love with Eleanor Roosevelt. Hickok was the first woman bylined on the front page of the *New York Times* and covered 1932's biggest story for the Associated Press: the Lindbergh baby kidnapping.

A woman in a man's profession, Hickok stood five feet eight inches tall with a heavy build and dark hair. She preferred wearing pants but adopted the skirt and blouse of a professional woman. She was the first female sports reporter in Minneapolis and a lifelong baseball fan. She smoked, drank bourbon, and played poker with the boys, but also loved opera and was a good cook.

Like Eleanor, Hickok had experienced romantic betrayal. After eight years of being together, her lesbian lover had left her for the stability of a heterosexual marriage.

Historians can debate whether Eleanor and Lorena were physically intimate, but the women's letters reveal an emotional affinity. During months of separation, Lorena wrote: "Most clearly I remember your eyes . . . and the feeling of that soft spot just north-east of the corner of your mouth against my lips" (Steitmatter 1998, 52). Hanging up the phone after a conversation with Hickok, Eleanor wrote how she had longed to whisper *"je t'aime et je t'adore"* (I love you and adore you), but her son had been within hearing (Steitmatter 1998, 17).

After Eleanor's death, Esther Lape recalled how she and Lorena burned the most indiscreet letters. The surviving correspondence was sealed in a box and donated to the FDR Presidential Library with instructions to keep it sealed until ten years after Hickok's death. In 1998, a collection of the provocative letters was finally published, allowing the public to consider for themselves the relationship between Eleanor and Lorena.

Further Reading

Streitmatter, Rodger, ed. 1998. *Empty Without You: The Intimate Letters of Eleanor Roosevelt and Lorena Hickok*. New York: The Free Press.

with managing the White House. Eleanor was determined to maintain her autonomy. The morning after the election, she returned to her students at Todhunter School. Eventually, she would have to resign, but she would teach for as long as possible.

Franklin would not be sworn in as president for four months. Eleanor invested that time in her own priorities. Bolstered by Lorena Hickok's encouragement, she worked on two books. She reconnected with her father and celebrated his early life by editing letters from his round-the-world adventure: *Hunting Big Game in the Eighties: The Letters of Elliott Roosevelt, Sportsman.*

She also drafted *It's Up to the Women*—a call for women to participate in their communities through political activism. She urged women to become the change they wanted to see in the health and education of their families. Working through her own disillusionment with Franklin, she wrote, "If you are going to be discouraged by finding that people do not always measure up to what you expect of them" or discovering that some individuals are not as honest as you would hope, "the sooner you get over that discouragement the better" (Roosevelt 1933, 211).

Eleanor Roosevelt also took to a microphone with her own radio show sponsored by Pond's cold cream. Each Friday night, she filled part of a half-hour broadcast speaking about family, children, and women's issues. To her surprise, people actually listened. Helen Keller (1880–1968), revolutionary advocate for the deaf and blind, wrote to Eleanor applauding "the ring of conscience and vision" in her broadcasts (Keller to Roosevelt, Feb. 19, 1933).

Eleanor Roosevelt's influence was increasing, but she also discovered how easy it was to be misinterpreted. Listeners misconstrued her advice that young women should know their limit for alcohol as an endorsement for girls to illegally drink liquor. Her position that women needed work outside of the home for their own fulfillment endeared her to many professional women but caused others to label her as destructive to American culture.

She was criticized for having a high-pitched voice and a per-program salary equivalent to what most workers made annually. She wrote back to a particularly chastising Mr. Graves from Toledo, Ohio: "I knew when I agreed to broadcast for Pond's Extract Company that I would be subjected to criticism of all kinds." People from across the country had been writing to her for financial help. She couldn't assist all of these people, but she could donate her "proceeds to help the unemployed" and she hoped that would "far out-balance the criticism." She realized that once her husband was sworn in as president she would have to cease her radio broadcasts, but until that time "I am a private citizen and have the right to decide for myself what is wise and what is unwise. I am sorry indeed to offend you" (Roosevelt to Graves, Jan. 25, 1933). A contrite Mr. Graves apologized.

In the whirl of attention over her increased public profile, Eleanor received a letter from Katy Mann and her son Elliott Roosevelt Mann. They congratulated her on becoming the First Lady of the country. Even if Eleanor knew Elliott Mann was her half-sibling, she made no comment. She responded only that it was interesting that he had been named after her father. Had she sought to uncover the truth, an investigative journalist like Hickok would have known where to look for answers. Eleanor Roosevelt embraced her father as she wished to remember him and chose to remain blind to his flaws, even if that meant never acknowledging her half-brother.

The friendship between Eleanor Roosevelt and Lorena Hickok, or "Hick," intensified quickly. At Christmas, the gruff reporter presented her new friend with a ring: a sapphire surrounded by small diamonds. It had been given to Hickok by an opera diva appreciative of a good review. Hick gave the cherished ring to Eleanor as a token of her affection. Eleanor slipped the ring on her finger and wore it on her left hand for the next four years.

WOMEN IN POWER

On January 1, 1933, Eleanor Roosevelt closed the door on another home. The family's belongings were temporarily moved from the governor's mansion back to New York City.

The presidential inauguration remained two months away. FDR spent January in Warm Springs recuperating and planning out his administration. When Eleanor wasn't with family, she and Hick dined out at a favorite Armenian café or spent the evening attending a play, a concert, or an opera. Some nights they cherished the simplicity of a quiet dinner at Hick's apartment. During the day, ER worked. She wrote, taught, scripted her broadcasts, and determined how she would be relevant as First Lady.

Old reform allies threw a party at the Waldorf Astoria in Eleanor's honor. Despite the chilly January night, Aunt Corinne fought through her arthritis and a lingering respiratory illness to attend. She was proud to celebrate her niece's achievements. Elliott's daughter proved to be the Roosevelt most like her Uncle Ted—politically courageous and determined to improve the lives of all Americans.

Eleanor Roosevelt humbly accepted the accolades from the women she admired, but she worried about Franklin's presidency. His new advisers were a tight group of male professors from Columbia University with similar affluent backgrounds and viewpoints. Louis Howe was sidelined, and her own influence felt diminished.

So many intelligent, talented women had come together to work on FDR's campaign. If there was going to be real reform, these female leaders needed to be in the rooms where decisions were being made. Women and children without power only had one true champion: women in power.

Every week, ER met with Molly Dewson to go over the names and abilities of women they hoped to have appointed to federal agencies. Women in bureaucratic positions would have true influence over governmental policy.

Dewson worked the political angle: these women were no different than the men; they had been crucial to the Democratic Party's success and now they deserved positions in the new administration. When necessary, she used Eleanor's endorsement as leverage. Dewson also approached FDR directly. Eleanor was able to deny influencing her husband's decision to appoint the first woman to a cabinet-level position because it was Dewson who had pressed the president-elect to make history by appointing Frances Perkins as U.S. secretary of labor.

Eleanor Roosevelt worked her personal connections. Elinor Morgenthau's husband, Henry Morgenthau III, was chosen for secretary of the treasury; ER suggested several women for high-level positions in his department.

Historian Susan Ware points out that ER and Dewson didn't see themselves as feminists; they were social reformers working to improve conditions for men and women. However, they stridently believed women in government tended to work for social good, while most men sought personal power and self-aggrandizement. ER and Dewson were intent on placing as many women as possible in positions of governmental power.

While they worked behind the scenes, an older generation of social reformers took note. Systemic change meant lasting change. Carrie Chapman Catt wrote to Eleanor Roosevelt that her walls had previously held portraits of statesmen. Now she was building a new collection of stateswomen, "and you are at the center of it all" (Catt to Roosevelt, August 15, 1933).

Roosevelt and Dewson believed that successfully integrating social reform into New Deal policy required the expertise and passion of the women who had spent their lives creating and instituting such programs. Social policy experts like Perkins and Esther Lape had well-developed progressive ideas waiting for implementation.

ER couldn't personally be in the rooms where policy was being determined, but through her network of women she would have a voice and an ear.

MOLDING THE PERSONA OF FIRST LADY

In 1928, Eleanor Roosevelt had written that women had to play the game of politics like men. They had to face undesirable facts and respond practically. As she prepared to become the nation's First Lady, she accepted that appearances mattered.

The backlash against her radio broadcasts demonstrated that many Americans were not ready for a woman in a position of authority. Aspersions were cast that she was an unelected adviser and had undue influence on the future president. If the public viewed her negatively, Franklin would distance himself. She might work proactively behind the scenes, but the image of the First Lady needed to be purposeful.

Lorena Hickok and Eleanor crafted a public persona for First Lady Eleanor Roosevelt. There were no mentions of servants or cooks. She drove her own car, answered her own mail. There would be no dwelling on her blueblood ancestry or abilities to speak multiple languages. First Lady Roosevelt was like other American women: she was a helpmate running a household, disinterested in politics but determined to support her

WOMEN IN POWER

The women Roosevelt and Dewson promoted into civil service shared certain goals and backgrounds. Most were over fifty, white, and college-educated; half of them held graduate degrees. As nurses or volunteers during World War I and the flu pandemic, they had witnessed social inequity. They fought for the right to vote to influence change. They honed their organizational skills advocating for labor rights, gender equity, and social justice. The majority were also wives, sisters, or daughters of politicians; they understood politics and how to communicate with men in power.

They all agreed: a qualified, talented woman in the right position would open doors for others, but a woman who failed would negatively impact them all. Their interwoven network informed, supported, and depended on each other.

Secretary of Labor Frances Perkins was the model, populating her department with capable and assertive women.

Nellie Tayloe Ross, former governor of Wyoming, became the first female director of the Mint, and Josephine Aspinwall Roche was appointed assistant secretary of the Treasury. Assistant Treasurer Marion Glass Banister paved the way for nearly a century of women in the position of U.S. Treasurer.

At the State Department, Ruth Bryan Owen became the first female U.S. ambassador, and Florence Jaffray Harriman served as U.S. minister to Norway.

Mary Harriman Rumsey and Hilda Worthington Smith led New Deal advisory boards or programs. Other network members were elected to Congress.

The women's network embraced the mission to educate voters. They published articles and spoke publicly on government programs and services. They built support for new ideas and recruited more women into civil service.

Male historians, who claim female suffrage and social activism failed to have long-term impact, disregard how this generation of women influenced FDR's New Deal. For the first time in American history, women served in leadership positions within government bureaucracy and led the way for others to follow.

Further Reading

Ware, Susan. 1981. *Beyond Suffrage: Women in the New Deal*. Cambridge, MA: Harvard University Press.

husband. They wove a veil of domesticity behind which ER cloaked her political activity for the rest of her life.

Hickok had become Eleanor's closest adviser. Esther Lape and Elizabeth Read found Hick a bit rough around the edges, but they delighted in Eleanor's personal happiness. Nancy Cook and Marion Dickerman immediately disliked the blunt mid-westerner. They resented Hickok's influence and didn't trust a reporter in the Roosevelt inner circle. Hickok returned their distain.

Cook and Dickerman had long been political advisers to both Roosevelts. Hickok, however, put Eleanor first and imagined a more visionary role for the First Lady. She proposed a revolutionary idea: The First Lady's Press Conference.

Women reporters were the first to be fired when newspapers made Depression cutbacks. If the First Lady held a weekly press event limited to female journalists, media outlets hungry for insider information would be forced to keep at least one woman on staff. Established journalist Ruby A. Black became the first woman hired by the *United Press* for the sole purpose of covering the First Lady's Press Conferences.

Hickok understood that these female reporters would be invested in the First Lady; her success would be their success. If they were treated with professionalism and respect, they would accurately convey First Lady Roosevelt's voice. The weekly events would keep Eleanor in the news and establish her as a person of authority worthy of being covered in the mainstream press.

ER could highlight issues important to women and thereby raise the profile of these issues in the general media. She could also support the administration by bringing in female officials, like Perkins, to speak on programs or about their role in the administration. She might also showcase notable women in literature and the arts.

Eleanor Roosevelt regarded her role as First Lady as a job. She pulled in her administrative team from the Democratic Party to staff her White House office. Tommy would act as her full-time private secretary. Others would work as secretaries and run the White House switchboard. A full-time social secretary would handle etiquette and events.

Aunt Corinne, who had cheered Eleanor just six weeks earlier, did not live to see her enter the White House. A new network of women gathered around Eleanor Roosevelt. Helen Keller sent a corsage for Eleanor to wear at the inauguration. Teams of women prepared to step into positions in various government offices and agencies.

When Eleanor Roosevelt walked into the White House as First Lady, Lorena Hickok was at her side. Together they would shape a forward-thinking ideal of what a modern American First Lady should be.

SOURCES

Cook, Blanche Wiesen. 1992. *Eleanor Roosevelt, Volume 1: 1884–1933*. New York: Viking Penguin.

Lash, Joseph P. 1971. *Eleanor and Franklin: The Story of Their Relationship Based on Eleanor Roosevelt's Private Papers*. New York: W.W. Norton & Company, Inc.

Letter from Carrie Chapman Catt to Eleanor Roosevelt. August 15, 1933. Franklin D. Roosevelt Presidential Library and Museum. http://www.fdrlibrary.marist.edu/_resources/images/ersel/ersel017.pdf

Letter from Eleanor Roosevelt to Mr. Graves of Toledo, Ohio. January 25, 1933. "Letters to (and from) Eleanor Roosevelt." American Radio-Works. https://www.americanradioworks.org/segments/letters-to-and-from-eleanor-roosevelt/

Letter from Helen Keller to Eleanor Roosevelt. February 19, 1933. American Foundation for the Blind. https://www.afb.org/about-afb/history/helen-keller/letters/eleanor-roosevelt/letter-eleanor-roosevelt-helen-keller-0

Perkins, Frances. 1946. *The Roosevelt I Knew.* New York: Viking Press.

Roosevelt, Anna Eleanor. 1933. *It's Up to the Women.* New York: Frederick A. Stokes Company.

Roosevelt, Eleanor. 1961. *The Autobiography of Eleanor Roosevelt.* New York: Harper Perennial.

Woloch, Nancy. 2017. *In Her Words: Eleanor Roosevelt on Women, Politics, Leadership, and Lessons from Life.* New York: Black Dog and Leventhal Publishers.

8

People's Advocate in the White House (1933–1936)

The Roosevelts entered the White House with a sense of urgency. Economic crisis engulfed the country; nearly four out of every ten workers were unemployed. In the week before Franklin D. Roosevelt's inauguration on March 4, 1933, 75 percent of the states closed their banks, fearing they would fail. Still, the White House was exhilarated, ready to get to work and save the country. "What was interesting to me about the administration," Eleanor Roosevelt wrote, "was the willingness of everyone to co-operate . . . that pulled us out of the depression" (Roosevelt 1961, 173).

Initially, however, Eleanor was not included in that cooperation. Franklin shut her out from his inner team of advisers, leaving her to manage the White House domestic staff and plan social events.

The blockbuster movie *King Kong* premiered that first week. It was as if the men in the White House believed they could subdue the economic monster without the intelligent women who had helped put them in office. Eleanor and her network needed partners in reform, not protectors.

Franklin felt it was political folly to lead public opinion, but Eleanor believed they should use the office to lead the public. She would use print, radio, and public appearances to grow her relationship with the American people and nurture their support for Progressive reforms.

As the new administration faced America's economic challenge, it failed to appreciate the perilous changes transpiring around the world. The day after Franklin D. Roosevelt was sworn in as president of the United States, Adolf Hitler and the National Socialist Party won election in Germany. By the end of the month, Japan announced its withdrawal from the League of Nations, Hitler assumed authoritative powers and usurped Bavaria, and the first German political prisoners were transported to a new prison at Dachau. The future was whispering in Eleanor's ear, but she kept her focus on American economic despair.

FIRST DAYS IN THE WHITE HOUSE

Moving into the White House, everything seemed familiar; no structural changes had been made in twenty-five years. Even some of the staff had been around since her uncle's administration. They were delighted to see a Roosevelt back in the White House but startled to watch the First Lady step into the elevator and insist on operating it herself. Eyebrows rose even higher as she and Nan Cook hammered nails into the walls to hang family photos.

Many Americans were homeless or living in poverty; it was no time for a palatial White House. ER removed the formal butler at the front door. There would be no White House chef or elaborate cuisine. Meals would be simple and guided by nutritional science based on the new field of "home economics" from Cornell University. They would serve affordable meals that could be easily replicated in American homes. While a noble ideal, the White House under Eleanor became notorious for inedible food.

On day two of the administration, Eleanor Roosevelt held her first Monday morning First Lady's News Conference. Thirty-five women of the press were ushered into the Red Room. Some were established reporters, like Doris Fleeson (syndicated political columnist), Emma Bugbee (*New York Herald Tribune*), and Bess Furman (Associated Press). Others, like Margaret Chase Smith (1897–1995) and Martha Gellhorn (1908–1998), were young reporters just starting their careers.

ER promised to treat the journalists fairly and never scoop them in her own writings. She would leave politics to the president but provide them with an inside look at her role in the White House. During her first week, she met with Native Americans from the Sioux Nation, representatives from California, and the leadership of Girl Scouts, and initiated a weekly tea with the wives of Cabinet members.

Lorena Hickok planned the press conference to be informal with the goal of developing camaraderie between the First Lady and the journalists. Many were working mothers. Eleanor respected them and identified with them.

Hickok asked the Associated Press to transfer her, but they already had a female reporter at the Washington bureau. Eleanor called Hick, who was in New York, and described how well it had gone.

At the end of the long day, Eleanor sat down to dinner with Isabella Greenway. As always, they talked of politics and children. Eleanor confided that Arizona's lone congressman was joining Franklin's administration. The two friends hatched a plan: Isabella would run for his congressional seat.

The friends also discussed two of Eleanor's children: Anna's affair with a married man threatened to erupt into scandal. And Elliott was floundering—he had no career prospects and a baby on the way.

Isabella brought out the practical problem-solver in her old friend. In the following days, Elliott headed west to be mentored in business by Isabella. And

First Lady Eleanor Roosevelt on July 20, 1933. Four months after entering the White House, Eleanor was holding weekly press conferences, securing civil service positions for women, and about to publish her book, *It's Up to the Women*. (Library of Congress)

Eleanor went for a drive with John Boettiger; together they planned out how he and Anna would strategically divorce their spouses and then marry. Eleanor Roosevelt would not pressure her children to stay in unhappy marriages.

The following day was Lorena Hickok's birthday. The miles that separated them seemed unbearable. Eleanor wrote to Hick, "All day I've thought of you . . . I ache to hold you close. Your ring is a great comfort. I look at it and think she does love me, or I wouldn't be wearing it" (Streitmatter 1998, 19). She promised that the next year, on Hick's birthday, they would be together.

CARVING OUT HER PLACE IN THE WHITE HOUSE

Eleanor moved into the bedroom suite at the southwest corner of the White House's second floor. Her aunt and uncle had shared this room during Uncle Ted's presidency. The view of the Washington Monument brought Eleanor comfort. The white obelisk had been completed two months after her birth. The simple classic structure rising over the city appeared enduring and triumphant.

The large bedroom had a small sitting room. Eleanor swapped their functions; the side room became her bedroom and the larger room acted as her personal sitting room and workspace.

Her day started with walking her Scottish terrier and/or riding. Her staff gathered for a morning meeting in the large West Hall just outside her sitting room. The middle of the day was filled with appearances and meetings. Frequently she hosted an afternoon tea for various women's groups or visitors, determined to make the White House accessible to the American public. Her official day ended with an evening drive and informal meeting with Louis Howe. After dinner, she answered mail, wrote correspondences, and managed household and personal accounts, sometimes late into the night.

Eleanor Roosevelt set a personal goal to equal Franklin's $75,000 annual income as president. Her first month in the White House, *Scribner's Magazine* published her article advocating for equal pay for women and fair treatment in the workplace. In the first month of her husband's administration, she and Franklin were at ideological odds.

Franklin and his advisers had quickly passed the Economy Act to reduce federal spending. It downsized government agencies, cut education funding, and reduced benefits for veterans. Women were banned from federal jobs if they had a husband employed in government. Even if the woman was the primary wage earner, she was forced to resign. Some of the women Eleanor had fought to place in government positions were pushed out. Education cuts added 100,000 teachers, mostly women, to the unemployed.

The previous year, veterans had come to Washington opposing pension cuts. President Hoover had subdued the protestors with military on horseback bearing bayonets and deploying tear gas. Angry veterans responded by supporting Franklin D. Roosevelt at the ballot box. Now, the veterans felt betrayed and marched back to Washington.

Howe advised FDR to allow the veterans to gather at an old military base and to use relief funding to provide them with meals. The encampment swelled. Washington residents feared an unruly mob.

Howe asked Eleanor to join him for an early drive. Without security or letting her know where they were going, he drove to the veterans' encampment. After initial hesitation, ER talked with the veterans, ate with them, and listened to their complaints.

She understood these men and their challenges. They knew her brother and cousin as respected World War I pilots. Her presence diffused the men's anger and hopelessness. She suggested many might find work with the Civilian Conservation Corps and promised to take their concerns to the president. The veterans felt heard; they embraced Mrs. Roosevelt as their advocate.

By the next morning the press had picked up the story. To face an angry mob of veterans Hoover sent the military, but Roosevelt sent his wife.

At her weekly press conference, ER spoke sympathetically of the veterans and diffused the notion that they were dangerous. The demonstrators disbanded and went home. Howe reminded Franklin that his wife was his greatest political asset.

In an attempt to stabilize food and commodity prices, the Agricultural Adjustment Act paid farmers to stop raising crops or livestock that were considered abundant. The unexpected ramifications were extreme. Southern property owners evicted thousands of Black sharecropper families so they could claim relief payments for unplanted cotton and tobacco. A mass migration of African Americans poured out of the South. Tons of unprocessed cotton were discarded; "300 million bushels of wheat were destroyed . . . and over six million pigs were slaughtered" (Cook 1999, 82). The carcasses were buried or turned into the soil.

The wastage sickened Eleanor. Americans were hungry and without clothes. Hickok leaked the story to the women journalists. She claimed ER had phoned the secretary of interior, asking: Why can't the federal government buy these surplus commodities and disperse food and clothing through relief agencies to people in need? Behind the scenes, ER pressed the topic. A process was quickly created to enable the purchase of farm surplus so it could be distributed, rather than wasted. The female journalists closed ranks around Eleanor. They recognized that men in the administration were taking credit for the practical change that First Lady Roosevelt had demanded.

Eleanor was carving out her place in the new administration as the unfiltered critic, the observer in the field, and the voice for the underrepresented. Franklin reengaged his wife's advice. Informal Sunday evening dinners resumed. Eleanor placed letters, notes, or items she felt Franklin should see in a basket beside his bed. Reading them became part of his morning routine.

Franklin's academic male advisers found Eleanor overbearing—a problematic idealist. Some even considered her a meddler with unwarranted influence. Gradually, however, a select few realized the value of her insight and began working with her to bring ideas to the president.

AN ALPHABET SOUP OF PROGRAMS

Franklin D. Roosevelt's legislative agenda was staggering. Eleanor half-heartedly supported his immediate repeal of Prohibition, but she and the women's network cheered the National Recovery Administration (NRA), the Federal Emergency Relief Administration (FERA), and the Civil Works Administration (CWA).

Under the Department of Labor, the NRA established codes on worker treatment, wages, and product pricing. Perkins appointed WTUL leader Rose Schneiderman to the NRA Labor Advisory Board. Workplace standards, originally developed by the Consumers' League, codified humane working hours as well as safe and sanitary workplace conditions and banned labor by minors.

The day before President Roosevelt signed the NRA into law, Eleanor Roosevelt bolstered the program by inviting Schneiderman to speak at her June 15 weekly press conference. She spotlighted the WTUL and used her influence to explain the value of unions and collective bargaining: "Only where they are organized do women get equal pay for equal work" (Beasley 1983, 12).

Like the Consumers' League's white label nearly twenty years earlier, the NRA's Blue Eagle label identified products made in compliance with NRA codes for the ethical treatment of workers. Eleanor Roosevelt and daughter Anna proudly accepted the first two ladies' coats produced in a factory with the Blue Eagle label. ER joined workers at a hat factory and stitched in the Blue Eagle label on the first hat produced under the new codes. On her fingertip, she balanced a golden thimble presented to her by the Millinery Workers Union.

FLIGHTS OF FANCY

Being the people's advocate was becoming a full-time occupation, but Eleanor did find moments for personal joy. In April 1933, a White House dinner celebrated the Amateur Air Pilots Association and Amelia Earhart's successful solo transatlantic flight. After the meal, the first lady of the air and Mrs. Roosevelt shared a press opportunity. They took a night flight over Washington, D.C., and Maryland with reporters.

Eleanor loved the freedom of flying. Some sources say she considered flying lessons, but Franklin thought it too dangerous for her to pursue.

The night flight sealed a friendship between Eleanor Roosevelt and Amelia Earhart (1897–1937). They both envisioned opportunities for women in aviation.

Under the cover of campaigning for Isabella Greenway, Eleanor flew to Arizona to resolve a family crisis. Despite having a wife and an infant back east, Elliott was now in love with another young woman, who was pregnant with his child. Unhappily, Eleanor facilitated a second child's divorce, while trying to keep it out of the press.

Lorena Hickok was also hungry for attention. Geographically separated for months at a time, Eleanor and Hick maintained a steady correspondence.

Letter writing had always been the most direct path to Eleanor's romantic heart and sometimes the two women wrote more than once a day. Letters were private slices of personal time—no interruptions, no filters.

In an audacious move, First Lady Roosevelt planned a three-week driving vacation with Hick through New England and French Canada. Despite the fact that six months earlier an assassin's bullet had missed Franklin and killed the mayor of Chicago, Eleanor refused a security detail. To appease Franklin and the Secret Service, she conceded to keeping a revolver in the glove compartment of her car.

Earl Miller had taught her to shoot. She argued that she could protect herself. She failed to mention that the glove compartment was locked and there were no bullets in the gun. Besides, she insisted, who would take notice of two middle-aged women?

In her shiny new convertible Buick roadster, Eleanor and Hick motored north. They stayed in small country inns and luxury hotels. Eleanor felt an autonomy she hadn't known since her travels with Mademoiselle Souvestre.

The food and ambiance in Quebec felt like Europe. The two women drove along the Gaspé Peninsula, wandering a dirt road through picturesque villages with staggeringly beautiful coastal views. Only the blue sports car attracted attention. It was an idyllic adventure.

When they returned, however, their world was already changing. Hickok had resigned from the news service and, at Eleanor's suggestion, been hired by FERA to investigate the effectiveness of relief programs. Hick would travel the country writing detailed reports back to Washington, but she would no longer have a public audience.

Simultaneously, Eleanor's public profile was blossoming. Her new magazine column, "I Want You to Write to Me," premiered in the August 1933 issue of *Woman's Home Companion*. Readers were invited to write to her with their challenges, questions, and successes. Eleanor represented the approachable public face of the administration. If the First Lady acknowledged your needs, you felt heard; if she helped you, you felt valued. Each individual she engaged with then related their first-hand experience to their friends and family.

Within six months, her team was answering over 300,000 letters annually and Eleanor Roosevelt's approval numbers surpassed the president's.

A UTOPIAN IDEAL

Lorena Hickok's first FERA assignment was investigating conditions in the steel mills and coal-mining areas of western Pennsylvania and West Virginia. The depth of poverty she saw overwhelmed her. Hick wrote to Eleanor about families living inside abandoned steel-smelting ovens. In coal towns, where miners had been blacklisted for trying to unionize, families huddled in fraying tents. They used the same trickle of mine-waste runoff water for drinking, bathing, and sanitation. Children were malnourished, diphtheria was epidemic, and health care was nonexistent. Hick urged Eleanor to experience the area herself.

Within weeks, Eleanor Roosevelt was walking through West Virginian towns. She became FDR's eyes and ears among the people again. Toxic waste from the coalmines degraded the land, leaving nothing for the people to live on. Eleanor saw lives wasted in squalor and dreamed of revitalizing communities.

Traveling the French countryside and living at Hyde Park informed Eleanor's idyllic view of rural life. If mining families could be relocated to fertile land, they could grow healthy supplemental food. Augmenting that simple livelihood with an income from light industry or craftsmanship—like Val-Kill furniture—would enable the people to build their own thriving community.

"Arthurdale" was Eleanor Roosevelt's economic and social experiment, and the first project of FDR's Subsistence Homestead program. The president listened to Eleanor's firsthand account and shared her convictions. Within two months, the NRA purchased 1,028 acres of West Virginia farmland. The federal government would build 125 houses and the families would pay back the government through long-term loans. Private donors would finance the school.

It was a utopian ideal: people lifted out of poverty to lead productive lives—healthy, educated, and empowered. ER wasn't just an advocate for Arthurdale, she helped coordinate its building and became its number one philanthropic supporter.

She envisioned modest well-built homes with modern heating, electricity, indoor plumbing, and kitchens fitted with appliances and a refrigerator. Secretary of Interior Harold Ickes baulked at the costs, arguing that impoverished miners wouldn't know how to use such luxury. But ER stood her ground; running water and appliances would transform the lives of the community's women. Before the end of the year, construction began.

THE RISING NAZI STORM

Carrie Chapman Catt had been relaying reports to Eleanor from female activists in Germany. Eleanor conveyed to Franklin the descriptions of Hitler's followers destroying Jewish businesses, burning books, and racially segregating public housing. The administration found it difficult to condemn racism in Germany while Jim Crow laws in the South segregated and limited individual rights because of race. FDR needed the Southern Democrats to guarantee passage of New Deal legislation; he wouldn't risk losing their votes.

By August 1933, Catt and several professional women, who had recently fled Nazi Germany, met with ER to enumerate firsthand experiences. They described how Progressive women's organizations were forced to dissolve after defiantly refusing to oust their Jewish members.

Nearly one hundred years of the women's movement in Germany was erased almost overnight. The Nazi Party defined a woman's role as wife and mother. Women lost the right to vote, to participate in government, or to own businesses. Germany needed to increase its population. Birth control was outlawed. Women unable to reproduce were considered valueless. High-ranking Nazi officials were offered secondary wives to produce children.

Women unwilling to bear children were labeled mentally deficient and considered undesirables, as were members of the LGBTQ community and the physically disabled. They were taken away to prison camps. Hitler's fascism wasn't just a threat to democracy; for Eleanor and the women's network, it was a chilling example of how easily female personhood could be lost.

The women made their case to Franklin D. Roosevelt. He finally appreciated the gravity of the situation and reached out to the British prime minister. Unfortunately, previous failed diplomatic negotiations had fostered distrust. The British did not respond and for the next few years, they regarded the U.S. president as an unreliable ally.

Catt and others tried to engage the American public with facts about Nazi atrocities. At the same time, however, anti-Semitic Nazi propaganda flooded American communities.

Eleanor had grown up in a home where Jews—even those with wealth—were considered to be of a lesser social class. Elinor Morgenthau was Eleanor's close friend and political ally; the two women were riding companions most mornings. Yet, Eleanor admitted that the Morgenthau's were kept somewhat separate from other family friends. Morgenthau was not part of the women's network. Approaching her forty-ninth birthday, Eleanor Roosevelt began to seriously reevaluate her own prejudices.

A NEW DEAL FOR WOMEN

First Lady Roosevelt appeared to constantly come up with new creative ideas, but she didn't do it alone. Not only was Lorena Hickok editing some of her writing and helping shape her public persona, there was also a close circle of imaginative minds at the core of Eleanor's women's network. These women were a well of experience and collaborative creativity. Every other week, Frances Perkins, Mary Harriman Rumsey, and Lady Elizabeth Lindsay joined Eleanor Roosevelt for "air our minds" luncheons.

An eclectic mix, all were college educated except Eleanor. Perkins was working class, while the other three were New York heiresses. All were or had been married with children. Perkins and Rumsey were widows and had been living together since 1922. (Whether their relationship was emotional or financial remains a mystery.)

Lady Elizabeth Hoyt Lindsay (1885–1954) was the wife of British Ambassador Sir Ronald Lindsay, but she was an American who had grown up on Oyster Bay. Her friendship with Eleanor and Isabella Greenway went back to their debutante days. A botanist and trained landscape architect, Lindsay had been an executive with the Red Cross in Britain during World War I. A political insider, she brought wicked humor and international insight to Eleanor's innermost circle.

During their "air our minds" lunches, these women felt free to admit defeat and found ways to turn failure on its head. The New Deal was not benefiting women equally. After six months, work programs were employing millions of men, but only 50,000 women. The Civilian Conservation Corps (CCC) initially excluded women. ER suggested women could staff botanical nurseries and raise the trees the CCC men would plant, but the president's advisers appeared unable to imagine how to utilize women.

To brainstorm ideas and jumpstart programs targeting women, why not go back to the female minds that built the foundation of the Progressive Movement? ER and Molly Dewson organized a conference at the White House on the relief needs of women. The organizational participants all had direct links to Eleanor's "air our minds" friends: the National Consumers' League, League of Women Voters, Red Cross, WTUL, social workers, and private philanthropists.

The conference resolved that women could do more than be hired to work in sewing rooms. Those with experience as nurses, teachers, librarians, researchers, and even investigative reporters (like Lorena Hickok) should be employed in those fields. With the recommendations and connections from the conference, 300,000 women moved into government-subsidized work over the next few months.

It's Up to the Women wasn't just the title of the first book that Eleanor Roosevelt authored—it was her mantra. *Time* magazine put her on the cover of their November issue—praising her as an advocate for the American people. Projects vied for her personal touch. When Lorena Hickok returned for the Christmas holidays, she had expected to spend personal time with Eleanor. However, she soon grew impatient competing for Eleanor's attention.

FEMALE ENERGY IN THE WHITE HOUSE

Eleanor sat knitting in the gallery of the House of Representatives on January 3, 1934, watching Isabella Greenway being sworn in as one of four new female representatives. With 73 percent of the vote, Arizona swept Greenway into office as their first female congressperson. How far they had come from being misfit debutantes. The network now had another voice in Congress and Isabella filled a fifth seat at the "airing our minds" luncheons.

Female energy was coursing through the White House. At her weekly press conference, ER gave Molly Dewson a national platform to deploy the "Reporter Plan." Local chapters of women's organizations were asked to assign individuals as "reporters" on federal agencies. These women would investigate agency programs, policies, and resources so they could act as community experts—providing information on New Deal programs to their neighbors and the local press. Women were encouraged to research criticism as well as successes of an agency so they could speak to both with facts.

Dewson and ER were purposefully nurturing public support for New Deal policies and engaging the public in an election year. ER wrote in her autobiography that these female investigators helped shape the trend of government. Over the next two years, 15,000 women became Eleanor Roosevelt's eyes and ears across the country; they showcased New Deal successes and raised the alarm on failures. When failures came, they had fact-based suggestions for improvement. This army of female "reporters" was invested in New Deal policies and built the foundation for a stronger Women's Division of the Democratic Party.

ER solidified her personal network of women by hosting regular gatherings for women executives in government. Many of these female civil servants had never been invited to the White House. She acknowledged the value of their work and they recognized her influence in the White House.

That influence extended to the judiciary. The women's network suggested Ohio State Supreme Court Judge Florence Allen to FDR for a position on the U.S. Court of Appeals. Allen had run for Congress in Ohio in 1932 and lost, but she was known among lesbian intellectuals in New York—including Dewson, Lape, and Read—for her stalwart professionalism on the bench and her support for the World Court. The Senate unanimously approved Allen as the first woman to sit on the Court of Appeals.

SPOTLIGHT ON PUERTO RICO

In March 1934, the Federal Emergency Relief Administration deployed Lorena Hickok to investigate conditions in Puerto Rico. Hick envisioned a working Caribbean vacation and invited Eleanor to join her. Eleanor jumped at the opportunity to travel, but she envisioned that a First Lady's visit could publicize the desperate poverty of Puerto Rico's people.

Rose Schneiderman had already alerted Eleanor to the island's deplorable labor conditions. Women and children produced embroidery inside ramshackle homes. What good were Blue Eagle labels if little girls with no labor protections were stitching adornments to be appliquéd onto union-made clothing?

While Hick was imagining quiet strolls on the beach to celebrate her birthday, Eleanor was inviting reporters Ruby Black, Emma Bugbee, Bess Furman, and a photographer to accompany them. It would be the first time an American First Lady had traveled by air out of the country. Puerto Rico would be her first international media event.

Dressed all in white, from hat to shoes, Eleanor Roosevelt walked through San Juan's muddy slums. Trash floated in stagnant puddles. Hickok and two male officials escorted the First Lady past shacks pieced together from wooden debris and bits of tin. Barefoot children in torn clothing clustered around them. ER stopped and asked the photographer to take a few steps back so he could capture a wider view of the devastating poverty.

She had become media savvy. The photo ran on the front page of newspapers across the country. Stories hailed First Lady Roosevelt as the champion of the downtrodden. The president and the nation were forced to acknowledge the need for action.

With specific recommendations from ER and Hickok, federal management of Puerto Rico and all other U.S. territories and reservations was transferred from the War Department to the Department of the Interior. Minimum wage levels for female garment workers were established and federal funding transformed schools and prisons from wooden shacks to masonry structures. But as in the American South, large landowners protested that relief assistance for agricultural workers would drive up wages and destroy their plantation economy. ER suggested an Arthurdale-like homestead project to improve living conditions, but the idea was blocked.

Eleanor did set aside time in the Caribbean for morning swims and private dinners with Hick, but Hick's self-respect suffered. Photo captions in the newspapers identified the former journalist not as a FERA investigator but simply as "a friend" of the First Lady.

A BLACK NEW DEAL

When New Deal programs excluded African Americans, community leaders approached Eleanor Roosevelt. Initially, the CCC was closed to Black men. When it did open up to them, they were relegated to segregated units or pejoratively assigned as kitchen staff or janitors. An African American was needed in a leadership position at one of the New Deal agencies. The male leaders suggested a Black woman would be less threatening to the white-male power structure; Eleanor agreed and brought FDR on board.

She activated her network and made inquiries. Frances Perkins, at Labor, had no interest in race issues. Harold Ickes at Interior was integrating his department but had issues with outspoken women. Harry Hopkins (1890–1946) and his assistant Aubrey Williams at FERA were determined to help all Americans, regardless of race, and they already had strong women within their ranks. Hopkins embraced the idea of a woman to head Negro Affairs within FERA and asked the First Lady for her recommendation.

Mary Jane McLeod Bethune had been at the edge of Eleanor's activist circle since before Franklin's return to politics. Only ten years older than Eleanor, Bethune was the daughter of emancipated slaves and had grown up picking cotton in South Carolina. Like Eleanor, Bethune had become an educator and managed her own school for girls. The two shared a passion for women's education, politics, and social justice. They trusted each other and could speak openly.

Eleanor had introduced her husband to the older Black woman years earlier; Franklin considered Bethune intelligent and insightful. Leaders of the African American community informally gathered at Bethune's on Friday nights. Ideas to advance racial equality were born and fleshed out in her apartment. Through Bethune, Franklin had input from an unofficial "Black Cabinet."

While Bethune's position was being established, ER made a point of inviting her and Walter White (1893–1955), head of the National Association for the Advancement of Colored People (NAACP), to the White House. She also modeled racial inclusion by inviting African American singers and musicians to perform at the White House on a regular basis.

Despite her intellectual desire to be unbiased, Eleanor Roosevelt admitted she had to work through her own racial prejudices. She typically greeted her female friends with a hug and a kiss on the cheek. When she realized she hesitated to greet Bethune in this same manner, she felt ashamed. Eleanor worked through her learned prejudices until she treated Bethune equally.

ARTHURDALE—SUCCESS AND FAILURE

By June 1934, ER's rural utopia was taking shape. Eager families moved into Arthurdale's first fifty houses. The First Lady timed the publishing of an article on "Subsistence Farmsteads" to coincide with the community's opening. Isabella Greenway led congressional support for federal funding toward the settlement's furniture-making workshop and Nancy Cook acted as the expert consultant. Residents would be trained in metalwork, weaving, knitting, and furniture construction. They would learn their trade making goods for their own homes.

Bernard Baruch, the financier Eleanor had met on her honeymoon, was now one of FDR's economic advisers. Impressed by the pride of ownership the families felt for their new community, Baruch financially supported the school.

Arthurdale, unfortunately, was a flawed prototype. To cut costs, Louis Howe purchased prefabricated beach houses, which failed to align with the completed foundations and weren't insulated for snowy winters. Houses budgeted at $2,000 a piece ended up costing $8,000–$10,000. Others made the unfortunate choices, but overruns were publicly blamed on Eleanor. Critics claimed Arthurdale was socialism and labeled Eleanor Roosevelt a communist.

The U.S. Post Office had proposed a small factory to make mailboxes and furniture for postal facilities, but opponents cried foul. The government would be subsidizing one town to the detriment of others. Congress controlled the Post Office's budget and defunded the manufacturing idea. Retaining adequate employment plagued the community.

At the grand opening, Eleanor was startled to see only white faces among the families. The ideal had been diversity. Though chairperson of the selection committee, she had not participated in choosing the families. Quaker leaders and social workers from the University of West Virginia had selected only white Christians born in the United States. No immigrants, no Blacks, and no Jewish applicants had been selected.

Defiantly, Eleanor demanded that the second phase of applicants be more diverse. She urged that African Americans be included. The homesteaders, however, voted to keep their community "white only." Eleanor was crestfallen.

Despite Arthurdale's shortcomings, Eleanor Roosevelt remained committed to the experiment; a large percentage of her personal income went toward supporting the community. Fifty-two other homestead projects followed. She pushed for resettlement communities for Jewish needle makers and for African Americans, but the latter was never approved.

THE FIRST LADY AND RACE RELATIONS

Eleanor Roosevelt met regularly with Walter White regarding the NAACP's drafting of anti-lynching legislation. Twenty-eight men of color had died in the previous year in reported lynchings. The bill defined lynching as an illegal act and held local public officials accountable for not protecting all citizens.

In the South, relief jobs with the Civil Works Administration (CWA) offered subsistence wages. White landowners protested that Black sharecroppers wouldn't return to the fields if they could make more money

ARTHURDALE'S LEGACY

Arthurdale was more than a government experiment in housing and industry; it was a Progressive showcase in community.

Fifty percent of the original households were coal-mining families. Agricultural experts from the University of West Virginia assisted them with seed selection, livestock, and farming practices. Connecting farming families with academic experts was an innovation first implemented by female college students during World War I. The Arthurdale example supported 1936 legislation to establish soil and water conservation districts across the country. Today, conservation districts continue to bring public, private, and governmental agencies together to protect soil health and maintain best agricultural practices for preserving healthy water, air, and natural resources.

Eleanor Roosevelt not only helped finance Arthurdale's school, she brought in innovative educators from Bank Street College and Columbia University to implement hands-on curriculum. While school buildings were still under construction, students learned by building their own structures. The high school class of 1934 used the context of topographical surveying to learn math. Their final project was surveying the path for state highway Route 92 as it passed their community. Arthurdale's students engaged in Science Technology Engineering and Math (STEM) education nearly a century ago.

Eleanor Roosevelt and Bernard Baruch initially underwrote the services of a physician and nurse for the school. The community also needed health care. Residents paid a dollar each into a community medical fund to pay for access to the doctor. It became one of the first experiments with socialized medicine in the United States.

Arthurdale was a flawed prototype, but through it, many families were lifted out of generational poverty. The legacy of Arthurdale lives on in the programs that evolved out of it and the numerous charitable organizations that continue to improve futures for impoverished families by helping them find the security of a safe and healthy home.

Further Reading

Arthurdale Heritage, Inc, West Virginia. n.d. Accessed January 23, 2021. https://arthurdaleheritage.org/

doing relief work. The rural Southern economy depended on poverty wages for agricultural laborers. Those that benefited from the old system fought to preserve it. Facing pressure from Southern white Democrats, President Roosevelt terminated the CWA in 1934.

FDR's capitulation to the so-called Dixie-crats angered Eleanor. She joined the NAACP, becoming the first white member of the Washington, D.C. chapter, and publicly voiced her support for anti-lynching laws.

Death threats followed. At the FBI, J. Edgar Hoover added "social agita-tor" to his file on Eleanor Roosevelt. In an attempt to discredit her activ-ism, a rumor began to circulate that the First Lady was of mixed race.

Behind closed doors, Eleanor held on to her convictions, facilitating meetings between Walter White and the president. By mid-April, there were enough votes in the Senate to pass the anti-lynching bill. Franklin, however, refused to signal support for the legislation and it died in com-mittee, never receiving a vote.

Racial inequities had become a priority for Eleanor Roosevelt. Some his-torians believe Lorena Hickok did not share this awakening concern and it increased the friction in an already tenuous relationship. When the two women tried to recreate the previous summer's romantic escape by travel-ing to Yosemite National Park, they were both disappointed. Because Hickok's publicity plans had succeeded, people recognized Eleanor Roos-evelt wherever she went. The mainstream press followed First Lady Roos-evelt's every move. There was no privacy, no place for Hick. While they continued to be confidantes and friends for the rest of their lives, the inten-sity of their relationship cooled.

AN INFLUENCING FRIEND

In September 1934, Eleanor Roosevelt returned to live commercial radio. She presented views on current events during five primetime Tuesday-night variety programs for a mattress company. This was followed by six fifteen-minute broadcasts, themed "Americans of Tomorrow," sponsored by the typewriter industry.

Introduced as "your friend and neighbor, Mrs. Franklin D. Roosevelt," she casually chatted to the audience (S. Smith 2014, 43). She explained how New Deal policies stabilized the banks and how the League of Nations was an important institution for peace. She touched on sports and recent sci-entific discoveries, but also mentioned refugees streaming out of Germany and the need for countries to open their arms to displaced peoples.

She urged unions and manufacturers to negotiate responsibly and sup-ported rural farmers by encouraging listeners to drink more milk. Strate-gically, she initiated a national discussion about new ideas: New York's successful unemployment insurance and a public pension system for the elderly or physically disabled.

Eleanor Roosevelt was becoming a radio professional and one of a hand-ful of female news commentators. She may not have been on the air as frequently as well-known personalities, like Al Jolson and Will Rogers, but she became one of the highest paid women in radio. Companies paid her $3,000–$4,000 per weekly broadcast at a time when female garment work-ers were making $12 a week.

Through her published articles, columns, books, speaking engagements, and radio programs, she achieved her goal of equaling Franklin's presidential salary during the administration's first year.

Critics decried her efforts as demeaning the position of First Lady. They equated accepting money from commercial sponsors with product endorsement. Eleanor countered that she donated her personal income to the American Friends Service Committee (Quakers) for distribution to various philanthropic efforts (primarily Arthurdale).

Her argument was mostly true; her agent received a percentage and Eleanor retained funds to pay for expenses linked to the broadcasts. When questioned about the criticisms at one of her Monday press conferences, Eleanor stated off the record that she would continue to "get the money for a good cause and take the gaff" (Beasley and Belgrade 1985, 3).

The female journalists accepted her answer. Eleanor Roosevelt was a role model for working professional women—passionate about her work and unapologetic about her income. While over 80 percent of Americans in 1934 did not approve of a married women working by choice, the women of the press corps could relate to the First Lady. They did not pursue the inherent conflict of interest.

BACK ON THE CAMPAIGN TRAIL

As the midterm elections approached in 1934, Eleanor Roosevelt apprehensively watched the movement toward war in Europe and the rise of racism within the United States. Over 20,000 people gathered in Madison Square Garden to support the "New Germany" Nazi movement. Republicans, opposed to New Deal policies, tried to turn voters against each other by depicting union members as communists and un-American. Popular nationalism functioned as a mask for racial bigotry.

While ER struggled to stay out of presidential politics, she leapt to help Caroline O'Day run for the U.S. House of Representatives in New York. Not only was O'Day a longtime friend, their political priorities were completely aligned; there was no need to spin or obfuscate. She signed on as campaign financial chair; it was the first time a sitting American First Lady actively participated in a political campaign.

ER, Nancy Cook, and Marion Dickerman hit the campaign trail for O'Day, with Amelia Earhart occasionally joining them. Each day was an exciting challenge to change minds and reinvigorate voters. Eleanor loved it. She felt guilty when she missed a rendezvous with Hick, but the campaign took priority.

On Election Day, Caroline O'Day won her seat. In Arizona, Isabella Greenway was overwhelmingly reelected. The women's network had helped reverse the historical trend for midterm elections to favor the party that was out of power. The Democrats increased their majority and the women's network expanded its foothold in Congress.

The triumph of the 1934 election, however, was short-lived. Mary Harriman Rumsey was tragically killed in a horse-riding accident. The loss struck at the heart of the women's network—life was unpredictable and there was so much work to do.

CHAMPION FOR THE WORLD COURT

With the advantage of a super majority in Congress, ER and the women's network pushed for sweeping legislation: social security, U.S. admission into the World Court, and an anti-lynching law.

The Roosevelts' bedrooms were along the same White House corridor, yet they were living fairly separate lives. As they hurried off to New York for daughter Anna's marriage to John Boettiger, Franklin D. Roosevelt unexpectedly signaled the Senate that he would support the United States joining the World Court.

For the past year, Esther Lape, Carrie Chapman Catt, and peace advocates had been laying out the argument to the American people for U.S. participation in the World Court. ER had penned the first chapter in a book of essays, *Why Wars Must Cease*, edited by Catt. World Court supporters, like O'Day, had been enthusiastically elected across the country despite attacks from William Randolph Hearst's newspapers and arguments that America's participation in any international body would relinquish U.S. sovereignty. The American people now seemed to favor joining the World Court and the president followed their lead.

Once back from the wedding, Eleanor Roosevelt jumped into the fray. With votes from O'Day, Greenwood, and Mary Norton, the House passed a bill to ratify U.S. participation in the World Court. During the two weeks of Senate debate, ER published essays and spoke in public forums supporting the bill. She and Lape were confident they had the votes in the Senate.

Father Charles Coughlin (1891–1979), a Roman Catholic priest in Detroit, had gained national attention intertwining politics and religion on his "Hour of Power" radio broadcast. He had initially endorsed Franklin D. Roosevelt for president. Some historians believe Coughlin became vocally opposed to Franklin when he wasn't offered a position in the administration. Others feel Coughlin was motivated more by power than ideology—the more he leaned into bigotry and white nationalism, the greater his following grew.

The weekend before the Senate vote, Coughlin railed against the bill, spreading anti-Semitic propaganda that Jewish bankers manipulated the World Court. Coughlin summoned his millions of listeners to flood their senators with letters and telegrams against internationalism.

The night before the vote—Sunday, January 27, 1935—NBC radio show-cased a Democratic senator from North Carolina denouncing ratification and Eleanor Roosevelt explaining her support.

She reminded the American people that the world was a smaller place than they would like to think. Events in other parts of the world impacted their daily lives. Like a good teacher, she provided the factual history: Americans had initiated the World Court. Theodore Roosevelt, a Republican president, had used the international body to peacefully resolve a land dispute with Mexico. "In an arbitration," she explained, "both sides give up something and the result is a compromise." The World Court had success-fully arbitrated boarder disputes, ship collisions, and other conflicts, which might have compelled military action.

The Great War had wasted millions of lives and dollars. "I remember the war well," she said. "I have looked on the acres of cemeteries in other countries where lie our boys and the boys of other nations. These dead are the result of war!"

"I beg of you," she added, "to let your senators in Congress know that you want to join the World Court at once" (S. Smith 2014, 70–72).

Washington was deluged with letters and telegrams on both sides. The Senate vote was postponed for two days. Franklin D. Roosevelt chose to appear neutral. The bill needed a two-thirds majority to pass; it fell short by seven votes.

For Eleanor Roosevelt and Esther Lape, the loss was personal. Lape felt betrayed by FDR's silence. She and Elizabeth Read remained devoted to Eleanor, but they distanced themselves from the White House.

FDR's advisers labeled his wife a liability. Harold Ickes claimed the First Lady had become a detriment to the president; no one had voted for her, she had overstepped her position. The president also pulled his support from the anti-lynching legislation and the bill died in committee.

Backlash was swift. Lape's American Foundation was threatened with investigation and the loss of tax-exempt status. She was forced to step away from international issues.

ER had expected critics, but now she had a vocal enemy in Father Cough-lin. Franklin strongly urged his wife to avoid speaking on international issues. The State Department became so rabid to control her comments that when the government of the Netherlands honored the First Lady with an "Eleanor Roosevelt" tulip, she was not allowed to thank them directly. An official response had to be issued through the State Department.

THE FIGHT FOR SOCIAL SECURITY

Eleanor Roosevelt may have felt like stepping out of the political spot-light, but Social Security was on the line. Franklin had campaigned on a pension system to protect all Americans from "cradle to grave" and health insurance, but he had failed to move forward on these promises. Eleanor and the women's network had laid the foundation and were determined to see Social Security implemented. Perkins headed the Social Security working committee. Assistant Secretary of the Treasury Joanne Roche kept ER abreast of the committee's progress.

Franklin's compromise plan excluded farmers, laborers, and domestic servants from coverage. Mary McLeod Bethune alerted Eleanor that these exclusions would heavily impact African Americans. With each incident, Eleanor became more attuned to racial inequities.

Franklin wasn't listening to Eleanor's objections. She felt frustrated and helpless to shift the discussion on Social Security.

Despite the limitations of the legislation, the "public educational work" previously done by ER and members of the women's network proved "sufficient to insure wide backing" from the voting public (Perkins 1946, 297). The Social Security Act passed in August 1935. It reinvigorated middle-class voters to support FDR, but it initially abandoned civil servants (from city clerks to sanitation workers), public school teachers, workers at charities and nonprofits, as well as agricultural and domestic workers. Historians estimate that 80 percent of Black women, 60 percent of Black men, and 60 percent of all women were initially not covered by Social Security. It amounted to institutionalized racism and sexism. The national health-care provision was completely abandoned.

Eleanor Roosevelt had to remind herself to play politics like a man. She couldn't despair at what was lost; she had to accept the compromise. It was a beginning; it could be improved upon.

THE WORKS PROGRESS ADMINISTRATION

Stung by recent failures and partial successes, Eleanor leaned into her relationship with the more progressive members of FDR's administration: Harry Hopkins and his team at the newly forming Works Progress Administration (WPA). With the dissolution of FERA, Congress created the WPA to enable the federal government to hire unemployed people to work on small infrastructure projects—building roads, bridges, schools, museums, parks, and other public buildings.

Eleanor Roosevelt advocated for female jobs in public health, cataloging historical records, and library management, including transcribing books into Braille. She also lobbied for the arts. Across the United States unemployed artists and performers languished while many Americans had never experienced public art, live theater, or professionally performed music.

For the past year, ER had also been trying to bring attention to youth needs; they were becoming adults in an economy with little opportunity.

Hopkins and Williams shared her concern and suggested she propose a youth branch within the WPA to the president.

Eleanor wrote that she approached Franklin late one night with the idea of youth training and education. She claimed the president put aside potential political objections and agreed to a youth program because it was the right thing to do for the country's young people.

A magazine editor invited to dinner at the White House, however, recounted a different, "very unpleasant and bitter scene between President Roosevelt and his First Lady" (K. Smith 2016, 169). Mrs. Roosevelt briskly stated that young people were being left out of relief efforts. The president countered that unemployed men over forty felt left behind; she should refer young people to the CCC. Mrs. Roosevelt displayed open contempt, stating forestry had limitations as a marketable skill. The president glowered, personally slighted. Besides, Mrs. Roosevelt added, the CCC offered little or no opportunities for young women. The verbal arm wrestling continued until the president agreed to consider youth programs.

The dinner-table brawl may be more accurate than the congenial discussion, which fit into Eleanor's crafted public image of the Roosevelt marriage. Franklin frequently instigated debate-like sparring matches with his wife. He pushed her to factually support her ideas or actions. The tactic angered her, but her responses supplied him with answers to counter opposition. On several occasions, Eleanor was startled to hear the president use her arguments when he presented "his" new ideas.

A few weeks after their tense discussion, President Roosevelt signed an executive order adding the National Youth Administration (NYA) to the WPA. Just as Eleanor had hoped, programs focused on education: helping students stay in school, providing aid for college (including historic Black colleges), and training in marketable skills. The NYA included a Women's Office and Mary McLeod Bethune finally had a specific position as NYA's director of Negro Affairs.

The WPA rolled out both construction projects and positions for creative artists. It created more jobs for a diverse population than any other New Deal program. Through Eleanor Roosevelt's influence, WPA construction projects were decorated with public art: sculpture, mosaics, and murals. Theater productions and music projects gave opportunity to the next generation of artistic innovators.

Eleanor Roosevelt finally felt she had a niche in the administration. She acted as an unofficial advisor to the NYA, checking on youth programs.

ON THE ROAD

New Deal opponents attacked the WPA for paying commensurately high wages to people of color. They implied that African Americans paid as musicians would forget their place as underclass laborers. Opponents used the issue as further evidence that Eleanor Roosevelt was a radical leftist.

To escape Washington, Eleanor returned to touring the countryside checking on NYA and WPA programs. Early in the administration, a *New Yorker* cartoon had poked fun at the First Lady's travels. Two coal miners down in a dark tunnel looked up and exclaimed, "For gosh sakes, here comes Mrs. Roosevelt!" (June 3, 1933). Now she was invited to visit a coal mine in Ohio and she accepted.

Surrounded by journalists, ER stepped into the mine car to ride down into the coal mine. She witnessed the working conditions first hand and spoke directly with the miners. She visited a dam-building site in the Tennessee Valley, hopping onto a viewing platform lifted by a crane and swung out over the construction. Critics charged that a woman's priority should be home and family. They claimed First Lady Roosevelt was destroying the structure of the American family with her unwomanly behavior.

ER countered with an article in the *Saturday Evening Post*. Coal was an energy source in her home. To be an informed consumer, she wanted to know if the men mining the coal worked in a safe environment. The factory seamstress, the workers maintaining water systems, and the farmer growing the food she served her family—all of these people were connected to her home. A responsible woman had an interest in the health and welfare of everyone who provided products or services for her family. It was a hard argument to counter.

Lorena Hickok also went on the road investigating WPA projects. The two women continued to write to each other, though not as often or as intimately. Hick loved Eleanor's descriptions of her daily adventures in her letters and began brewing a new idea.

ER traveled to Detroit, Michigan, to open a federally built, low-income housing development. The new residents were mostly African American and during the festivities, a young Black girl officially presented the First Lady with a small bouquet of flowers. Eleanor Roosevelt was the grandmother of several children similar in age. She smiled warmly and leaned down to the little girl. She accepted the bouquet, then plucked out a single flower and handed the bloom back to the brave child.

Flashbulbs popped. The image of Eleanor Roosevelt handing a flower to a Black girl became a meme. Some regarded it as a warmhearted gesture. *Georgia Women's World* and the far-right American Liberty League created a propaganda piece labeling the First Lady a "negro-lover." They sought to negate her voice in the South and northern mid-West.

Eleanor was infuriated. She needed a retreat from the public fishbowl of life in the White House. For her fifty-first birthday, she rented the third-floor walk-up apartment in Elizabeth Read and Esther Lape's New York brownstone. The Greenwich Village apartment became her hideaway from Washington and the Secret Service. Beyond the control and judgment of others, she could spend a quiet evening with either Earl Miller or Lorena Hickok.

A First Lady with a private apartment where her husband could not physically go seemed suspicious to J. Edgar Hoover. He heightened FBI monitoring of the First Lady.

As the mainstream press focused more on Eleanor Roosevelt, it became harder to shape her own narrative. Hick proposed that Eleanor should chronicle her activities in a daily newspaper column, just as she did in their letters. It would give Eleanor control over her message rather than letting reporters interpret her actions.

Eleanor signed a contract with a newspaper syndicate to write "My Day," Monday through Saturday. She also joined the Newspaper Guild and became a union journalist. The first column appeared on January 1, 1936. Through her personal daily journal, Eleanor Roosevelt would speak directly to the American people.

THE COMING CAMPAIGN

In a presidential election year, Hickok's reports described growing pockets of disgruntled voters. Franklin D. Roosevelt's lack of support for anti-lynching laws and his repeated capitulation to Southern Democrats alienated African American voters. The women's vote was being taken for granted. Howe was seriously ill and unable to lead FDR's reelection campaign. The women's network worried the president's advisors were overly confident.

The United States was increasingly isolationist. Even Dr. Albert Einstein approached Eleanor Roosevelt seeking help to stop the deportation of Jewish German scientists back to danger in Nazi Germany. The woman's network worked behind the scenes trying to mitigate restrictive immigration laws. ER and Frances Perkins did their best to protect Jewish scholars, from rabbis to physicists, by extending work-related visas. Caroline O'Day attempted to pass legislation to stop the deportations, but failed.

When Louis Howe died in April 1936, Eleanor Roosevelt lost one of her closest friends and allies. As with many losses in her life, however, she pushed aside her true emotions. "[In] public life," she wrote, "you can have no private time for sorrow. Duties must be performed and your own feelings must be suppressed" (Roosevelt 1961, 186). The self-effacing little man, who shared her love of theater, who had helped shape her public voice and believed in her, was gone.

Howe had watched Eleanor and the women of the Democratic Committee change the Party from male bosses motivated by personal power and cronyism to issue-driven individuals supported by facts. The women had become better organizers, better at getting out the vote, and better builders of social institutions. He championed their efforts and knew how to deploy them in a campaign.

Without Howe, Eleanor initially avoided the campaign. She was conflicted about her husband's reelection. FDR's failure to address lynching or poll taxes in the South angered her and she was appalled by his silence on Hitler and Fascists threatening Spain's democratically elected government. But in the days before the Democratic National Convention, he helped pass legislation that provided a concrete step toward federal labor law and the abolishment of child labor.

To support Franklin D. Roosevelt's reelection, Molly Dewson activated the Reporter-Plan women to reinforce the benefits of New Deal programs in their communities. The Democratic Women's Division put 60,000 precinct workers and 10,000 local leaders to work talking to constituents. Eleanor Roosevelt had supported the individuals of her network and now these women pulled her forward through her indecision and personal gloom.

At the Democratic National Convention, the Women's Division placed innovative "rainbow flyers" on each delegate's seat. Flyers in eight different colors addressed factual talking points on specific topics: a red sheet detailed how Democratic actions had reduced utility costs while increasing rural access to electricity; a blue sheet highlighted successful labor protections; and a purple sheet explained Democratic steps to normalize trade. The yellow sheet asked voters and businesses to "Take Stock of Your Gains." Voters were asked to consider if they were better off now than they were four years ago.

Following the convention, Franklin sailed off on a vacation with his sons. The campaign wouldn't begin until August. While ER publicly claimed she didn't "take any particular part in the political activities unless I was specially asked" (Roosevelt 1961, 186), the facts are more complicated. From Campobello, she sat down and detailed what the campaign was lacking and what needed to be done. (See Primary Documents: *Eleanor Roosevelt Campaign Strategy Memo, July 16, 1936*.)

Despite her decisive memo days earlier, Eleanor wrote to Hick, "I have a feeling the tide is setting pretty hard against F.D.R. just now but there is time to turn it." The quiet isolation of the wind and waves at Campobello seemed to constantly reshape her resolve about the election. She told Hick she felt "Lord so *indifferent!*" (Streitmatter 1998, 190). Hick took Eleanor to task for the statement. From her place of privilege, Eleanor might question Franklin's reelection, but poor people across the country desperately needed him to be president.

Without Louis Howe, Eleanor's commitment became fragmented. The two voices from her childhood—her father's empowering support and her mother's crushing criticism—echoed in her head. Her female network regarded her as the bold leader. Molly Dewson called her "my wonder woman" (Ware 1981, 10). At the same time, opponents denounced her as a dangerous leftist.

To her intimate friends, Eleanor revealed ambivalence. She wrote to Hick: "I truly don't think that what I do or say makes much difference" (Streitmatter 1998, 193). In "My Day," she appeared to be wandering through life from one luncheon to another. She skirted real topics.

In the midst of the election, Hick suggested that Eleanor should write her autobiography. Writing about her childhood and her early married life grounded Eleanor in her own story. It validated her personal journey to overcome fearfulness and reclaimed her personal priorities.

A voice from her early life was also challenging her publicly. Cousin Alice Roosevelt Longworth staunchly supported Franklin's Republican opponent. Alice labeled New Deal policies as "Mollycoddle Philosophy," contending that Franklin had been pampered by others. She charged that the New Deal was weakening American society and making people dependent on the federal government.

Eleanor Roosevelt casts her ballot at Hyde Park, NY, in the November 3, 1936 reelection of her husband. Though the moment appears casual, Eleanor was surrounded by a crowd of photographers and film cameras. She flashed a smile and hid her annoyance at being made a spectacle. (National Archives)

Few people dared challenge Theodore Roosevelt's daughter, but Eleanor stepped forward and reminded voters that no one had mollycoddled Franklin through polio. Just as Theodore Roosevelt had rebuilt his physical health, Franklin D. Roosevelt had overcome his physical challenges. Eleanor's voice was strong and clear: No one "who really knew both men" could call Franklin a mollycoddle (Cook 1999, 386). Theodore Roosevelt had been a champion of the underserved, a Progressive, but the Republican Party had abandoned his goals. Seamstresses and farmers, coal miners and factory workers, were not mollycoddles; they were working people who deserved a government that cared about their sacrifices and strife.

On Election Day, Franklin D. Roosevelt carried every state except Vermont and Maine. Democrats held three out of every four seats in Congress. The number of women voting for the Democrats increased dramatically and the African American vote solidified behind Roosevelt. Eleanor embraced Louis Howe's mantra: politics was compromise. There were four more years to get things right.

SOURCES

Beasley, Maurine, ed. 1983. *The White House Press Conferences of Eleanor Roosevelt*. New York: Garland Publishing.

Beasley, Maurine H., and Paul Belgrade. 1985. "Eleanor Roosevelt: First Lady as Radio Pioneer." Paper presented at Annual Meeting of the Association for Education in Journalism and Mass Communication (August 3–6). https://eric.ed.gov/?id=ED258200

Cook, Blanche Wiesen. 1999. *Eleanor Roosevelt, Volume 2: The Defining Years 1933–1938*. New York: Viking Penguin.

Perkins, Frances. 1946. *The Roosevelt I Knew*. New York: Viking Press.

Roosevelt, Eleanor. 1961. *The Autobiography of Eleanor Roosevelt*. New York: Harper Perennial.

Smith, Kathryn. 2016. *The Gatekeeper: Missy LeHand, FDR, and the Untold Story of the Partnership That Defined a Presidency*. New York: Simon & Schuster, Inc.

Smith, Stephen Drury, ed. 2014. *The First Lady of Radio: Eleanor Roosevelt's Historic Broadcasts*. New York: The New Press.

Streitmatter, Rodger, ed. 1998. *Empty Without You: The Intimate Letters of Eleanor Roosevelt and Lorena Hickok*. New York: The Free Press.

Ware, Susan. 1981. *Beyond Suffrage: Women in the New Deal*. Cambridge, MA: Harvard University Press.

9

Battles Large and Small: World War II (1937–1943)

"One of the greatest causes of trouble in the world today is the distrust we have for each other," Eleanor Roosevelt said, "which brings about fear, and fear is the basis of all our other evils." While paying tribute to Amelia Earhart at a *New York Herald Tribune* event (October 5, 1937), she found a way to speak about racism, nationalism, and Fascism. Fear of the other, fear of displacement, fear of opposition—Eleanor Roosevelt knew how fear could motivate the worst in humanity.

She hoped to inspire compassion and tolerance, but after eight years of economic insecurity, many Americans still feared hunger and homelessness. Meanwhile, as fear of war mounted in Europe and Asia, Americans tried to look away.

FRANKLIN D. ROOSEVELT'S SECOND TERM

Eleanor Roosevelt was now a sought-after, highly paid public lecturer traveling a multicity circuit through several states two or three times a year. She had trained herself to be comfortable speaking before live audiences of several thousand people and radio audiences of a million or more.

Since George Washington, U.S. presidents had traditionally held office for no more than two consecutive terms. She believed Franklin had run his last presidential campaign; she felt liberated to speak her mind. On a lecture tour from Pennsylvania to Michigan, she encouraged voter activism, including lobbying political officials to improve and expand Social Security. She threw her support behind federal aid for low-income housing and a new anti-lynching bill.

President Roosevelt's reelection and overwhelming Democratic control of Congress created political opportunity. Esther Lape had been collecting data on deficiencies in the country's delivery of medical care. She interviewed over 2,000 physicians and medical educators for *American Medicine: Expert Testimony Out of Court*. ER, Lape, and Elizabeth Read believed the moment was ripe to take on health care.

The threesome strategized over breakfast on the morning of Franklin D. Roosevelt's January 1937 State of the Union address. At the Cabinet dinner following the speech, they would ease the conversation toward health care.

Public-managed health care had been removed from the 1935 Social Security Act because of opposition from the American Medical Association (AMA). Lape and Read now had evidence that a broad spectrum of the medical community actually favored a nationalized medical delivery system.

The three women knew that Franklin would need evidence of tangible public support before he would consider challenging the powerful AMA. They approached him with a proposal. If their network of women presented the benefits of a public health-care system to the American people and won the people's support, would the president back the legislation? Franklin said "No."

A conservative Supreme Court repeatedly overturned New Deal programs, declaring them unconstitutional. FDR's attention turned entirely to countering the court. Without hearing opposing opinions, he announced his intention to amend the U.S. Constitution and add Supreme Court Justices. Suddenly, Eleanor felt the crushing absence of Louis Howe. She had become the only voice in the White House willing to question or criticize the president and he no longer sought her advice.

Opposing public opinion came swiftly. Elizabeth Read counseled Eleanor that Franklin's plan posed a serious attack on the Constitution and its balance of governmental power. The congresswomen in Eleanor's network felt the president was overstepping his authority. Eleanor opposed Franklin's action, but she found herself publicly explaining the president's motivation.

Franklin spent months flailing against the Supreme Court. ER appealed to Democratic Party leaders: She and the Progressives had brought African American voters to the Democratic Party, but to keep this new constituency, anti-lynching legislation, unemployment, and racial inequality in health care needed to be addressed. Eleanor and her network of progressive-minded women watched the opportunity to pass national health care and the new anti-lynching bill slip away.

LAUGHING AT HERSELF

Despite disappointments, Eleanor maintained her appreciation for fun. The male press corps held an annual Gridiron Dinner where they lampooned the president and men of the administration. First Lady Roosevelt countered with the Gridiron Widows Dinner—an event for female journalists, women of the administration, and wives of public officials.

Eleanor and Elinor Morgenthau typically acted out a song or a comical skit. At the 1937 dinner, the newswomen presented a humorous skit of the "First Lady" engaged in a sit-down strike. Picketers marched across the stage with signs demanding: "Union hours for First Ladies" and "No more than 300 handshakes a day." Picket signs denounced teas and demanded limits on public events (Lash 1971, 652). Frances Perkins came on stage to negotiate between the striking "First Lady" and organizations desiring her attention. The "First Lady" character refused to negotiate or move. The rest of the evening's entertainment had to go on around her.

Eleanor Roosevelt laughed heartily. The camaraderie and mutual respect between the First Lady and the female press corps had grown unshakeable.

THE POWER OF WORDS

In the spring of 1937, Eleanor Roosevelt's autobiography *This Is My Story* was serialized in the *Ladies' Home Journal* magazine. She bravely exposed the loneliness and inferiority she had felt as a child. She chronicled her lack of preparation for motherhood and the trials of Franklin's recovery from polio. For the first time, an American First Lady published an autobiography while still in the White House. Her revelation of vulnerabilities and failings made her even more approachable.

Her new devotees in the African American community, however, were startled to read the term "darky" in her references to Black servants. When challenged, Eleanor Roosevelt became defensive. She argued that her Great-Aunt Gracie had used the term affectionately. She dismissed accusations that the word was an offensive racial pejorative.

Negative letters, however, kept coming and similar outrage flared when she used the word "pickaninny." Eleanor was forced to reevaluate her family's attitudes and acknowledge that her father's mother and aunt had used these terms in reference to enslaved Black people. Both words cast African Americans as subhuman.

Eleanor Roosevelt struck the term "darky" from her autobiography before it was published as a book. She eliminated the two words from her vocabulary and required her staff to do the same.

Her personal story reinvigorated the *Ladies' Home Journal* and the book quickly became a bestseller. ER earned the equivalent of the president's annual salary for *This Is My Story*. The nation proved eager to learn how the first couple had met and married. Women in the administration bought copies for their sisters and daughters. Even critics praised the First Lady's personal candor.

While ER laid bare her failures and dark moods, Isabella Greenway knew she had strategically omitted some truths. "Eleanor *my* dearest" she wrote, "you have in your own way . . . found such a perfect middle path for *narrative*." Eleanor's good friend didn't challenge her for leaving out Franklin's infidelity or admonish her for downplaying her own political acuity. There was much in the book to help other women and Greenway added: "your example of . . . translating bitterness to triumph thro interpretation—will help many a person" (Miller and McGinnis 2009, 250).

However bold Eleanor Roosevelt had been in revealing her personal foibles, she maintained the persona she and Lorena Hickok had crafted: a devoted wife, a mother, and an apolitical helpmate.

BETWEEN A WEDDING AND THE SPANISH CIVIL WAR

Journalist Martha Gellhorn, Eleanor Roosevelt's friend, was becoming a renowned war correspondent covering the Spanish Civil War. Francisco Franco Bahamonde's insurgent Nationalist fighters were crushing the democratically elected Communist government of Spain.

American capitalists, including Franklin D. Roosevelt's advisers, were so threatened by communist philosophy, they endorsed the United States placing a trade embargo on trade with Spain. American companies, however, continued selling oil, steel, and components for making munitions to Nazi Germany. Hitler in turn supplied Franco.

Eleanor was incensed; Franklin's policies enabled Hitler's military expansion and assured Franco's Fascist takeover of Spain. The unfortunate reality was that commodity sales to Germany were reviving the American economy.

Martha Gellhorn returned to the United States with her partner and fellow writer, Ernest Hemingway. Hemingway and a Dutch film director had made an exposé documentary, *The Spanish Earth*. Gellhorn reached out to Eleanor for a meeting with the president, but no invitation was forthcoming.

Newspapers carried Gellhorn's articles about 500 Spanish orphans seeking refuge in the United States. Eleanor Roosevelt used her "My Day" column to encourage charity toward the children but she stopped short of advocating for their asylum.

The Roosevelts' son Franklin Jr. was marrying Ethel du Pont, the daughter of one of America's wealthiest industrialist families. British media hailed it a "Romeo and Juliet" wedding. The son of America's leading liberal Democratic family was marrying the daughter of Eugene du Pont Jr., the financial support behind the American Liberty League, the conservative group that had attacked Eleanor for supporting racial equality.

The Du Pont Company represented everything Eleanor Roosevelt opposed. It was one of the world's largest producers of munitions and military equipment. It employed thugs to violently suppress striking workers. The Du Pont Company and its subsidiary General Motors were actively building petroleum refineries, munitions, and vehicles in Germany in partnership with the Nazi government.

Eleanor Roosevelt had resolved not to intrude into her children's private lives, but she and her husband questioned Franklin Jr.'s choice of bride.

An extravagant wedding, when so many Americans faced extreme poverty, put the Roosevelts in a precarious position. President Roosevelt brushed off press inquiries regarding the cost, glibly answering that traditionally the bride's family paid for the wedding.

On the big day, film crews took newsreel footage of the American society wedding of the year. The Delaware National Guard provided security at the du Pont estate for over a thousand reception guests. As the champagne flowed, Eleanor withdrew. She had no appetite to watch Franklin toast with his political foe. She left the reception to deliver her weekly radio broadcast.

On route to Hyde Park the following day, Eleanor heard over the radio that Amelia Earhart was missing, believed lost at sea while attempting her round-the-world flight. The news was devastating. Eleanor had helped her friend negotiate landing permissions in difficult countries. She regarded Earhart as an icon of bravery.

The loss prompted Eleanor to embrace her own courage; she contacted Martha Gellhorn. They screened *The Spanish Earth* for the president and the filmmakers made their case, but President Roosevelt did not lift the embargo. Even humanitarian and medical supplies for Spain remained blocked.

Within days, the July 12, 1937 issue of *LIFE* magazine featured a photo of bride Ethel du Pont Roosevelt with her ten yards of tulle veil flowing

around her. On the facing page images depicted striking steel workers and
WPA artists protesting layoffs. The story preceding the society wedding
was "Death in Spain: The Civil War Has Taken 500,000 Lives in One Year."
Images of dead children on Spanish streets killed by German artillery were
a page turn from the Roosevelt wedding.

The magazine's editors had critically juxtaposed President Roosevelt in
a protected bubble of extravagance against the economic realities of working people and the atrocities facing civilians in distant lands. The story
haunted Eleanor Roosevelt.

THIS TROUBLED WORLD

A few months later, Eleanor wrote to Hick that she wanted to write an
article on peace. She had remained silent on foreign policy for nearly a
year.

Eleanor and Hick had remained confidantes, but when they actually
spent time together, it frequently ended in hurt feelings and shattered
expectations. Eleanor had had a hurtful falling out with Nancy Cook and
Marion Dickerman. She had dissolved her business partnerships and co-
owned properties with them. Her correspondences with Hick were an
emotional lifeline.

Lorena Hickok had considered covering the war in Spain, but Eleanor
talked her out of it. The once successful reporter had traded her journalistic identity for a relationship with the First Lady. Now, she had neither the
relationship nor the career. Though depressed, Hick continued to champion Eleanor Roosevelt.

Be brutally honest, Hick advised Eleanor. Write exactly what you think
and what's in your heart. What began as a magazine piece became a book-
bound essay: *This Troubled World.*

Advocating for peace applied not only to relations between nations,
Eleanor Roosevelt wrote, but also to relations between workers and business, racial groups, and economic classes. Americans needed to be mind-
ful of peace every day, in every aspect of their lives. "We must reach a point
where we can recognize the rights and needs of others, as well as our own
rights and needs" (Roosevelt 1938).

She reevaluated her blue-blood heritage. "The people who settled in
New England came here for religious freedom," she wrote, "but religious
freedom to them meant freedom only for their kind of religion.... Like our
forebears we want freedom for ourselves, but not for those who differ from
us." She chastised the U.S. government for its "bullying, patronizing attitude" toward Central and South American countries (Roosevelt 1938).

She took isolationists to task: oceans wouldn't protect them in a modern world and inaction wouldn't bring peace. To her pacifist friends, she explained that Fascism was a threat to democracy; the United States needed a standing peacetime military. Only an electorate informed with truth could make the choice to enter into military engagement. The people should demand a free press untainted by special interests.

She pointed at greedy arms dealers selling munitions and encouraging war, fully aware that her in-laws, the du Ponts, were selling munitions to Germany, Italy, and both sides in Asia. She also called for the public to hold profiteers accountable for their actions.

The League of Nations had failed because countries, like the United States, refused to endow it with confidence as an honest mediator. "To say that we cannot find a way [to mediate between nations] is tantamount to acknowledging that we are going to watch our civilization wipe itself off the face of the earth" (Roosevelt 1938).

Looking forward, she described an international body of nations empowered with a policing and inspection capability to hold aggressor governments accountable without punishing civilians. The American government might raise an embargo against Spain and Japan, but economic sanctions would only be successful when adopted by a collective group of nations.

"We will have to want peace," Eleanor Roosevelt wrote, "want it enough to pay for it, pay for it in our own behavior and in material ways. We will have to want it enough to overcome our lethargy and go out and find all those in other countries who want it as much as we do" (Roosevelt 1938).

She gave Franklin a copy before the manuscript went to the printer and claimed he made no changes. World tensions brought them closer; they conferred at least once a day. President Roosevelt finally spoke out against Germany's anti-Jewish policies. Secretly, he attempted to arrange a meeting, but Britain's leaders ignored his overtures.

When *This Troubled World* hit bookstore shelves in January 1938, it sold well. Audiences across the country gave Eleanor Roosevelt a standing ovation when she spoke on peace efforts. Carrie Chapman Catt and other activists rallied to her side, even supporting President Roosevelt's budgetary increase to modernize the military.

Despite Eleanor's renewed influence, President Roosevelt continued the embargo on Spain. German and American propaganda depicted Spain's communist government as anti-Catholic. Father Coughlin falsely portrayed Franco as the defender of Christian civilization. Coughlin also denounced Jews as the founders of the Communist Party and incited hatred by claiming Jews were responsible for slaughtering millions of Christians. He called for a "Christian Front" to defend America from communism. President Roosevelt feared supporting Spain would cost Democrats their Catholic constituents.

THE COMMUNIST SCARE RETURNS

Father Coughlin's anti-communist megaphone empowered politicians opposing New Deal programs. Social Security and the WPA were labeled "socialist" or "communist."

Actual communist ideals had been circulating in the United States since 1917. The Communist Party had been active in unions and labor disputes, and supported racial equality. Conservative politicians exploited the fear of communists overthrowing the government to vilify individuals and influence voters against communist philosophy.

Texas Republican Martin Dies chaired the House of Representatives' Un-American Activities Committee (HUAC) to investigate "communist" activities. Dies described national health care and governmental housing assistance as gateways into Marxist Communism.

In the tumultuous summer of 1938, Eleanor Roosevelt and her women's network led the passage of the Fair Labor Standards Act. Frances Perkins carefully drafted the legislation specifically applying its measures to companies engaged in interstate commerce. The federal government held constitutional authority over commerce across state borders; therefore, the Act was safe from court challenges.

The Act extended protections for maximum daily work hours and minimum wages. It treated male and female workers equally and prohibited labor by children under the age of sixteen. It was the success Eleanor Roosevelt and the women of the Consumers' League had been working toward for decades.

If the Fair Labor Standards Act couldn't be challenged, the woman who wrote it could be attacked personally. The Dies Committee targeted Secretary of Labor Perkins. ER knew Dies was popularizing himself, so he could run for president and "Miss Perkins was the easiest victim" (Lash 1971, 680). Eleanor enlisted Franklin to shield Perkins.

Dies couldn't go after the First Lady, so he attacked programs and people important to her. He turned his attention to the WPA arts programs, accusing the theater companies of producing communist propaganda.

ER had become a supporter of the American Youth Congress. HUAC subpoenaed the youth activists. ER conceded that some individual participants were communists, but others were socialists, or members of labor unions. No single philosophy dominated the group. Opponents denounced the First Lady as too naïve to see she was being used by communist agitators.

Eleanor Roosevelt with labor advisor Rose Schneiderman and David Dubinsky, International Ladies' Garment Workers' Union president, at a 1938 performance of *Pins and Needles*. The musical revue, created by union workers, championed labor issues and used satire to counter personalities, like Eleanor's nemesis—anti-Semitic Catholic priest Father Coughlin. Eleanor's media influence helped make the production a Broadway hit. (Library of Congress)

Dies alleged the First Lady was a communist threat and the promoter of "Eleanor Clubs"—groups of organized Black maids rumored to exist in Washington, D.C., and throughout the South. Similar to social media conspiracies of the twenty-first century, rumors spread that African American cooks were gathering in groups and being indoctrinated into communism at Eleanor Clubs. It was alleged that these Black women were going to rise up and demand to eat at their white employers' dinner table or quit and leave the families without a cook. Eager to find salacious material on the First Lady, J. Edgar Hoover sent the FBI to investigate. Agents found all the allegations were heresy and without factual origin.

ADDRESSING RACISM

If democracy was to survive, Eleanor Roosevelt believed it had to truly provide equal treatment, protection, and representation for all people. She and Mary McLeod Bethune traveled to the Southern Conference on Human Welfare in Birmingham, Alabama. The racially integrated organization worked to address the educational, economic, and voting inequities in the American South.

In an effort to stop the conference, officials sent police to enforce Birmingham's public segregation laws. Participants were forced to sit in racially segregated sections in the meeting hall: whites on one side and African Americans on the other.

Eleanor Roosevelt knew whatever she did would echo through the press. She could comply with segregation or violate the law. She picked up her chair and moved it into the center aisle between the two sections. Her act of defiance spoke loud and clear without breaking the law.

Fear of the other had become pervasive across the United States. When director Orson Welles broadcast a dramatized version of H. G. Wells's *War of the Worlds* over the radio during Halloween 1938, Americans were willing to believe space aliens were invading the country. In an article titled "Keepers of Democracy," ER responded: "[W]e have allowed ourselves to be fed on propaganda which has created a fear complex" (Roosevelt 1939, 117).

Eleanor Roosevelt presents opera singer, Marian Anderson, with the NAACP's Spingarn Medal for African American achievement in 1939. Eleanor hoped public accolades and the White House's invitation for Anderson to sing before the British king and queen would open minds, but the DAR maintained their racist policy barring Black performers from Constitution Hall in Washington, D.C. (Library of Congress)

Fear was toxic. She recounted her uncle Theodore Roosevelt saying: "[W]hen you are afraid to do a thing, that was the time to go and do it. Every time we shirk making up our minds or standing up for a cause in which we believe, we weaken our character and our ability to be fearless" (Roosevelt 1939, 118).

In February 1939, Eleanor Roosevelt took those words to heart. Since becoming First Lady, she had invited musicians and performers of all races and nationalities to perform. African American opera singer Marian Anderson had sung in the White House several times.

Anderson had been scheduled to perform on Easter Sunday in Washington's Constitution Hall. However, the Daughters of the American Revolution (DAR) owned the hall, and they refused to grant permission for a Black singer to perform on their stage.

Eleanor was outraged. She had never been active in the DAR, but she had been a member most of her life. She wrote a letter resigning from the organization and chastised them for failing to "lead in an enlightened way" (February 26, 1939).

Then she strategically wrote about her dilemma in her February 27 "My Day" column: "To remain as a member implies approval of that action, and therefore I am resigning."

Cousin Corinney responded immediately. "I want you to know how proud I was of you the other day . . . You are the First Lady of the land in your own right!" (Caroli 1998, 280).

Eleanor Roosevelt couldn't shame the DAR into reversing their stance, so she facilitated another stage for Anderson. Secretary of the Interior Harold Ickes shared ER's commitment to racial equality and held jurisdiction over National Monuments. Behind the scenes, the First Lady helped arrange for Anderson to sing on Easter morning in front of the Lincoln Memorial. Instead of 3,000 people, Anderson sang to an audience of 75,000. The powerful image of the African American singer performing in front of Abraham Lincoln's statue made a political statement, inspiring future leaders of the Civil Rights Movement.

RESCUING REFUGEES

The inevitability of American involvement in the war continued to grow. Eleanor's eldest son, James, enlisted as a captain in the Marine Corps Reserve. Elliott was a pilot volunteering on a general's staff within the Army Air Force. The two younger boys were still at Harvard, but Franklin Jr. was in Naval Reserve Officer Training.

Hundreds of thousands of refugees were fleeing Europe, but in January 1939, only a quarter of Americans supported even allowing refugee children into the country. After failing to help the Spanish orphans, ER founded the U.S. Committee for the Care of European Children, with a goal of rescuing 20,000 refugee children.

With German bombs falling on Britain, the Committee would first transport British children to safety in the United States and then increase their effort to those escaping Europe. Carrie Chapman Catt and other advocates arranged host families. Chicago department store tycoon, Marshall Field III, oversaw fundraising while ER worked on immigration legalities. The U.S. State Department refused to offer permanent asylum. The children would be admitted on visitor visas and required to return to their country of origin after the war.

The effort transported 800 refugee children from England before ship travel became too dangerous. The last group included 350 Jewish children. Thousands remained stranded in Britain.

Masses of people were fleeing France just ahead of advancing Nazi troops. French Jewish actor Marcel Dalio and his actress wife Madeleine Lebeau escaped via Lisbon, Portugal, on August 8, 1940 on the SS *Quanza*. Of the 317 passengers, 251 were refugees. When the ship arrived in New York City, they were among the 121 refugees denied entrance into the United States. The ship traveled to Veracruz, Mexico, but ultimately 86 refugees remained stranded on board. With forged or inadequate immigration papers, no country would allow them entry. The ship was ordered to refuel at Norfolk, Virginia, before returning to Europe.

The refugees began to panic; persecution awaited them in Nazi-occupied Europe. Friends and family reached out to government officials. At Hyde Park on September 10, Eleanor Roosevelt received a telegram pleading for help from the women on the *Quanza*.

Eleanor personally called Assistant Secretary of State Breckenridge Long, but he refused to intervene. Eventually, she convinced the president to send a representative from his Advisory Committee on Political Refugees to interview the passengers.

The interviewing inspector declared all of the asylum claims valid. Assistant Secretary Long rushed to stop the refugees from being permitted into the country, but he was told that it was impossible; they had already left the ship.

Within eighteen months, Dalio and Lebeau were portraying refugees stuck in a German-held North African outpost in the classic movie *Casablanca*. Dalio was the only member of his Jewish family to escape death in the concentration camps. Lebeau's heartbreaking rendition of the French anthem, "La Marseillaise," was grounded in her reality as a refugee. The film helped Americans empathize with victims of Nazi Germany.

Eleanor Roosevelt had rescued 86 individuals, but the State Department tightened immigration restrictions. The *Quanza* reinforced Eleanor's belief that decision-makers at the State Department were purposefully turning away Jewish refugees.

She began working behind the scenes with a small group of individuals—the Emergency Rescue Committee. Privately, they facilitated the evacuation of notable artists, authors, scholars, politicians, and labor leaders out of German-occupied France.

UNITING A POLITICAL PARTY

As the 1940 presidential election approached, Franklin D. Roosevelt failed to signal support for either his vice president or the chairman of the Democratic Party who planned to run for the Democratic nomination. At the party convention, a surreptitiously planned chanting of "We want Roosevelt!" manipulated the delegates into a public demonstration of support to nominate FDR for an unprecedented third term. Chaos erupted.

Frances Perkins phoned from the Chicago convention urging President Roosevelt to send the First Lady to calm the situation.

The Women's Division had been diminished. Many in the women's network baulked at the notion of a third presidential term. Isabella Greenway had retired from Congress, but as a delegate she refused to support a third term. Esther Lape and Elizabeth Read questioned Franklin's motives.

Franklin made the case to Eleanor that he was the only candidate able to beat the Republican challenger and guide the nation through the global crisis. She stood by his decision and flew to Chicago. No other acting First Lady had addressed a national party convention before. Her words to the delegates on July 18, 1940, defined the situation succinctly: "This is no ordinary time." For the sake of the nation, she rallied the Democrats to come together. By a slim margin, Franklin D. Roosevelt won reelection for a third term.

PREPARING THE COUNTRY FOR WAR

Three days after the election, Eleanor wrote to Hick: "No, I don't look forward to the next four years" (Streitmatter 1998, 234). Her own career was being placed on hold, again. New Deal programs were waning as industrial production for the war reinvigorated the economy. She felt sidelined.

Eleanor still believed education could motivate Americans to oppose Fascism. She helped James distribute a film—*Pastor Hall*—that fictionalized the life of an actual German minister who stood up for Jewish residents in his town and was tortured in a Nazi concentration camp. Several large cities, including Chicago, banned the film for being too shocking.

She tried a softer approach and wrote *Christmas; A Story by Eleanor Roosevelt* (1940). The holiday parable fit in a child's hands and was illustrated with elegant line drawings. The story of Fascism as an evil force stalking innocent families was too dark. Americans struggled to identify with the crisis in Europe.

If nothing else, she could lead by example: Eleanor Roosevelt picked up her knitting needles. She worked with the American Red Cross, again, to motivate the knitting of socks and mufflers for refugees and soldiers overseas.

If Americans entered the war, women would be needed in the workforce. Unplanned motherhood was a major impediment for working women. In the spring of 1941, ER brought together government agencies and the National Birth Control Federation. She had long supported birth control and openly pressed the surgeon general to fund state programs to assist women with spacing births in a healthy manner.

Isabella had married Harry O. King before returning to Arizona. Out west, Isabella Greenway King chaired the American Women's Voluntary Services (AWVS). Women learned to fight fires, provide first aid, drive and repair vehicles. They trained to facilitate air-raid procedures and operate radios. Isabella's action reinvigorated Eleanor. She highlighted the AWVS in her column, hoping to inspire other like-minded women.

THE FIRST STEP TOWARD NONDISCRIMINATION

During the election, ER allied with African American labor unions. She had championed the training of African American pilots at the Tuskegee Institute and demonstrated her faith in their aviation ability by taking reporters to document her flight with one of the Black pilots.

But Franklin D. Roosevelt's promises of opportunity in the military and defense industries evaporated after the election. Black labor leaders and the NAACP planned a July 1941 march on Washington. They were tired of Black sailors and soldiers being assigned to food service positions regardless of education or experience. They demanded equal pay and opportunity.

President Roosevelt sent the First Lady to diffuse the situation. The deal she struck was Executive Order 8802. It was neither a law nor a promise to desegregate the military, but for the first time an American president prohibited discrimination on account of race or ethnic origin. It was one of Eleanor Roosevelt's most satisfying accomplishments; EO 8802 set precedent and initiated a foundational change toward racial equality. (See Primary Documents: *Executive Order 8802: Prohibition of Discrimination in the Defense Industry.*)

A TIME OF LOSS

During the summer of tense negotiations, Missy LeHand, Franklin's longtime personal secretary, suffered a debilitating stroke. LeHand and Eleanor had maintained a friendship and respected each other's position.

Eleanor Roosevelt takes to the air in a Piper Cub aircraft with Charles Alfred "Chief" Anderson, March 1941. Anderson was an instructor for the Tuskegee Institute's all-Black Civilian Pilot Training Program. Using visual media, Eleanor challenged racial stereotypes and conveyed her trust in African Americans as able pilots. (U.S. Air Force)

Now, other secretaries and women in Franklin's circle vied to be close to the president. Eleanor retreated to Campobello and her cottage at Val-Kill.

Over the course of three weeks in September 1941, both her mother-in-law and her brother died.

Eleanor Roosevelt's relationship with Sara Delano Roosevelt had evolved from intimidation, through opposition, to respect. At fifty-seven years of age, Eleanor finally felt she could make decisions without being criticized or subverted by Franklin's mother. At the same time, she appreciated how important the matriarch was to her husband and their children.

Immediately after Sara Delano Roosevelt's funeral, Eleanor rushed to her brother's bedside. Hall was dying from alcohol-related liver failure. For two weeks, she kept vigil at his side. Hall struggled to breathe, to form a thought, to find peace. She loved him as a brother and cared for him like a son, but she judged him as undisciplined. She never understood substance use as a disease. Eleanor saw only wasted potential that echoed the death of her father.

Shared loss rekindled Eleanor and Franklin's bond of shared life experience. Throughout the fall, they made time to be together. They provided solace for each other's pain. Their children saw moments of intimacy between them—a hug, a kiss—which they had not seen in years.

THE WAR BEGINS

Eleanor needed a purpose to override her sorrow. Franklin supported her appointment as assistant director of the Office of Civilian Defense (OCD). For the first time, Eleanor Roosevelt officially held a government position. She threw herself into the job, drawing upon her network and coordinating efforts with Isabella and the AWVS.

In October, she initiated a new Sunday evening radio broadcast. She would prepare American women for war by visiting defense installations, talking about managing food rations, and explaining why the U.S. Navy escorted merchant ships crossing the North Atlantic with supplies for Great Britain.

On December 7, 1941, all plans changed. Japanese aircraft bombed Pearl Harbor, Hawaii. President Roosevelt entrusted the First Lady to address the nation during her radio program and calm public fears.

When she went to Franklin's room late that night, he seemed relieved. War was upon them, there was only one road forward: winning the war. In her own heart, she felt despair. There was a high probability that at least one of their sons would not survive the fighting.

Within hours of President Roosevelt's request for Congress to pass a formal declaration of war, Eleanor Roosevelt flew to the west coast with Fiorello La Guardia, the director of the Office of Civilian Defense and mayor of New York City. They would coordinate civilian defense measures from California to Washington.

They arrived in Los Angeles amid confusion and anxiety. Rumors flew of Japanese forces bombing San Francisco. While La Guardia organized civilian firefighters and medical responses, ER coordinated volunteers. Members of Isabella's AWVS met the First Lady and drove her to various California locations.

After a full day of organizing response teams, ER boarded a train north. "It was a queer sensation," she wrote, "to be on a train with all of the lights concealed—even the headlight on the locomotive was dimmed—and no lights to be seen outside" (Roosevelt 1961, 229). The west coast was in blackout.

After a week, calm prevailed, but Eleanor had witnessed growing animosity and suspicion toward different ethnic groups. In her "My Day" column, nine days after the attack, she addressed ethnic tensions and assured readers that the FBI and Secret Service were investigating individuals sympathetic to hostile governments. People merely descended from German, Italian, or Japanese heritage "must not feel that they have suddenly ceased to be Americans." In the United States, people of different races and cultures lived together peacefully with equal protection under the law. She added that "if we can not keep in check anti-semitism [*sic*], anti-racial feelings as well as anti-religious feelings, then we shall have removed, from the world, the one real hope for the future on which all humanity must now rely" (December 16, 1941).

Some Americans read her words and rallied to aid their immigrant neighbors. Others cut the column out of the newspaper and sent it to the FBI as evidence of Eleanor Roosevelt's suspicious and un-American behavior.

A STEP TOWARD THE UNITED NATIONS

Before the end of the year, British prime minister Winston Churchill (1874–1965) secretly visited the United States to confer with President Roosevelt. Churchill intended to sign an agreement of alliance between Britain, the United States, the Soviet Union, and China, which would delineate them as the world's superpower nations.

Eleanor Roosevelt found Churchill to be a colorful character, but she distrusted him because of his drinking and his growing influence over Franklin. She confided to Hick that Churchill was "a forceful personality." His "stress on what the English speaking people can do in the future worries me a little" (Streitmatter 1998, 241).

The influence of Mademoiselle Souvestre in England during the Boer War and Britain's behavior following World War I caused Eleanor to question British imperialist motives. She worried that when victory came, small countries and ethnic groups would be sidelined by decisions favoring the superpowers.

The negotiations occurred in all-male meetings, but the First Lady maintained access to the president. She reminded Franklin of the vision he had once believed in: the League of Nations. When Churchill proposed an alliance of "Associated Powers," President Roosevelt countered with a Declaration of the United Nations. In addition to the larger powers, India and twenty-two individually named smaller nations would sign the document independently, thereby creating the Allied Nations against Germany and Japan.

After Churchill returned to Britain, the Roosevelts' interlude of confidence faded. ER resumed her work with the OCD. A quarter of young men brought before military draft boards showed symptoms of malnutrition or nutrition-related health problems—rickets, tooth loss, and pellagra. ER regarded nutrition as integral to civil defense and advocated for a federal nutrition program, privately hoping it might also create a foundation for national health care after the war. The president and his advisers, however, refused to divert war funds for nutrition.

In her eagerness to put OCD programs into action, ER hired people she knew. She believed dancing could be an important form of exercise and that theater offered a stimulating avenue of recreation.

Political opponents pounced on the First Lady for creating wasteful programs. They attacked her for hiring personal friends and alleged communists. Congressional investigations challenged the morality of dancing. The First Lady became a target for every politician seeking attention or opposed to New Deal programs.

SILENCED

On February 19, 1942, President Roosevelt signed Executive Order 9066. American citizens of Japanese heritage and their immigrant parents, who had been barred by law from applying for citizenship, were now also forbidden from living in western coastal states, which were deemed military exclusion zones. It served as legal cover for rounding up Japanese Americans and confining them in "relocation centers." Without any evidence of them having committed criminal acts, approximately 122,000 men, women, and children were stripped of their civil liberties because of their racial heritage.

Shocked and angry, Eleanor confronted Franklin. Innocent people were losing their homes, property, and businesses. Their bank accounts were being frozen. Franklin claimed she didn't understand the national security issues.

Eleanor wanted to know who stood to profit by acquiring the thousands of acres of quality farmland owned by Japanese families.

Franklin was done discussing. For five months he had protected her position at OCD. The accusatory noise had risen too high. He suggested she resign. A silent wall came down between them. Eleanor resigned from the Office of Civilian Defense.

Quietly, she tried to reconnect Japanese internees with their financial savings. She attempted to keep relocated families together. She even reached out to the attorney general to see if the president's action could be legally challenged.

Eleanor's secretary Tommy wrote to Esther Lape that she and Eleanor talked less than usual. The First Lady would sink into dark moods. She worried about her sons and the sons of mothers around the world; the war felt like a "slow death" (Roosevelt 1961, 251).

Over the summer, Britain violently subdued demonstrations in India against colonial rule; thousands of civilians died. Pro-independence leaders Mahatma Gandhi (1869–1948) and Jawaharlal Nehru (1889–1964) were arrested and jailed. Eleanor Roosevelt and several cabinet members longed to speak out in support of Indian independence, but Britain was America's ally. President Roosevelt demanded their silence. ER continued to write her daily column and magazine articles, but she felt ineffective.

WOMEN AND THE WAR EFFORT

Early on, Eleanor implored Franklin to allow women to volunteer for the military or for war work. She felt the administration was making the same mistake it had initially made with the New Deal—they were leaving out women.

Army chief of staff, General George C. Marshall (1880–1959), agreed. Every able-bodied man was needed on the battlefield. The Army already enlisted nurses, but women could also fill positions as clerks, secretaries, drivers, and office staff. Eleanor Roosevelt supported legislation forming the Women's Auxiliary Army Corps (WAAC) and assisted Dr. Margaret Chung in creating a women's branch of the U.S. Naval Reserve: Women Accepted for Volunteer Emergency Service (WAVES).

After a summer of Hitler's advances and Britain's suppression of India, Americans questioned sending their sons to fight in Europe. With mounting losses in the South Pacific, voices were calling for a redirection of American resources.

American criticism angered Winston Churchill. British and American military forces had difficulty melding together. Franklin needed Eleanor's diplomatic skills to reassure Churchill and rally American troops. In October 1942, the president asked the First Lady to travel to embattled Britain.

Thankful for an assignment, Eleanor longed to see how women were integrated into the British civil defense and military. In between three weeks of diplomatic events, she hoped to visit schools, factories, shelters, military bases, and hospitals.

First Lady Roosevelt and Tommy flew to Britain under strict security. ER toured London's bombed-out neighborhoods with King George VI and Queen Elizabeth. She described streets of destroyed homes to her readers and detailed British gratitude for American aid.

The press corps followed at her heels snapping photos and writing stories for the American papers. Lorena Hickok was "simply delighted with the press [Eleanor] was getting" (Streitmatter 1998, 246). Images of First Lady Roosevelt sitting with individual American soldiers made their mothers at home feel their government cared about their sons. ER wrote in her

November 6, 1942 "My Day" column: "[E]very American soldier I see is a friend from home and I want to stop and talk with him."

She shared the precious moments seeing her son Elliott before his unit deployed. She described barracks to reassure American families and reported on the good spirits of American sons and husbands. She, purposefully, mentioned seeing Black troops and the training of Black non-commissioned officers. Privately, she made notes of racial disparities.

First Lady Roosevelt befriended everyone from the Queen Mother to children relocated to country care centers. At a private dinner party, however, she stood her ground when Winston Churchill toasted American support supplying Franco's newly installed government in Spain. ER protested: Fascism in Spain had emboldened Hitler. Churchill bellowed, but his wife agreed. Lady Clementine Churchill ended the meal and Eleanor Roosevelt embraced a new friend.

Lady Churchill (1885–1977) shared Eleanor Roosevelt's belief that the purpose of government was to help the people. She was active in civil defense, especially in making air-raid shelters clean and safe. The two women developed a relationship of respect and admiration as they toured programs overseen by women.

ER pointedly told her readers how British women were helping win the war. At one airplane factory alone, nearly a quarter of the workers were women. The government provided services to enable female participation in the workforce: daycare and hot lunches for workers and school children.

Women in the British military trained as plotters—mapping troop and asset movements—communication coders, and radio experts. Women in motor transport units drove vehicles—including ambulances and trucks—and provided routine service and repair.

American aviator Jacqueline Cochran (c. 1906–1980) had approached the Roosevelt administration about coordinating a female air corps, but she was turned away. In Britain, she was coordinating female pilots who ferried planes to locations where they were needed. Eleanor noted Cochran's successes and put a female air corps at the top of her list for the president.

Before departing, First Lady Roosevelt addressed the British and American people over the radio. She noted their shared values of freedom and tolerance. She acknowledged the sacrifices of both and the shared objective of "winning the war as quickly as possible so that we may save as many lives as possible" (Smith 2014, 225).

Prime Minister Churchill and President Roosevelt applauded Eleanor Roosevelt's ability to unite the two nations. When Eleanor landed back in the United States, she was surprised to see Franklin's car waiting on the tarmac. He acknowledged a job well done and expressed his happiness to have her home safely. She honestly felt he had missed her.

CREATING OPPORTUNITIES FOR WOMEN AND MINORITIES

President Roosevelt confided that he had been reading Eleanor's column every day while she was in Britain. Following her full report, he expanded the nascent Women's Auxiliary Ferrying Squadron into a full-scale military air corps—the Women's Airforce Service Pilots (WASPS) directed by Cochran.

Eleanor's insights expanded WAVE assignments into supply, weather, photography, and even aviation ordnance support. At the Naval Communications Annex in Washington, D.C., WAVES typed top-secret decoded messages and delivered them directly to President Roosevelt.

ER reinvigorated the National Youth Administration with programs training young men and women in defense industries. Women became skilled as welders, machinists, and riveters. They were known as Rosies after "Rosie the Riveter," an iconic World War II image of an empowered woman doing equal work alongside men to support the war effort. Manufacturer Henry J. Kaiser took note of the First Lady's suggestions and structured his Kaiser Steel shipyards to provide daycare, health care, and access to necessities for working mothers.

In Britain, American soldiers complained to the First Lady about terrible delays in their mail. Across Europe, war had impacted postal systems. Mary McLeod Bethune had become an assistant with the WAACs. She approached ER on behalf of African American military women who were seeking roles in line with their training. ER pushed for the formation of the Army's 6888th Central Postal Directory Battalion. Led by Major Charity Adams Earley (1918–2002), the highest-ranking African American woman in the Army, the all-female African American battalion deployed to unravel a backlog of undelivered mail.

Eleanor had seen African American soldiers denied access to eating areas on American bases and forced to sit behind German prisoners at movies. She took her observations directly to General Marshall and Secretary of War Henry L. Stimson. While Stimson regarded the First Lady as a thorn in his side, General Marshall valued her observations. Historian Blanche Wiesen Cook claims that General Marshall dedicated two staff members to investigate and resolve correspondence from First Lady Roosevelt.

The Tuskegee Airmen had been trained, but Eleanor heard the Black pilots remained at their base in Alabama. She wrote directly to Secretary

ENLIST IN THE WAVES

U.S. NAVY

RELEASE A MAN TO FIGHT AT SEA

Apply to your nearest
NAVY RECRUITING STATION OR OFFICE OF NAVAL OFFICER PROCUREMENT

This 1943 poster urged young women to join the U.S. Naval Reserve's WAVES (Women Accepted for Volunteer Emergency Service). Eleanor Roosevelt lobbied the president and the Congress to include women in all branches of the U.S. military. She felt military service offered opportunity and professional training to women of all backgrounds. (Library of Congress)

Stimson, urging that the aviators be allowed to participate in the war effort. This time Stimson obliged. The 99th Pursuit Squadron deployed to North Africa to begin its exemplary record of performance in combat.

RACIAL STRIFE

Renewed by her successes, Eleanor Roosevelt returned to racial issues at home. In the spring of 1943, she traveled to the Japanese Internment Camp at Gila River, Arizona. She arrived with a photographer, unannounced and accompanied by government officials who supported closing the camp. She toured the camp and posed for photos with Japanese internees. She chronicled the hardships they had endured and gave an interview to a national newspaper. She had been silent too long.

She pressed President Roosevelt for the internees' release but made no headway.

That same April, 25,000 white workers in Detroit, Michigan, went on strike opposing the addition of three African American men to their assembly line. Race riots erupted over the summer. White mobs burned homes and businesses. Thirty people died and hundreds were injured.

President Roosevelt advised the First Lady to stay away from the conflict in Detroit, but she accepted the local NAACP's invitation to speak. White rioters threatened to take over a newly completed federal low-income housing project designated for African Americans. Eleanor Roosevelt spoke out: Why were Americans fighting against each other?

THE MANHATTAN PROJECT

While some in the Roosevelt administration were trying to shut out the First Lady, a group of physicists saw her as their best hope. Irving S. Lowen (1911–1949), a research associate on the top secret "Manhattan Project," had been chosen by his coworkers to contact the First Lady. Lowen had a colleague at Washington Square College who knew Eleanor Roosevelt. In a frantic attempt to circumvent military bureaucracy, he used that connection.

Until Lowen walked through the door of her new apartment on Washington Square in July 1943, Eleanor knew nothing of the secret project to build a nuclear weapon. The young physicist laid out the project's ultimate objective—a single bomb that could potentially destroy an entire city.

Lowen prevailed upon the First Lady that the scientists working on the project believed the War Department and the Du Pont Company, which was constructing the reactors for the project, failed to appreciate the necessity of speed. The physicists believed their German counterparts were closing in on success. The more desperate Hitler became, the more likely the Germans would be to use this destructive weapon. In this race, there was no coming in second.

Lowen gave the First Lady the names of the scientists the president should speak with, including the top minds behind the Manhattan Project: Leo Szilard (1898–1964), Enrico Fermi (1901–1954), and J. Robert Oppenheimer (1904–1967).

Eleanor called the president in Washington, D.C., and then personally typed a letter to him (July 27, 1943). She wrote on the back: "I hope you see Lowen—He impresses me with his own anxiety." The president saw the young physicist the next day and then relayed a sense of urgency to the project's supervisors. He, however, requested that Lowen communicate with him directly through his secretary in the future.

Lowen followed President Roosevelt's directions but maintained contact with the First Lady, updating her on the secret weapon.

VISITING THE TROOPS IN THE SOUTH PACIFIC

President Roosevelt needed a trustworthy firsthand account of the Pacific theater. He also wanted to distance the First Lady from conflict in Detroit and the Manhattan Project. He convinced her to visit troops in the South Pacific. Wearing the simple blue-gray American Red Cross uniform, she would also officially evaluate hospitals and facilities.

On August 17, 1943, Eleanor Roosevelt boarded a military plane with a small suitcase and a portable typewriter. She was headed into a battle zone. She left all of her personal jewelry, including her engagement ring, behind with instructions as to who was to inherit them if something should happen to her. Her only escort was a military journalist. Tommy wrote to Esther Lape that she had an uneasy feeling watching the First Lady board the plane alone.

Without her loyal secretary at her side, Eleanor Roosevelt kept a trip diary as reference for her daily columns. Each night or sometimes on an airplane during a flight, she typed her column to be wired back to the United States. She intended, as she told her "My Day" readers, to provide insight into the daily lives of their sons and sweethearts so far away.

Her plane landed on tiny atolls and islands with exotic names, such as Aitutaki and Tutuila. A major on the island of Bora Bora told her she was the first white woman he had seen in ten months. A female representative from the Red Cross accompanied her for a few days, but most of the time, she was alone with her transport team. Gazing down at the Pacific Ocean as she skipped from one island to another, her thoughts may have wandered to her friend Amelia Earhart, lost somewhere in this blue vastness.

Her son James advised her to eat with the enlisted men, because they would give her the inside scoop on conditions. She followed his advice and was pleased to see that in the remoteness of exotic islands, soldiers of all colors seemed to work and eat side by side.

When she got off the plane on New Caledonia, Admiral William Halsey Jr. (1882–1959) was obligated to meet her. He had no time for another government official looking to tour facilities, especially a middle-aged woman who required an escort. The admiral knew the First Lady was reviewing hospitals and Red Cross facilities and that she was visiting the governments of New Zealand and Australia. He was not expecting the envelope she handed to him. The letter from President Roosevelt instructed the admiral to allow the First Lady to visit the island of Guadalcanal, if he deemed it safe and possible.

For months, Guadalcanal had been a strategic location battled over by the Americans and the Japanese. Only recently had enemy troops withdrawn. The Japanese continued to bomb Guadalcanal, hoping to regain a foothold. Halsey looked at the letter and said "No." It was too dangerous.

Over 25,000 American and Japanese men had lost their lives fighting over the jungle island. Eleanor felt she needed to look into the face of war. She felt that if she couldn't experience Guadalcanal her journey had been for nothing. She dashed off a letter to Tommy: "I am discouraged & really sorry that I came," she wrote. "I simply will never face another hospital at home" (Roosevelt to Thompson, August 26, 1943).

Yet, early the next morning, Eleanor Roosevelt headed out for twelve hours of visiting injured men in three hospitals. She camouflaged her despair and offered compassion. She visited an officers' recuperation facility and met with the 2nd Marine Raider Battalion. James had been an officer with the Raiders during a major conflict on Espiritu Santo. She was heartened to hear their regard for her son. She spoke to soldiers, attended a reception, and went to a dinner in her honor. Then she spent several hours typing up her column and writing correspondences.

Admiral Halsey watched the First Lady all day. She walked for miles without complaint and gave equal time to every injured soldier and sailor. Her mental stamina and ability to look beyond gruesome injuries impressed him.

Halsey marveled as battle-hardened soldiers transformed to homesick boys in the warmth of her tranquil blue eyes. She gave them comfort and hope. The admiral became one of Eleanor Roosevelt's ardent supporters. After she completed the diplomatic leg of her trip, he would reassess the possibility of her visiting Guadalcanal.

Eleanor Roosevelt toured remote island outposts and large hospitals in New Zealand and Australia. "Malaria is almost as bad as bullets," she wrote to Hick (Streitmatter 1998, 250). Too often the men lacked adequate opportunities for recreation. She reported to President Roosevelt that the Red Cross was understaffed and the Navy and Marine Corps needed to improve their cooperation with each other.

She made friends with New Zealand's Indigenous Maori people and spoke before an audience of 3,000 Australians. First Lady Roosevelt united the Allied Nations and won over the military. Her transport pilots from the 13th Troop Carrier Squadron invited her to become an honorary squadron member. They named her transport C-47 aircraft "Our Eleanor," complete with nose art of a globe mapping her island hopping and a figure of the intrepid First Lady carrying her own small suitcase.

When she returned to New Caledonia, Admiral Halsey granted permission for her to go to Guadalcanal. Overnight, bombs fell on her destination, but in the dark of early morning, Eleanor boarded her transport to the battlefield.

GUADALCANAL

Guadalcanal was jungle, mud, and men on the move. As she stood waving to troop trucks headed down the road to battle, she heard an amazed soldier holler, "Gosh, that's Eleanor." She tried to look into as many faces as possible; she knew some would not return.

The makeshift hospital stood beside a field cemetery. The rows and rows of grave markers became etched into her memory. She wrote in her diary of helmets and mess kits balanced on crosses; names and religions carved into the wood: " . . . how united these boys had been in spite of difference in

religion and background" (September 20, 1943). Just after she left, Guadalcanal was bombed again.

She had one more stop: Espiritu Santo, Vanuatu. She stood alone on the
pier looking out over the clear turquoise water. Palms rustled in the sea
breeze. Gentle waves lapped against the pier. On this spot, James had been
decorated for his service in battle. She closed her eyes and for a breath, she
stood beside him. Her sons were spread around the world, but here she felt
connected to them.

Over nearly six weeks, she had traveled 25,000 miles, stopping at Hawaii,
New Zealand, Australia, and seventeen Pacific Islands. First Lady Eleanor
Roosevelt interacted with an estimated 400,000 members of the military.
She had raised morale in the field and at home.

Political opponents attacked her for costing the taxpayers, interfering in
a war zone, and wearing a Red Cross uniform. Admiral Halsey countered
these criticisms, stating: "She alone had accomplished more good than any
other person . . . who had passed through my area" (Sparrow 2016).

The trip left its mark on Eleanor as well. Independently, she had sought
out the places and people she felt were important to see. Her activity was
uncensored by political expectations. She rubbed noses in greeting with
her Maori guide and publicly shared an ice cream cone with an African
American soldier.

When she returned to Washington, her close friends sighed with relief.
Franklin listened intently to her experiences and observations. She spoke
of how the Australians had education programs for returning soldiers to
reestablish them in careers. Her suggestions led to the Servicemen's Read-
justment Act of 1944 (commonly known as the G.I. Bill of Rights). She
conveyed to the president how the mental strain was crippling men in
combat zones; he ordered the military to provide more frequent rest and
rehabilitation time for fighting troops in the Pacific.

Encountering Japanese Americans in Hawaii had reinforced her belief
in their patriotism toward the United States. Her support for Japanese
American nurses and the all–Japanese American 442nd Regimental
Combat Team influenced the inclusion of Japanese American volunteers
in the Military Intelligence Service and the general draft. By the end of
1943, a third of Japanese internees had been released into war-related
positions.

However, the trip had been strenuous. She lost thirty pounds and felt
exhausted. Witnessing so many broken and damaged bodies left its own
post-traumatic stress. Settling back into normalcy at the White House was
difficult. She would lie awake at night thinking of the wards of traumatized
boys and the men sleeping in entrenchments waiting to put their lives on
the line.

GOING FORWARD

Touring shelters in Britain and field hospitals in the Pacific, Eleanor Roosevelt had one reoccurring thought: how do we begin preparing for peace? Lasting international peace required international partners.

She had watched the League of Nations die. She had fought and lost the battle to engage the United States in the World Court. But on November 9, 1943, Eleanor Roosevelt's hope for the future was reignited.

She and Tommy peaked in the doorway of the White House's East Room. The flags of forty-four nations marked the chairs for their diplomatic representatives. Eleanor watched each man take his seat and hoped with all her heart that this time, before the battles ended, "we have the vision . . . to realize that there is much work to do and preparation by the peoples of the United Nations" to secure a lasting peace. Her "My Day" column brimmed with hope. The mere fact that an American president was sitting at the table was "a promise that we shall not repeat our past mistakes" ("My Day," November 10, 1943). Eleanor Roosevelt envisioned a peaceful future and she had no intention of turning back.

SOURCES

Caroli, Betty Boyd. 1998. *The Roosevelt Women.* New York: Basic Books.

Lash, Joseph P. 1971. *Eleanor and Franklin: The Story of Their Relationship Based on Eleanor Roosevelt's Private Papers.* New York: W.W. Norton & Company, Inc.

Letter from Eleanor Roosevelt to Malvina Thompson. August 26, 1943. Eleanor Roosevelt Papers Project. Columbian College of Arts and Sciences. Washington D.C. https://erpapers.columbian.gwu.edu/eleanor-roosevelt-malvina-thompson-august-26-1943

Miller, Kristie, and Robert H. McGinnis, eds. 2009. *A Volume of Friendship: The Letters of Eleanor Roosevelt and Isabella Greenway 1904–1953.* Tucson: The Arizona Historical Society.

Roosevelt, Eleanor. 1938. "This Troubled World." H.C. Kinsey and Company. In *Courage in a Dangerous World: The Political Writings of Eleanor Roosevelt,* edited by Allida M. Black, 86–100. New York: Columbia University Press.

Roosevelt, Eleanor. 1939. "Keepers of Democracy." *The Virginia Quarterly Review,* Winter. In *Courage in a Dangerous World: The Political Writings of Eleanor Roosevelt,* edited by Allida M. Black, 117–120. New York: Columbia University Press.

Roosevelt, Eleanor. 1961. *The Autobiography of Eleanor Roosevelt.* New York: Harper Perennial.

Smith, Stephen Drury, ed. 2014. *The First Lady of Radio: Eleanor Roosevelt's Historic Broadcasts*. New York: The New Press.

Sparrow, Paul M. 2016, August 25. "A First Lady on the Front Lines." Franklin D. Roosevelt Presidential Library and Museum. https://fdr.blogs.archives.gov/2016/08/25/a-first-lady-on-the-front-lines/

Streitmatter, Rodger, ed. 1998. *Empty Without You: The Intimate Letters of Eleanor Roosevelt and Lorena Hickok*. New York: The Free Press.

10

The United Nations and a Foundation for the Future (1943–1962)

Flickering light and shadow played across the vast movie screen as an audience of National Geographic members watched the film of Eleanor Roosevelt's triumphant South Pacific tour. She heard her voice describe Quonset huts nestled between palms, but her thoughts kept returning to Franklin.

Somewhere in the dark of the Atlantic Ocean, he was being secreted away by the U.S. Navy for strategic Allied negotiations in the Middle East. She wanted to accompany him, but Franklin had said "no."

She knew little about Soviet premier Joseph Stalin (1878–1953), but she worried that Winston Churchill would manipulate Franklin. Questions filled her head, questions she felt their British allies needed to answer. Why should Americans defend democracy in Britain while Britain imprisoned independence leaders in India? Why was Churchill delaying the establishment of a second front in Europe? Each day that the Allies waited to invade Germany more lives were lost on the Eastern Front and in Nazi concentration camps.

The moving images on the screen documented First Lady Roosevelt as an American diplomatic envoy to Australia and New Zealand. If she had been an asset in the Pacific, why was she now a liability? To be left behind in Washington felt like failure.

Informed observers saw the First Lady's potential squandered by the minimal role Franklin D. Roosevelt allowed her. Journalist Ruby Black concluded in her book—*Eleanor Roosevelt: A Biography*—that once the First Lady was released "from the restrictions and the duties of the wife of a public official, she [was] likely to reveal sides of her nature and her ability which have been suppressed" (1940).

CHANGING ALLEGIANCES

Between public events, Eleanor retreated to the Connecticut country home of Esther Lape and Elizabeth Read. She was weary of pretense and of playing the role required of her. With her old friends, she could admit her frustrations and loneliness.

She confessed to Lape that "respect and affection" summarized her relationship with Franklin (Cook 2016, 493). She and Hick still cared for each other, but Lorena had a new romance. Eleanor admired the lifelong love and devotion of Esther and Elizabeth. At fifty-eight, she felt the only person who had truly loved her had been her father.

When Franklin returned from Tehran in December, he was dogged by fatigue and a variety of illnesses. His malaise was compounded by a top-secret internal report from Treasury Secretary Morgenthau detailing "the utter failure of certain officials in our State Department" to act on behalf of "persecuted minorities of Europe who could be saved" (January 16, 1944). It was everything that Eleanor had warned of. Racism and anti-Semitism were entrenched at the highest levels of the Roosevelt State Department.

The harsh truth forced the president to ripple changes throughout the State Department and establish a War Refugee Board. Relieved to have him engaged in refugee issues, Eleanor missed the signs of his declining health.

Since Missy LeHand's stroke, other secretaries and a circle of female flatterers—especially, Franklin's cousins Laura "Polly" Delano (1885–1972) and Margaret "Daisy" Suckley (1891–1991)—had surrounded the president. Yet, his office lacked a strong manager. Daughter Anna moved back into the White House while her husband was deployed overseas. She became her father's personal assistant, vetting his appointments, monitoring his diet, and serving as an unquestioning ear at the end of a long day.

Anna facilitated FDR's cocktail parties and acted as White House hostess when her mother was away. Surreptitiously, she arranged for Lucy Mercer Rutherfurd to visit the president in the White House.

Anna became her father's confidante and protector. She determined if the president was too busy or too tired to be confronted by his wife. The friendship that mother and daughter had worked to build, eroded.

THE FOURTH TERM

Determined to finish the war, Franklin D. Roosevelt planned to run again in the 1944 presidential election. Eleanor was ambivalent. She had concerns about his health but seemed unaware that he had been diagnosed with congestive heart failure. By June, a healthier diet and medication gave him a rosy appearance. Eleanor Roosevelt assumed doctors had approved Franklin's running for a fourth term.

Anna and Daisy Suckley kept the president's persistent cough and his intermittent trouble with digestion and pain a secret. Modern theories suggest Franklin D. Roosevelt may have had melanoma. Though a darkened patch of skin above his left eyebrow was removed four years earlier, metastatic skin cancer may have contributed to his declining health.

Superficially, the president appeared improved. Eleanor believed he was buoyed by news of American troops successfully crossing the British Channel on D-Day and landing on the beaches of German-occupied France.

A fourth term wasn't guaranteed; the Democratic National Convention was contentious. The massive industrial effort building "Victory Ships" and airplanes had revitalized the economy. The newly wealthy opposed Depression Era tax levels on the rich. Both Republicans and Democrats challenged President Roosevelt's leadership.

To secure support for his reelection, the president acquiesced to Democratic moderates and jettisoned his Progressive vice president, Henry Wallace. He embraced a candidate some referred to as the "Missouri Compromise"—Missouri senator Harry S. Truman (1884–1972).

Eleanor Roosevelt knew little of Truman, but she agreed that continuity of leadership was necessary to win the war and establish a strong foundation for future peace. She campaigned for Franklin.

By August, Allied Forces had liberated Paris. Germany's defeat seemed inevitable.

NEGOTIATING THE END

A month after Eleanor Roosevelt's sixtieth birthday, Franklin Roosevelt won election to a historic fourth presidential term. The wartime inauguration in January 1945 was austere—no pomp, no parade, no balls.

Two days later, President Roosevelt left for diplomatic meetings at Yalta, in the Soviet Union. Despite or because of the First Lady's knowledge of international issues, he left her behind, again. The rejection felt especially bitter because FDR took Anna as his companion.

Beyond her personal feelings, Eleanor Roosevelt worried that the president's characteristic jovial nature had become a thin veneer. He would get agitated very quickly. He no longer seemed able to juggle the personalities in the room or play the necessary political poker to bluff his way to a win. He fumbled over words. His hand trembled. For the first time, he made no attempt to hide his dependence on a wheelchair. She worried Churchill and Stalin would take advantage of his frailty.

With the president overseas, the First Lady maneuvered against a conservative takeover at the State Department. She also met quietly with Dr. Leo Szilard, leading physicist on the Manhattan Project. Szilard feared military control over a weapon the generals didn't understand; he insisted that she impress upon the president that the potential destruction would be unfathomable. ER promised to convey Szilard's written warning to the president.

Because of the project's top-secret nature, she could speak to no one but the president. Even she did not know that Vice President Truman had been left out of all discussions on war strategy, including the development of the atomic bomb.

The initial news from Yalta was elating. Franklin D. Roosevelt had negotiated the first meeting of the United Nations for April 27, 1945, in San Francisco, California. "[It] is a stroke of genius," Eleanor wrote to her husband (Cook 2016, 530). But as more details came to light, she was shattered. Franklin had conceded the Baltic nations—Estonia, Latvia, and Lithuania—to the Soviet Union in exchange for Stalin's promise to join the fighting against Japan. Three nations of people delivered into Soviet control without opportunity for self-determination. Elections in Poland were postponed indefinitely.

When Franklin returned, they argued. She quickly realized, however, that the president wasn't countering her challenges. He became frustrated and unable to carry on a discussion. Eleanor saw Franklin as he was: tired and sick. After delivering his report to Congress, he left for Warm Springs. He had secured the best deal he could from Stalin and Churchill. She prayed he would rest. There had been no opportunity to pass on Szilard's warnings.

THE LAST DAY

On April 12, 1945, Eleanor Roosevelt convened her morning press conference, excited to take questions on the United Nations (UN) and the upcoming meeting in San Francisco. "When we say 'we' on international questions in the future," she exclaimed, "we will mean all the people who have an interest in the question" (Lash 1971, 927). The president was fulfilling the promise of Theodore Roosevelt, Woodrow Wilson, and all those who had worked for world peace.

She met briefly with a State Department representative advising the American delegation to San Francisco. For the first time, female voices would participate in discussing the structure of the UN. Eleanor felt confident Mary McLeod Bethune and the contingent from the LWV would move the men beyond talk to a drafted Charter.

Mid-morning, she learned that Franklin had fainted at Warm Springs, but his doctor reassured her and suggested she continue her scheduled engagements. She gave a speech at a local charity luncheon but was urgently called back to the White House.

Eleanor Roosevelt summoned Vice President Truman from the Capitol, and he was ushered into her sitting room. Eleanor put a hand on the vice president's shoulder. "Harry," she said. "The president is dead."

Truman stood silently. After a moment, he asked if there was anything he could do for her.

Eleanor Roosevelt looked him in the eye. "Is there anything *we* can do for *you*?" she emphasized. "For you are the one in trouble now" (McCullough 1992, 342).

She telegrammed her sons engaged in different battlefronts: "DARLINGS PA SLEPT AWAY THIS AFTERNOON. HE DID HIS JOB TO THE END AS HE WOULD WANT YOU TO DO. BLESS YOU. ALL OUR LOVE. MOTHER."

President Roosevelt had suffered a cerebral hemorrhage and had died several hours later. He had been sitting for a portrait commissioned by Lucy Mercer Rutherfurd.

Eleanor Roosevelt knew none of the details as she flew to Georgia. She only knew what she had seen in Harry Truman's eyes: the nation believed one man would lead them through the war and that man was gone. Lorena Hickok expressed "bewilderment and terror" (Streitmatter 1998, 267). A sense of shock spread across the nation.

The country needed a moment to grieve, an opportunity to say "farewell"—as Uncle Ted remembered saying farewell to Abraham Lincoln and as she remembered Britain's farewell to Queen Victoria. Eleanor Roosevelt's final act as First Lady would be to provide the nation with closure.

The president's body could have been flown back to Washington, D.C. Instead, Eleanor requested that the Presidential Train travel at twenty-five miles an hour: a slow funerary procession. From Georgia to Washington, over twenty-three hours, the train rolled past silent respectful crowds.

Somewhere during the journey, Polly Delano unloaded on Eleanor every hurtful secret she knew about Lucy Mercer: Lucy at Franklin's side when he fell unconscious, Lucy just out of sight at every inauguration, invitations to the White House, and frequent visits with Franklin at Warm Springs. Eleanor Roosevelt had no privacy for her personal emotions.

When the train rumbled into Washington, D.C., a solemn military parade escorted the president's flag-draped coffin on a simple black caisson pulled by six white horses. Grief-stricken faces of all colors and ethnicities lined the route to the White House. Newsreels captured a mourning nation and projected the ceremony befitting a beloved leader to the American people and the world.

Franklin's coffin lay in state overnight in the East Room. They had been married forty years. They had known warm affection and painful betrayal, shared joys and sorrows. "He might have been happier with a wife who was completely uncritical," she wrote, but she was not that person (Roosevelt 1961, 279). Others claimed she was Franklin's social conscience. She hoped she had helped him attain his life's purpose.

The next day, a thousand uniformed military men saluted along the pathway from the train to Sara Delano Roosevelt's Hyde Park rose garden. Three hundred mourners attended the "intimate" ceremony. Journalists, film crews, and radio reporters documented the twenty-one-gun salute and military plane flyover as the United States laid its Commander-In-Chief to rest.

If Eleanor Roosevelt felt personal betrayal about Lucy Mercer, she said nothing. She wrote nothing. She was consumed with practical matters: securing Franklin D. Roosevelt's presidential legacy, comforting the nation, and conveying American unity to the world.

TRANSFERRING POWER

The following day (April 17, 1945), Eleanor Roosevelt's "My Day" column spoke directly to Franklin's effort to establish the United Nations. "[A] leader may chart the way, may point out the road to lasting peace" she wrote. But to complete that effort "many peoples must do the building." She called on the American people to honor their fallen president and work toward the realization of the United Nations.

Over the next two days, Eleanor, her secretaries, and the White House domestic staff opened thousands of personal condolences and packed up twenty crates of Roosevelt belongings. Millions of pages of official memos, correspondences, and documents were shipped off to Franklin D. Roosevelt's Presidential Library.

In the midst of personal loss and the complete upheaval of her life, Eleanor Roosevelt realized her voice was needed to steady the country. It was the first time an American President had died in the midst of war. Harry S. Truman had not become a household name, nor was he the first choice of Roosevelt's Cabinet.

Casually, at first, ER mentioned taking Mrs. Truman on a tour through the White House. She emphasized that Truman values aligned with Roosevelt values: "It was good to find Mrs. Truman so appreciative of the things that I have loved" ("My Day," April 18, 1945).

Rumors spread that Eleanor Roosevelt planned to run for office, be appointed to a Cabinet position, or act as a delegate to the UN conference. She quickly squashed any notion questioning a complete handover of power to Truman. She proclaimed to the press that she was done with politics. She confided to the women's press corps that it wasn't "goodbye" because she planned to join their ranks as a journalist.

Doubts swirled in the press and in the administration about Truman's ability to fill Franklin D. Roosevelt's shoes. It had been twelve years since U.S. presidential power had passed to a new leader. Eleanor Roosevelt sensed hesitation in the public; she sensed the fragility of democracy. As she prepared to leave the White House, her column spoke lovingly of Franklin, with an inside peak at his human foibles. He wasn't a god; he was a man.

Now, a new man would lead the country. Eleanor Roosevelt reassured the nation that President Truman was gaining the "same type of support and confidence which sustained my husband in all he did." Then like a mother admonishing her children to behave, she added: "There is no question that President Truman, because of his attitude, will command the friendship and loyalty of the men who were closely associated with my husband" ("My Day," April 20, 1945). The Cabinet had publicly been put on notice.

Eleanor Roosevelt spent her last night in the White House alone. "I have always looked out at the Washington Monument from my bedroom window the last thing at night." The sight of it, she wrote in "My Day" (April 21, 1945), "has often made me feel during this war that, if Washington could be steadfast through Valley Forge, we could be steadfast today in spite of anxiety and sorrow."

A sudden change of leadership was difficult in a time of war. "There was consternation and grief but, at the same time, courage and confidence in the ability of this country and its people to back new leaders and to carry through the objectives to which the people have pledged themselves" ("My Day," April 21, 1945).

She left no space between the lines for interpretation. American democracy depended on a peaceful and orderly transfer of power. She reassured citizens across the nation, Americans in uniform battling toward Berlin and storming the Philippines, as well as international allies that President Truman had the full confidence of the government and the military. She fully supported President Truman and the American people should too.

It had been eight days since Franklin's death. She had comforted the country and helped facilitate a calm transition. Then she stepped out of the public arena.

AN UNCERTAIN FUTURE

Eleanor Roosevelt left the White House with "a feeling of melancholy and something of uncertainty" (Roosevelt 1961, 283). Rooms, which had hummed with possibility, stood silent. A transformative slice of American history had ended.

For the first time, she faced life on her own. She had always perceived her world as controlled by someone else: her grandmother, her mother-in-law, her husband. Now, a sense of deep freedom washed over her. She wasn't quite sure what she wanted, but she knew what she didn't want.

She was done with big elaborate houses. The family donated Spring-wood Mansion at Hyde Park to the federal government as a museum. Her cottage at Val-Kill and apartment in Washington Square would be her home. Both had a private room for Tommy, who would continue as her private secretary.

When the two women arrived at Eleanor's New York apartment, Lorena Hickok was already there. She had arranged the profusion of sympathy flowers and organized the cards to be answered.

Eleanor Roosevelt, also, didn't want to feel old. She had discovered a new vitality working with young people. She believed she still had a purpose.

Eighteen days after Franklin's death, Allied Forces bombed Berlin to submission and Adolf Hitler committed suicide. On May 8, 1945, Germany's full and unconditional surrender rang throughout the United States. Eleanor stood in New York's Times Square watching the paper confetti shower down on a jubilant crowd.

PRESIDENT TRUMAN'S CONFIDANTE

Though a private citizen, Eleanor Roosevelt still communicated with the authority of a First Lady. She continued her "My Day" column and magazine articles. She publicly applauded President Truman's Victory-in-Europe radio address and privately thanked him for graciously mentioning Franklin D. Roosevelt. Truman felt the former First Lady was the only person in the world who understood the weight of his daily responsibilities. He respected her understanding of global issues and appreciated her knowledge of international leaders. They began a trusted and confidential correspondence.

President Truman conveyed to the former First Lady the details of "the surrender arrangements with Germany" (Glendon 2001, 82). She offered insight into how to flatter Winston Churchill, just enough, to gain his confidence. She voiced her concern that oil resources in the Middle East would complicate mediation between Muslim residents and Jewish refugees seeking safety in Palestine. They discussed China and the complexities of American involvement in the conflict between Chinese leader Chiang Kai-shek and the Chinese Communist Party. Eleanor Roosevelt developed a more open relationship on international policy with President Truman than she had had with her own husband. They didn't always agree, but they admired each other's straightforward honesty.

Eleanor Roosevelt's personal interactions with Dr. Leo Szilard and other nuclear scientists gave her a unique understanding of the atomic bomb's dangerous potential. When news came of Truman's use of a nuclear weapon against Hiroshima, Japan, on August 6, 1945, she was neither surprised nor complacent. She gave voice to the dire ramifications; humanity had two choices: "destruction and death—or construction and life!" ("My Day," August 8, 1945).

When Japan surrendered on August 14, following a second atomic explosion over Nagasaki, Eleanor Roosevelt spoke to the nation on CBS radio. Americans were thankful for the war's end, but peace had come through a new destructive power that was "partly understood but not, as yet, completely developed and controlled" (Smith 2014, 242–243). Giving voice to Szilard's warning, ER questioned further military use and became one of the first Americans to speak out against nuclear weapons.

President Truman valued Eleanor Roosevelt's international experience and long-held aspiration for world peace. He recognized her as a bridge between foreign leaders and everyday Americans. She "believed the United Nations to be the one hope for a peaceful world" and was committed to its success (Roosevelt 1961, 299). If anyone could inspire faith in American participation in the UN, it was the former First Lady.

Truman asked Eleanor Roosevelt to serve on the American delegation to the first meeting of the UN in London. She hesitated, but family and friends urged her to accept.

Armed with advice from Esther Lape and a list of priorities from the LWV and the NAACP, Eleanor Roosevelt approached her appointment to the UN delegation strategically: Set a practical goal. Listen, educate, build consensus, and get it done.

AMERICA'S LONE FEMALE VOICE

In the black of night on December 30, 1945, Eleanor Roosevelt boarded the RMS *Queen Elizabeth* for London. She was alone and filled with trepidation. "I was simply terrified," she wrote to a friend. "I felt that I was going to do a job that I knew nothing about" (Glendon 2001, 25). Thick fog shrouded the ship, just as it had on that ill-fated voyage of her childhood. Eleanor gathered up her courage. As Mademoiselle Souvestre had taught her, she dug in and committed herself to learning about her new position. She studied the State Department documents, took notes at the daily briefings, asked questions, and prepared to be the best delegate she could be.

She was unaware that her male colleagues had vehemently opposed her appointment. Republican John Foster Dulles (1888–1959) regarded her as a far-left liberal unable to competently represent State Department policy. Others alleged her presence showed a lack of U.S. professionalism and seriousness. The *Los Angeles Times* called her appointment a mistake. The newspaper proclaimed she lacked "a guarded tongue"; diplomacy was beyond her capabilities. "Good judgment and good taste appear alike alien to her make-up " (Baritono 2017, 26).

Without consulting her, the men assigned her to Committee Three—social, cultural, and humanitarian topics. They must have thought, she wrote, "Ah, here's the safe spot for her . . . She can't do much harm there!" (Roosevelt 1961, 303).

Arriving in London, Eleanor feared that the legitimacy of her appointment to the U.S. delegation would be questioned. She soon realized, however, that it was her male counterparts who were liabilities. Foreign delegates considered Mr. Dulles and Senator Arthur H. Vandenberg arrogant. Secretary of State James F. Byrnes adopted a strategy of taking no specific stance. Foreign counterparts considered him untrustworthy. Roosevelt knew her position: "be fair and stand for what we believe is right" (Glendon 2001, 29).

Eleanor Roosevelt sits at a head table between Bertha Lutz of Brazil (left, standing) and Minerva Bernardino of the Dominican Republic (right) at a gathering of female delegates to the United Nations in London, in 1946. These women initiated the international discussion that women's rights are human rights. (Corel)

News services and radio broadcasts sought out the former First Lady. She gave interviews in English, French, German, and Italian. Her celebrity status irritated her male counterparts.

Just as the "airing our minds" luncheons had been a catalyst for building a women's network, Eleanor Roosevelt began inviting the other sixteen women participants at the United Nations' initial session to her room for tea. These casual gatherings of female delegates, alternates, and advisers coalesced the women from eleven countries behind shared goals and gave birth to an open letter addressed to the women of the world.

On February 12, 1946, Eleanor Roosevelt read the letter into the minutes of the General Assembly: "[W]e call on the Governments of the world to encourage women everywhere to take a more active part in national and international affairs, and on the women who are conscious of their opportunities to come forward and share in the work of peace and reconstruction as they did in war and resistance."

Delegations were asked to take the letter home and communicate it to their people. In addition, the French urged all nations to increase the number of women on their delegations.

AMERICA'S FOREMOST DIPLOMAT

In the final hours of the UN's first session, the Third Committee submitted a resolution for a General Assembly vote. The resolution protected the right of thirteen million war refugees to find safety in a country of their choice.

The Soviet Union had opposed the resolution in committee. They sent their lead debater, Andrei Vishinsky, before the General Assembly to argue for an amendment. Vishinsky was Stalin's attack dog, the prosecutor who convicted his political opponents. He authoritatively took the podium and proposed that war refugees must return to their country of origin. Individuals who refused, Vishinsky argued, did so because they were Nazi sympathizers or collaborators—traitors trying to avoid punishment.

In actuality, Stalin's government had begun persecuting pro-democracy activists in countries that had come under their influence after the war: Poland, Hungary, Czechoslovakia, Ukraine, other Eastern European countries and the Baltic States. Displaced peoples opposed to Soviet Communist Party rule, including Jews, were choosing not to return to their country of origin to avoid continued persecution.

As a supporter of the resolution, the U.S. delegation was called to address Vishinsky's amendment. It was the first public postwar challenge between the United States and the Soviet Union. The American men huddled in consultation, each unwilling to challenge Vishinsky. Dulles turned to Eleanor and suggested she should speak; she was on the Third Committee and most informed about the issue.

Eleanor Roosevelt calmly took the podium, though internally, she "trembled at the thought of speaking against the famous Mr. Vishinsky" (Roosevelt 1961, 308). She spoke succinctly and without notes. Most refugees were neither traitors nor collaborators, she countered. They were people seeking a safe place to resume their lives. Surely, Mr. Vishinsky wasn't proposing that refugees be forced to face persecution? Would the Soviet delegation send communist opponents of Franco's government back to Spain to face imprisonment? She drew in the South American delegations by referencing their hero of democracy: Simón Bolívar. Strategically, she solidified a coalition and the resolution passed without amendment.

Shortly after one in the morning, as ER wearily climbed the stairs to her hotel room, Mr. Dulles called out to her. He and Senator Vandenberg apologized for opposing her appointment; they said they were honored to work beside her. She felt a rare moment of appreciation and pride.

Newsreels hailed Eleanor Roosevelt as the most accomplished American diplomat at the UN. When the other American delegates headed home, she traveled to Germany. She needed to witness the refugee camps firsthand.

DEFINING HUMAN RIGHTS

Lorena Hickok was single again and hoping to spend time with Eleanor, but Eleanor embraced her new calling. The UN leadership invited the former First Lady to serve as one of nine delegates on a special commission to devise the structure and functions of a permanent Commission on Human Rights.

The other members chose ER to lead the organizational group. They decided that the Commission would have representatives from the five permanent nations of the Security Council plus thirteen countries on a rotating basis. The Commission would clarify what human rights were, establish accountability for nations, and create a process for complaints to be heard.

At the full Commission's first meeting in January 1947, they elected Eleanor Roosevelt chairperson. She believed the Commission's first goal must be to define human rights. Without an internationally accepted definition, there could be no accountability or adjudication. Her challenge was to inspire collaboration between individuals from different cultural backgrounds with conflicting philosophies, perspectives, and priorities.

Communist Party officials from the Soviet Union and Yugoslavia valued the state over the individual. Lebanese philosopher Dr. Charles Habbib

Malik (1906–1987) championed individual autonomy. Dr. Peng-Chun Chang (1892–1957), a Chinese scholar and diplomat, brought an Eastern philosophy: the rights of others were equivalent to the rights of self—one was not possible without the other. Chilean judge Hérnan Santa Cruz (1906–1999) championed socioeconomic rights. The only other woman on the Commission, India's Hansa Mehta (1897–1995), emphasized clear language and practical implementation of rights. René Cassin (1887–1976), a French Jew and legislative lawyer, had survived Nazi occupation by escaping to Britain. Roosevelt assigned Cassin to draft an outline, which he drew from his greatest influence: the *1789 French Declaration of the Rights of Man.*

Around the world, the name Eleanor Roosevelt was synonymous with aid to those in need. As chairman of the Commission on Human Rights, she began receiving pleas for assistance.

Ukrainian women, taking refuge in Austria, described their homeland as "streaming rivers of blood" (Ukrainian Women to Roosevelt, June 21, 1947). The Soviet Union was swallowing up their country. The signatures of 2,000 desperate women cried out to Eleanor Roosevelt, but her fledgling Commission had no authority to provide assistance.

A telegram on behalf of 5,000 exiles from the Dominican Republic begged Roosevelt "to do something, to mediate before President Trujillo" tortured "men and boys jailed in Santo Domino" (Ducoudray to Roosevelt, June 25, 1947). Their crime was seeking free and fair elections. Eleanor Roosevelt penciled a note on the bottom of the telegram for Tommy to draft a response: "The only thing I can do . . ." is to pass on the information to the UN Secretariat " . . . the HR [Human Relations Commission] is not a court."

She could have succumbed to despair; instead, she pushed the working group forward.

Throughout 1947, the Commission went back and forth over various drafts. Five to six months of the year, she attended meetings either in New York, Switzerland, or France. Meticulously, they weighed every word. Eleanor Roosevelt approved using "all men" as a reference to humanity, but Hansa Mehta objected. There were places in the world where women would be denied the rights in their declaration if the word "women" were not spelled out. Mehta prevailed. (See Primary Documents: *United Nations Universal Declaration of Human Rights.*)

DRAFTING THE DECLARATION

In May 1948, the Human Rights Commission gathered in New York to consolidate notes on the current draft. Threat of armed conflict was mounting in the Middle East over the establishment of a Jewish state carved out of existing Muslim-controlled lands in Palestine. The post World War II window of international goodwill was narrowing.

Eleanor Roosevelt employed all of her managerial skills to keep the commissioners working together. Malik and Cassin stood on opposite sides of the Palestinian/Jewish state conflict, yet they continued refining passages and growing in their admiration for each other.

Soviet leader Stalin actively opposed the *Declaration on Human Rights*, regarding it as an assault on national sovereignty—a stance shared by many American senators. Each session, Stalin replaced the Soviet representative in an attempt to disrupt progress.

The newest Soviet delegate was explicitly instructed to use any tactic possible to stop the Declaration's completion. He failed to get the group to start over, so he proposed amendments to each article. The editing process came to a crawl.

Between UN sessions, Eleanor Roosevelt returned to American radio. She and daughter Anna renewed their relationship, hosting a weekday interview program. ER used the broadcast to familiarize Americans with international issues and nurture support for the UN.

As the UN General Assembly convened in Paris in October 1948, the world felt precarious. The Chinese Communist Party was taking control of China. The UN's Middle East negotiator had been assassinated. The Soviet Union was blockading Allied access to West Berlin; the Americans were airlifting food and coal into the city. The Soviets were demanding that the United States relinquish its atomic weapons. Roosevelt, Malik, Cassin, and Chang believed that if they didn't successfully bring the *Declaration on Human Rights* to a vote during this session, the moment would be lost.

Eleanor Roosevelt was driven. She packed every free moment with informal negotiations. She wrote to Hick: "The work is hard now & high tension but it is coming to an end" (Streitmatter 1998, 279).

UNIVERSAL DECLARATION OF HUMAN RIGHTS

Throughout October and November, as the full Third Committee finalized the document, Roosevelt's committee fought off threats to amend or dilute the articles. They embraced a single amalgamated vision and worked together to nurture a larger consensus. The process dragged on, but Eleanor found hope in the expanded discussion; the more the contributing voices, the more nations would consider themselves stakeholders.

December 10, 1948, was the last day of the UN General Assembly session. The Soviet delegate submitted amendments and tried to postpone the vote on the Declaration to the next session. The moment was slipping away.

Late in the day, Eleanor Roosevelt took the podium before the General Assembly. She spoke directly to the proposed Soviet amendments.

Fifty-eight nations had come together and agreed on these specific words. The *Universal Declaration of Human Rights* was a statement "of basic principles of human rights and freedoms," she said. A vote of support from the General Assembly would enable the Declaration "to serve as a common standard of achievement for all peoples of all nations." There should be no last-minute changes. The moment had come to vote.

Then, she took a great risk. "This must be taken as testimony of our common aspiration . . . to lift men everywhere to a higher standard of life and to a greater enjoyment of freedom." It was imperative that no nation oppose the Declaration (Roosevelt, December 10, 1948).

Discussion roiled around the room. Some Muslim countries objected to Article 18, which stated that everyone has the "freedom to change his religion or belief." Some claimed it dishonored Islam, but the Muslim leader of the Pakistani delegation took the floor and defended the wording.

Minutes before midnight, the roll call vote began. Saudi Arabia abstained on religious grounds, but all of the other Muslim countries voted in favor.

South Africa abstained.

Eleanor Roosevelt feared the Soviets would vote "no." The six countries of the Soviet bloc refused to vote in favor, but they abstained rather than vote it down. The Declaration passed.

The president of the General Assembly commended the representative from the United States of America, Eleanor Roosevelt. The entire Assembly rose for a standing ovation.

"For the first time in history, the organized community of nations had issued a common declaration of human rights and fundamental freedoms" (Glendon 2001, 171). The *Universal Declaration of Human Rights* set a precedent as an international document establishing equal rights for men and women. It created an understanding that protecting human rights was not solely the responsibility of governments but also of communities and families. It was "Universal" because it applied not only to UN member governments and people within those societies but to all people.

Initially, the Declaration was not accompanied by a covenant or treaty to legally bind participant nations, but it was a moral pronouncement for a more equitable future. It provided a foundation for establishing the International Criminal Court and influenced the constitutions of new nations emerging in the later part of the twentieth century.

The Declaration identified racial discrimination as a violation of human rights. It unmasked the pretense that South African apartheid and Soviet totalitarianism were acceptable methods of maintaining social order and economic stability. It focused a spotlight on racial inequities in the United States and renewed the Civil Rights Movement.

Eleanor Roosevelt viewed the passage of the *Universal Declaration of Human Rights* as her most important personal contribution to a better

FEMALE VOICES AT THE UN

Most female delegates to the UN were appointed to the Sub-Commission on the Status of Women or other subgroups within the Third Committee. Their voices were not included in the *Universal Declaration of Human Rights* until the entire Third Committee reviewed the document. These women influenced Eleanor Roosevelt's evolving view of women's roles and challenges in the world. She, in turn, empowered them.

The Latinx delegates from Central and South America vocally championed women's equality. Minerva Bernardino from the Dominican Republic established the United Nations' ethos in 1945 by pressing for language in the Preamble of the UN Charter specifying "the equal rights of men and women." Lakshmi Menon of India proposed that these words also be included in the Preamble of the Declaration.

Equal application of human rights depended on inclusive wording. Marie-Heléne Lefaucheux of France called for a specific statement against sex-based discrimination. With strong support from Bernardino, Bertha Lutz of Brazil, and Isabel de Vidal of Uruguay, "sex" was included in the list of nondiscrimination distinctions in Article 2.

Denmark's Bodil Betrup proposed specific gender-neutral and inclusive language throughout the document. "Every man" and "mankind" became "all peoples," "all human beings," "every individual" and "everyone."

Child marriage and forced marriage threatened women in many countries. Begum Shaista Ikramullah of Pakistan championed Article 16 establishing equal rights for women entering, in, or leaving a marriage.

Economic rights were strongly raised by communist and socialist countries. Evdokia Uralova of Byelorussia argued for Article 23's inclusion of "Everyone, without any discrimination, has the right to equal pay for equal work."

Further Reading

Glendon, Mary Ann. 2001. *A World Made New: Eleanor Roosevelt and the Universal Declaration of Human Rights*. New York: Random House.

United Nations. n.d. "Women Who Shaped the Universal Declaration." Accessed January 23, 2021. https://www.un.org/en/observances/human-rights-day/women-who-shaped-the-universal-declaration

world. She wrote that working within the UN was "one of the most wonderful and worthwhile experiences in my life" (Roosevelt 1961, 299).

INFLUENCER AS ACTIVIST

As Eleanor Roosevelt turned sixty-five, her "My Day" column modeled modern political activism. She highlighted specific legislation, like a bill allowing Native American reservation lands to be sold to nonindigenous developers. She detailed the history of federal assaults on tribal sovereignty and explained how selling fragments of tribal lands would dismantle

Circa 1950, Eleanor Roosevelt holds a copy of her proudest achievement: the United Nations' *Universal Declaration of Human Rights* (adopted December 10, 1948). She felt this document would take its place in history beside the Magna Carta and the U.S. Constitution for its long-term impact on humanity. (Corel)

Native American culture and self-government. She urged her readers to voice their opposition to their congressional representatives and she successfully influenced President Truman to veto the bill.

In February 1950, ER dove into the latest technology: television. Only 20 percent of American homes owned a television, but ER and son Elliott produced a Sunday news program for NBC: *Today with Mrs. Roosevelt.*

She was the second American woman to host a television news forum. In her first episode, she boldly discussed the development of the hydrogen bomb with Albert Einstein, J. Robert Oppenheimer, and other leading physicists. Her next episode examined the potential of nationalized health care. Discussing everything from U.S. tax structure and rent control to foreign policy and statehood for Alaska and Hawaii, it was a trailblazing effort to bring consequential policy issues into American homes.

She returned to Paris for the UN General Assembly meeting that autumn and passed the chairmanship of the Human Rights Commission on to Charles Malik. She also expanded her international radio influence by broadcasting a weekly program in French on the French National Network. Through the *Voice of America*, these programs extended her influence into Belgium, Switzerland, Eastern Europe, and North Africa. Internationally, she was the voice of American compassion.

Back in the United States, Eleanor Roosevelt returned to NBC radio from October to August 1951. She co-hosted a weekday interview broadcast with Elliott and strategically linked it with a Sunday television program: *Mrs. Roosevelt Meets the Public*. She was in American homes six days a week, both in print and through live media. She brought trusted information to an audience that sought her expertise and ability to explain complicated topics.

With racially biased Jim Crow laws continuing in the South, she turned her attention to human rights at home. On January 1, 1952, Eleanor Roosevelt reminded her readers of the atrocities against African Americans that had occurred in the past year. A mob of 4,000 white rioters had demolished an apartment on the south side of Chicago because a Black family had moved into the all-white neighborhood. In Florida, a sheriff shot two Black men in cold blood. The NAACP leader who had been trying to bring the white sheriff to trial was murdered in a bombing.

While others looked away, Roosevelt's voice on civil rights was unrelenting. The Ku Klux Klan put a $25,000 bounty on her head. Letters poured into the FBI calling for Mrs. Roosevelt to be investigated. Opponents charged that she was spreading Russian propaganda and instigating racial strife.

TRAVELING THE WORLD

When General Dwight D. Eisenhower (1890–1969) became president, Eleanor Roosevelt tendered her resignation as a UN delegate to his Republican administration. Following her last day in the General Assembly in January 1953, Eleanor smiled to her secretary and said, we're in Paris, "why not go home the long way—around the world. We've already got a good start" (Roosevelt 1961, 324). Travel was the Roosevelt tonic; adventure would guide her path forward. Her UN colleagues happily arranged connections for her, each eager to have her experience their country.

She visited Malik's Lebanon and flew to Syria. She found the Palestinian refugee camps in Jordan "distressing beyond words" (Roosevelt 1961, 326). She had long advocated for the establishment of Israel and admired the wild optimism of newly arrived Jewish refugees. In sharp contrast, the displaced Palestinians appeared hopeless. She admitted that the situation was more complicated than she had originally comprehended.

The All Pakistan Women's Association greeted her with open arms. India's Prime Minister Nehru extended his personal invitation for her to visit his country. Eleanor Roosevelt walked with the people and toured newly established medical facilities and schools. The two nations were vibrant with their newly won independence from Britain.

In both the Pakistan-India border dispute and the Israel-Arab conflict, Eleanor saw that "fear of one's neighbor resulted in spending for defense huge sums badly needed for health, housing, education" and vital social needs (Roosevelt 1961, 328).

She drew a comparison to the economic collapse in Germany following World War I, which had spawned Nazism, and economic disparity, which had empowered communism in the Soviet Union and China. Conflict erupted out of the dark corners of inequity.

Using her platform as a former UN delegate, she published *India and the Awaking East*. In many emerging nations, she explained to her American audience, freedom from hunger was a greater driving force than personal freedoms. If Communism could more quickly remedy widespread hunger and homelessness, many young countries would turn to it. Democracy, with its struggle for compromise, was often slow to produce measureable change.

One of her most memorable moments abroad, however, was personal. Long ago, her father had told magical tales of India. Elliott Roosevelt had impressed on his young daughter that she must experience the Taj Mahal beneath a full moon. He painted an ethereal image of a bench beside a still pool and the reflection of the white dome bathed in mystical moonlight.

Eleanor Roosevelt sat on a bench that was just as her father had described and she witnessed the vision he had found unforgettable. Time transcended. She felt her father beside her. "I will carry in my mind the beauty of it as long as I live" (Roosevelt 1961, 322).

Setting a new path, she went on to Yugoslavia as a journalist and interviewed President Josip Broz "Tito" for *Look* magazine. The Eisenhower administration was engaging with the Yugoslavian dictator. Roosevelt directly questioned President Tito about suppressing his opponents. She felt the American people should judge his answers for themselves.

When she returned to New York, the former UN delegate walked into the nonprofit American Association for the United Nations and volunteered to help grow the organization. The group's mission was to raise understanding of how the UN worked and why it was important. She had just authored *UN: Today and Tomorrow*. Eleanor Roosevelt joined the Association's board and for the rest of her life, devoted herself to promoting the UN around the world and facilitating student participation in model UN exercises to develop international understanding and diplomatic skills.

BACKLASH AGAINST WOMEN

The booming 1950s economy made it possible for households to prosper on a single income. Though many women still needed employment, they were seen as taking men's jobs. Under Eisenhower's administration, women in the State Department were expected to resign when they married.

Opportunities for women in civil service evaporated; only one woman served in Eisenhower's Cabinet. (She would be the last woman in a presidential cabinet until 1975.)

Eleanor Roosevelt felt the backlash herself. She continued writing columns and books, but increasingly wrote to the norms of the time—highlighting her maternal and wifely role, downplaying her independent actions, and veiling her political influence.

Male-controlled media, especially in television, depicted women as happy suburban housewives—as in *The Adventures of Ozzie and Harriet* and *Father Knows Best*—or child-like characters who became entangled in predicaments and needed to be rescued by a husband or father—as in *I Love Lucy* and *My Little Marjorie*. Marilyn Monroe was the highest paid woman in films, valued for portraying sexy female characters that did not threaten male authority.

Eleanor Roosevelt and Lorena Hickok tried to reinvigorate female interest in politics by coauthoring *Ladies of Courage* (1954). The book celebrated women, Democratic and Republican, who influenced modern American democracy; it concluded with a chapter on "How To Break Into Politics." They tempered their call for political activism, however, by suggesting women could contribute while fulfilling their primary obligations in the home.

ER, however, seldom stayed home. She traveled internationally and traversed the country for several months each year as a paid public speaker, giving as many as 150 lectures annually. On the eighth anniversary of Franklin's death, she lost her favorite traveling companion, Malvina Thompson. Tommy had been her loyal secretary for nearly thirty years. The death of her friend was a deep loss.

Her network of women was shrinking. She and Hick remained confidantes, but diabetes was stealing Hick's eyesight and health. Elizabeth Read had passed away, but Esther Lape remained close. Molly Dewson had retired to the country due to ill health. Isabella Greenway King suffered a heart attack. Eleanor longed to see her old friend, but Arizona never seemed on her busy itinerary. "Our friendship is such an old one," Eleanor wrote, "that time and distance have never made any difference" (Miller and McGinnis 2009, 227). Isabella passed away before Eleanor could see her one last time.

SENATOR MCCARTHY AND THE "COMMUNIST MENACE"

From 1950 on, the specter of communism was used to scare voters away from progressive reforms and draw them toward conservative policies. A vocal group of Republicans charged that internationalists and civil rights leaders were "communists." Eleanor Roosevelt received letters calling the UN "Satan's work" ("My Day," January 22, 1953).

Seeking to promote his reelection, Wisconsin senator Joseph McCarthy (1908–1957) alleged that 205 officials in the Truman State Department were communist spies. Unable to substantiate his accusation, McCarthy put forward the names of nine State Department employees, including Dorothy Kenyon (1888–1972).

Kenyon was a judge, a longtime member of ER's extended women's network, and an adviser to the UN Sub-Commission on the Status of Women. Roosevelt and Kenyon were not personal friends, but the attack on a distinguished woman at the UN demanded response. Roosevelt publicly defended Kenyon. Senate investigations denounced McCarthy's allegations as a "fraud and a hoax." The Tydings Report determined the senator's purpose was to "confuse and divide the American people" (July 14, 1950).

Still, Senator McCarthy continued instigating fear and attracting media attention. The more outrageous his allegations, the more his following increased. President Eisenhower failed to curtail McCarthy. State Department libraries around the world were scrubbed of books alleged to have a communist leaning or questionable authors. In some cases, books were burned, inspiring author Ray Bradbury to write *Fahrenheit 451* in 1953.

McCarthy blackmailed government officials with evidence of their marital infidelity or homosexuality that had been provided by J. Edgar Hoover. McCarthy's power over people led some to bear false witness. McCarthyism poisoned America with fear. In response, playwright Arthur Miller used the early New England witch trials as an allegory and wrote *The Crucible* (1953).

While others avoided McCarthy's attention, Eleanor Roosevelt called him out. "Apparently you must agree with Senator McCarthy," she wrote "or you are liable to be his enemy. This is the way a dictator behaves" ("My Day," March 5, 1954).

Even McCarthy knew he couldn't directly accuse Eleanor Roosevelt. He fed statements to conservative groups like the Citizen's Committee to Combat Communism. The organization published "Eleanor's Red Record," eighty-eight citations of alleged communist connections, including the Women's Trade Union League, the American Youth Congress, and the American Civil Liberties Union. The purported "evidence" included her donations to abolish poll taxes, support legal aid for actors subpoenaed before HUAC, and charitable contributions for refugees in Spain and Yugoslavia.

McCarthy struck a flanking blow at Eleanor Roosevelt by claiming former members of the Communist Party would attest that Judge Kenyon had been assigned by communist organizations to influence Mrs. Roosevelt's writings and positions. McCarthy intended to vilify Kenyon to discredit Eleanor Roosevelt.

Roosevelt answered the senator's accusations publicly in "My Day" (August 16, 1954). While she had known Judge Kenyon for years, the two worked in different circles at the UN. "I have never discussed her ideas or mine on most important subjects," she said, "so there is no way in which she could have influenced everything I ever wrote." She added, "I have a great respect for Judge Kenyon's ability and have always found her honest and courageous."

She knew the bullying McCarthy would not call her before his investigative committee because he wouldn't want to share the television screen with her. She concluded with: "I can testify to the fact that the part of the accusation which said she [Kenyon] was assigned to influence my writings cannot be true, because in no way did she ever attempt to do so."

Senator Joseph McCarthy had gone too far. Voices began to rise up against him. By the end of 1954, the Senate censured the Wisconsin senator.

RECLAIMING POLITICAL POWER

In addition to McCarthyism, Eleanor Roosevelt felt President Eisenhower's failure to address racial discrimination discredited American democracy. She spoke against segregation in Southern hospitals and supported the 1954 Supreme Court decision in *Brown v. Board of Education of Topeka* to desegregate American schools. She pointed out to her readers that school segregation was a symptom of a greater problem: housing segregation. Integrated neighborhoods would naturally create diversity in public schools. She raised donations to support protestors during the Montgomery Alabama bus boycott. Civil rights were drawing her back into national politics.

Americans of color were being denied their basic right to vote. State laws might enable segregation, but Roosevelt was adamant: the federal government could protect voting rights. At seventy-one, Eleanor Roosevelt drafted the Democratic Party's civil rights platform for the 1956 election.

She strongly backed Illinois governor Adlai Stevenson II (1900–1965) in his second presidential run against Eisenhower. She had admired Stevenson as a State Department envoy to the UN and encouraged him to run for the Illinois governorship.

It was a long shot for Stevenson to defeat the incumbent president, but Eleanor Roosevelt hit the campaign trail. The Stevenson campaign proposed a televised presidential debate. Eisenhower refused, but the two campaigns compromised on a debate between surrogates. Two days before the election, Eleanor Roosevelt and Senator Margaret Chase Smith appeared on *Face the Nation* to debate on behalf of the two presidential candidates. It was the first televised presidential debate.

Eisenhower defeated Stevenson, but ER's efforts helped sweep in Democratic majorities in both the House of Representatives and the Senate.

From her reclaimed position in the Democratic Party, she weighed in on the pending Civil Rights Act. She voiced disappointment to Senate Majority Leader Lyndon B. Johnson (1908–1973); the legislation didn't ensure equal voting rights for African Americans. She argued that Southern states would still determine who was a "qualified voter" and thereby disenfranchise people of color.

In a personal letter to Johnson, she wrote: "[I]t would be fooling the people to have them think that this was a real vital step toward giving all our people the right to vote or any other civil rights" (Black 1999, 281). She agreed with the NAACP that the legislation capitulated to the Southern Democrats. It was mildly better than nothing. She would support the 1957 Civil Rights Act only if Johnson cooperated with Republicans and "put back many of the foreign aid cuts, if not all." Leaning in with the power of her influence, she stated she was going to write in her column that Johnson was "too statesmanlike" to allow funding for UN programs and foreign aid to be cut.

THE POWER OF MEDIA

Eleanor Roosevelt strongly believed education and access to diverse viewpoints were vital to a healthy democracy. In August 1957, in the midst of the Cold War, she traveled to the Soviet Union to write a series of articles for the *New York Post*. While she found the cities joyless, she pointed out that communism had secured food stability, education, and health care for the Soviet people. "The people are not free, but they are better off materially every year" (Roosevelt 1961, 385).

In a journalistic coup, she became the first American to interview Nikita S. Khrushchev (1894–1971), boldly questioning the new Soviet leader. Why had the Soviet Union refused to reduce its military forces and weapons? Was bilateral disarmament possible with international inspection? Roosevelt provided Americans a view of the Soviet Union and its leader without U.S. government filters.

While their discussion was sometimes heated, Roosevelt and Khrushchev agreed that cultural exchanges might reduce misunderstandings between the United States and the Soviet Union. Fear only exacerbated hostility.

Two years later, Khrushchev became the first Soviet premier to visit the United States and he stopped at Val-Kill Cottage. A steady stream of foreign leaders, from Ethiopian emperor Haile Selassie to a young Indira Gandhi, journeyed to Eleanor Roosevelt's home to discuss international issues. The American public needed to hear these different points of view, too. Eleanor proposed returning to television but was warned that commercial sponsors regarded her as "fanatically disliked" (Roosevelt 1961, 416).

A British company, however, approached her to do a television commercial. She weighed the potential criticism of a former First Lady selling margarine on TV against the proposed income. The money could positively impact 6,000 lives through her various philanthropies. She filmed the commercial and braced herself for controversy.

Many Americans valued Eleanor Roosevelt's endorsement and, to everyone's surprise, the margarine sold. Suddenly, she was offered a variety of high-paying television spots.

On her seventy-fifth birthday, she premiered *Prospects of Mankind*—a news and issues television program. Produced for a prototype of public television in collaboration with Brandeis University, each episode highlighted a critical topic. Host Eleanor Roosevelt initiated questions and directed discussion between three to five experts (including public officials, foreign diplomats, scientists, journalists, and scholars). No topic was too controversial or intellectual—international arms control, foreign aid, even perceptions of Americans abroad.

She made complex topics comprehensible and relevant, while her personal contacts provided access to foreign leaders and international experts. International policy students around the world studied *Prospects of Mankind.*

INFLUENCING THE FUTURE

In 1960, Eleanor Roosevelt was as busy as she had ever been. Initially, she didn't support Senator John F. Kennedy (1917–1963) as the Democratic presidential nominee. She felt he had avoided taking a stance on Senator McCarthy and prioritized winning the South over enacting civil rights.

Kennedy visited her at Val-Kill and convinced her of his determination to expand New Deal programs such as Social Security. She actively joined Kennedy's campaign and helped deliver several states in a very close election.

As President Kennedy set up his administration, ER noticed his first 200 appointees included only 9 women. She knocked on the White House door with a three-page list of women qualified for major administrative posts. She also pressed Kennedy to create a Presidential Commission on the Status of Women in America. He did and asked her to lead the effort.

Roosevelt embraced Kennedy's Peace Corps program and conducted the first televised interview of a sitting president to promote the idea on *Prospects of Mankind* (March 1961). She advocated for the Peace Corps across her media platforms, believing public service to international communities would be the "most fruitful [way] . . . of sharing our American Dream with others" (Roosevelt 1961, 407).

In April 1962, she interviewed President Kennedy again. Her hair had gone white and her skin was like porcelain. The Commission on Women was still investigating, but the two discussed early findings on the marginalization of women in the workplace, pay inequity, and the need for more women in professional degree programs. The popular ideal might be white middle-class housewives, but women of all colors made up a third of the workforce. Data on the needs and challenges of working women was key to initiating a new cycle of positive change.

FINAL DAYS

For two years, Eleanor Roosevelt had lived with *aplastic anemia*—her bone marrow was not producing adequate new blood cells. Impatient with doctors and tests when she felt fine, she traveled to Europe, campaigned for John F. Kennedy, maintained her public speaking engagements, and spearheaded the Commission on Women. In the spring of 1962, she was actively advocating for the establishment of Medicare and planning future broadcasts of her TV program.

For the first time in her life, however, ill health infringed upon her activities. She required periodic blood transfusions, raising concern that she might have leukemia.

Between August and early October, Eleanor's health seemed to improve. Her "My Day" column continued to appear in newspapers until September 26, 1962. Few people realized she was severely ill.

She died on November 7, 1962, from a rare form of systemic tuberculosis—*miliary tuberculosis*. Her personal physician, Dr. David Gurewitsch, anguished that delayed diagnosis might have prevented antibiotics from saving her life. Controversy swirled around her death for the next forty years.

Eleanor Roosevelt was initially exposed to tuberculosis as a young woman. Modern investigation reveals that the tuberculosis bacillus, which spread through her body, was a newer antibiotic-resistant strain of the bacteria. She possibly encountered it during her travels to struggling nations, refugee camps, or even the area where she first engaged in philanthropy, New York City's Bowery neighborhood. In 1962, 15 percent of tuberculosis patients in New York demonstrated resistance to at least one antibiotic.

There is no evidence that medical error played a role in her death. Eleanor Roosevelt passed away in her New York apartment surrounded by her family.

Eleanor Roosevelt joins President John F. Kennedy at the White House on February 12, 1962, as part of the President's Commission on the Status of Women. Despite declining health, Eleanor played a vital role in the agenda and pushed the Commission to investigate why women were not fully participating in the economy or government. (Franklin D. Roosevelt Library)

FIRST LADY OF THE WORLD

News of her death sent shock and sorrow around the world. Adlai Stevenson, U.S. ambassador to the UN, addressed a special session of the General Assembly on November 9, 1962. "The United States, the United Nations, the world has lost one of its great citizens," he said. Eleanor Roosevelt's aspiration for world peace would forever make the UN her memorial. "She breathed life into this organization."

Stevenson quoted his friend: "We must build faith in the hearts of those who doubt. We must rekindle faith in ourselves when it grows dim, and find some kind of divine courage within us, to keep on, till on earth we have peace and goodwill among men."

Looking out across a sea of faces of all races, religions, and cultures, he concluded, "The issues that we debate in this hall are many and grave. But I don't think that we are divided in our grief at the passing of this great and gallant human being who was called 'The First Lady of the World.'"

Thousands of tearful Americans, as well as several sign-carrying detractors, lined the road as Eleanor Roosevelt returned one last time to the rose garden at Hyde Park. For the first time in history, a sitting president attended the funeral of a former First Lady. President John F. Kennedy and First Lady Jacqueline Kennedy stood beside former presidents Truman and Eisenhower. From Vice President Lyndon B. Johnson to Chief Justice Earl Warren, the political leaders of the nation paid their respects as the funeral was broadcast to the world.

There was one notable absence—Eleanor's cousin Alice Roosevelt Longworth. While the press publicized her absence as a final familial snub, the Washington matriarch simply stated that she had no intention of deflecting the spotlight from Eleanor.

After the family, dignitaries, and cameras had gone, a lone mourner stood beside the grave. Lorena Hickok laid a small bouquet of wildflowers on the fresh earth.

Each hand Eleanor Roosevelt had touched, each individual she had valued, made a positive difference. Every experience, painful or joyous, had prepared her for the challenges and opportunities of her life. In her final days, she drafted *Tomorrow Is Now.* "We face the future fortified only with the lessons we have learned from the past," she wrote. "It is today that we must create the world of the future" (Roosevelt 1963, xv).

SOURCES

Baritono, Raffaella. 2017. "Eleanor Roosevelt at the United Nations: 'Diplomacy from Below' and the Search for a New Transatlantic Dialogue." *European Journal of American Studies Spring 2017: Special Issue—Eleanor Roosevelt and Diplomacy in the Public Interest.* https://doi.org/10.4000/ejas.11920

Black, Allida M., ed. 1999. *Courage in a Dangerous World: The Political Writings of Eleanor Roosevelt.* New York: Columbia University Press.

Cook, Blanche Wiesen. 2016. *Eleanor Roosevelt, Volume 3: The War Years and After 1939–1962.* New York: Viking Penguin.

Glendon, Mary Ann. 2001. *A World Made New: Eleanor Roosevelt and the Universal Declaration of Human Rights.* New York: Random House.

Lash, Joseph P. 1971. *Eleanor and Franklin: The Story of Their Relationship Based on Eleanor Roosevelt's Private Papers.* New York: W.W. Norton & Company, Inc.

Lerner, B. H. 2001. "Revisiting the Death of Eleanor Roosevelt: Was the Diagnosis of Tuberculosis Missed?" *The International Journal of Tuberculosis and Lung Disease* 5 (12): 1080–1084.

Letter from Feliservio Ducoudray to Eleanor Roosevelt. June 25, 1947. United Nations Digital Archive. https://archives.un.org/sites/archives .un.org/files/UDHR/dominican_rep.pdf

Letter from Ukrainian Women to Eleanor Roosevelt. June 21, 1947. United
    Nations Digital Archive. https://archives.un.org/sites/archives
    .un.org/files/UDHR/s-0472-0071-0002-00001_uc.pdf

McCullough, David. 1992. *Truman.* New York: Simon & Schuster.

Miller, Kristie, and Robert H. McGinnis, eds. 2009. *A Volume of Friend-
    ship: The Letters of Eleanor Roosevelt and Isabella Greenway 1904–
    1953.* Tucson: The Arizona Historical Society.

Morgenthau, Henry. 1944, January 16. "U.S. Policy During WWII: Mor-
    genthau Documents State Department Inaction." Jewish Virtual
    Library. https://www.jewishvirtuallibrary.org/morgenthau-documents
    -state-department-inaction-january-1944

Roosevelt, Eleanor. 1935–1962. "My Day Index." *The Eleanor Roosevelt
    Papers Digital Edition* (2018). Edited by George Washington Uni-
    versity. https://erpapers.columbian.gwu.edu/my-day-index

Roosevelt, Eleanor. 1948, December 10. "Speech on the Adoption of the
    Universal Declaration of Human Rights." American Rhetoric.
    https://www.americanrhetoric.com/speeches/eleanorroosevelt
    declarationhumanrights.htm

Roosevelt, Eleanor. 1961. *The Autobiography of Eleanor Roosevelt.* New
    York: Harper Perennial.

Roosevelt, Eleanor. 1963. *Tomorrow Is Now.* New York: Harper & Row,
    Publishers.

Smith, Stephen Drury, ed. 2014. *The First Lady of Radio: Eleanor Roos-
    evelt's Historic Broadcasts.* New York: The New Press.

Streitmatter, Rodger, ed. 1998. *Empty Without You: The Intimate Letters of
    Eleanor Roosevelt and Lorena Hickok.* New York: The Free Press.

Timeline: Events in the Life of Eleanor Roosevelt

October 11, 1884	Anna Eleanor Roosevelt (ER) is born in New York.
September 29, 1889	Brother, Elliott Roosevelt, Jr. is born.
July 1890	Family travels to Europe.
June 28, 1891	Brother, Hall Ludlow Roosevelt is born in France.
August 1891	Her father enters a French sanatorium and the family returns to New York.
December 7, 1892	Her mother, Anna Hall Roosevelt, dies from diphtheria.
May 25, 1893	Her brother, Elliott, Jr., dies from diphtheria.
August 14, 1894	Her father, Elliott Bulloch Roosevelt, dies from complications of substance use disorder.
Autumn 1899	ER attends Allenswood school in England.
September 14, 1901	ER's uncle, Vice President Theodore Roosevelt, Jr., becomes U.S. president following William H. McKinley's assassination.
August 1902	ER returns to New York and comes out in November as a debutante.

1903	ER volunteers at College Settlement and joins National Consumers' League.
November 22, 1903	ER and Franklin Delano Roosevelt become secretly engaged.
March 17, 1905	ER marries Franklin Delano Roosevelt (FDR).
May 3, 1906	ER's first child, Anna Eleanor Roosevelt II is born.
December 23, 1907	Second child, James Roosevelt is born.
March 18, 1909	Third child, Franklin Delano Roosevelt, Jr., is born.
November 8, 1909	Baby Franklin Jr. dies from complications following influenza.
September 23, 1910	Fourth child, Elliott Roosevelt, is born.
January 1, 1911	FDR takes office as a New York state senator and family moves to Albany.
April 1913	President Woodrow Wilson appoints FDR assistant secretary of the Navy and family moves to Washington, D.C.
Spring 1913	ER hires Lucy Mercer as personal secretary.
August 17, 1914	Fifth child, Franklin Roosevelt, Jr., is born.
March 13, 1916	Sixth child, John Aspinwell Roosevelt, is born.
April 6, 1917	United States enters World War I.
1917–1918	ER volunteers with the American Red Cross and at navy hospitals during World War I.
September 20, 1918	ER confronts FDR regarding his affair with Lucy Mercer.
November 11, 1918	World War I ends.
November–December 1918	Influenza pandemic peaks in the United States.
January–February 1919	ER travels with FDR through war-torn Europe.
August 18, 1920	Nineteenth Amendment to the U.S. Constitution grants women the right to vote.

September–November 1920	ER participates in FDR's unsuccessful campaign for vice president.
April 12, 1921	ER attends League of Women Voters' second national conference and becomes politically active.
August 10, 1921	FDR is struck with polio.
Spring 1922	ER joins Women's Trade Union League and the Women's Division of the Democratic State Committee.
October 1923	ER's first professional article appears in *Ladies Home Journal* in connection with American (Bok) Peace Prize.
January 1924	ER gives her first public radio address: "Women in Politics" on NBC radio.
January 23, 1924	Esther Lape and ER testify before a Senate committee investigating American (Bok) Peace Prize.
June 24, 1924	ER leads the women's delegation at the Democratic National Convention in New York City.
March 1925	ER is editor of the first published issue of *Women's Democratic News*.
1925	FDR builds Val-Kill Cottage for ER, Marion Dickerman, and Nancy Cook and the women start Val-Kill furniture factory.
1926	ER purchases Todhunter School for Girls with Dickerman and Cook.
July–November 1928	ER directs Democratic National Committee's Bureau of Women's Activities with Molly Dewson and campaigns for Al Smith for president.
January 1, 1929	FDR sworn in as governor; ER becomes First Lady of New York.
October 29, 1929	U.S. stock market crashes and Great Depression begins.
October 1932	ER and Lorena Hickok establish a relationship during FDR's presidential campaign.

March 4, 1933	FDR inaugurated as 32nd U.S. president; ER becomes First Lady.
March 6, 1933	ER convenes initial weekly First Lady's Press Conference.
Fall 1933	ER initiates Arthurdale community resettlement project.
October 1933	ER publishes her first authored book, *It's Up to the Women.*
March 7–17, 1934	ER takes a press detail to Puerto Rico to reveal poverty and labor abuses.
June 1935	ER helps establish National Youth Administration within the Works Progress Administration.
August 1935	Women's network helps pass Social Security Act.
January 1, 1936	First "My Day" column appears in newspapers.
January 8, 1938	ER's book *This Troubled World* is published.
February 26, 1939	ER resigns from the Daughters of the American Revolution to protest discrimination against African American singer Marian Anderson.
July 18, 1940	ER sets precedent for a sitting First Lady to address a national political party presidential nominating convention.
November 5, 1940	FDR elected to third term as U.S. president.
June 25, 1941	ER successfully negotiates FDR's signing of Executive Order 8802—precedent for future antidiscrimination laws.
September 1941	ER's mother-in-law, Sara Delano Roosevelt, and her brother, Hall Ludlow Roosevelt, both die.
November 1941	ER is appointed assistant director of the Office of Civilian Defense.
December 7, 1941	ER addresses the nation on the radio after the Japanese bomb Pearl Harbor. The United States enters World War II.

February 22, 1942	ER is forced to resign from the Office of Civilian Defense.
October 21–November 17, 1942	ER visits Britain to bolster U.S. relations and support American troops.
August 17, 1943	ER begins five-week tour visiting U.S. troops in the South Pacific war zone.
November 7, 1944	FDR elected to fourth term as U.S. president.
April 12, 1945	FDR dies; ER informs Harry S. Truman he is president.
May 8, 1945	Victory in Europe is declared; Germany signs an unconditional surrender.
August 14, 1945	Japan surrenders after atomic bombs are dropped on Hiroshima and Nagasaki.
January 10, 1946	ER is the only female American delegate at the opening session of the United Nations in London.
January 1947	ER is elected chairperson of the UN Human Rights Commission.
December 10, 1948	The *Universal Declaration of Human Rights* is ratified by the UN General Assembly.
October 1, 1950	TV program *Mrs. Roosevelt Meets the Public* runs in tandem with a daily radio program.
January 1953	ER's tenure as U.S. delegate to the UN ends.
August 16, 1954	ER publicly takes on Senator Joseph McCarthy's witch hunt for "communists."
November 4, 1956	ER and Senator Margaret Chase Smith act as surrogates for Gov. Adlai Stevenson and President Dwight D. Eisenhower in the first televised presidential debate.
August 1957	ER interviews Soviet leader Nikita S. Khrushchev for the *New York Post*.
October 11, 1959–June 3, 1962	ER hosts groundbreaking public policy TV series *Prospects of Mankind*.

January 1961	President John F. Kennedy appoints ER to lead the Presidential Commission on the Status of Women in America.
March 12, 1961	ER conducts first television interview of a sitting president, John F. Kennedy.
November 7, 1962	Eleanor Roosevelt dies.
1963	Her book *Tomorrow Is Now* is published posthumously.

PRIMARY SOURCE DOCUMENTS

Theodore Roosevelt's Letter to Anna "Bye" Roosevelt, June 7, 1891

In the summer of 1891, a family crisis swirled around Eleanor's father. Elliott Roosevelt was completely overwhelmed by alcohol and opiate substance abuse. The family was in France and Eleanor's mother, Anna, was approximately eight months pregnant. Elliott's older sister "Bye" had come to help manage the conflict between husband and wife and care for the two children. Six-year-old Eleanor was too young to understand the seriousness of the situation but old enough to feel abandoned when she was sent away for periods of time.

Elliott Roosevelt's behavior was erratic. During an outburst, he violently pushed his pregnant wife. Anna was temporarily hospitalized and Bye wrote home. Letters were streaming across the Atlantic Ocean daily, between Bye and brother Theodore Roosevelt. No one realized they were rushing toward a defining moment that would change the future of Eleanor's immediate family.

Eleanor's uncle Theodore was dealing with allegations from Katy Mann, a former housemaid, who was also about to give birth to a baby fathered by Elliott. Theodore Roosevelt had recently risen to be head of the U.S. Civil Service with a mandate to clean up corruption. His career was rising while his brother was sinking. The Mrs. Carow he refers to in this letter is his mother-in-law. He has sent her to the family's country estate, Sagamore Hill at Oyster Bay (O.B.), where his wife Edith is also expecting a child in August. His friend "Bob" is Robert Munroe Ferguson.

689 Madison Avenue.
June 7th 91 [1891].

My own darling Byne,

I have just come in to town to meet Mrs. Carow and family, who are much worked up over your appearance when they saw you at Paris; I have sent them out to O.B. and am now here with dear Bob. Polo at Orange is largely over and he is now coming down to stay at Sagamore.

My own dearest sister, the strain under which you are living is like a hideous nightmare even to bear abroad—Your last letter in which you described Anna's hysterical attack due to Elliott's violence, is the most frightening of all. His curious callousness and selfishness, his disregard of your words and my letters, and his light heartedness under them, make one feel hopeless about him. Of course he never wrote me a word about the alleged Katy Mann letter. Now, one thing is definite, the present dreadful existence *must* not drag on beyond Anna's confinement and convalescence. Now you are doing a noble deed—the deed of a true, brave, loving woman—in standing between Anna and the horror of solitary association with Elliott. But you would be guilty of mere blameworthy folly if you permitted yourself to be lead [sic] the life a moment longer than it is absolutely necessary; that is a moment longer than Anna's health prevents her taking the children and coming home, leaving Elliott if he will not come home or go where he can be treated for a year and over. Anna herself must be made to understand that it is both maudlin and criminal—I am choosing my words with scientific exactness—to continue living with Elliott or suffering him to live with her, in the present fashion, a moment after she gets well enough to travel and take the children with her. Do everything to persuade her to come home at once, unless Elliott will put himself in an asylum for a term of years, or unless, better still, he will come too. Once here I'll guarantee to see that he is shut-up.

If Anna plays the fool, and is false to her duty and to her children, and persists in living with him as he now is—and it would be impossible to over paint the shameful immorality of ever continuing to live with him, and the cruel wrong she thereby does to the children *and to him*—then you must leave her to her fate and come home yourself.

Make up your mind it's one dreadful scene. Use this letter if you like. Tell him that he is either responsible or irresponsible. If irresponsible then he must go where he can be cured; if responsible he is simply a selfish, brutal and vicious criminal, and Anna ought not to stay with him an hour.

Do not care an atom for his threats of going off alone. Let him go. I wish most to see him in a retreat; but in any event I wish to see him separated from Anna and his children. If you can't get him into a retreat, then let him go off anyhow. What happens to him is of purely minor importance now; and the chance of probable scandal must not be weighed for a moment against the welfare—the life—of Anna and the children.

I enclose a letter to Anna; give it to her unless you deem it best not to do so; and choose your own time about doing it; Read it over.

If he can not be shut up and will neither go of his own accord, nor let Anna depart of his free will, then make your plans and go off some day in his absence. If you need me telegraph for me, and I (or Douglas if it is impossible for me to go on account of Edith) will come at once. But remember I come on but one condition. I come to settle the thing once for all. I come to see that Elliott is either put in an asylum against his will or not or else to take you, Anna and the children away, and to turn Elliott loose to shift for himself. You can tell him that Anna has a perfect right to a divorce; she—or you and I—have but to express belief in the Katy Mann story and no jury in the country would refuse a divorce.

Make Anna understand that if I am telegraphed for I come to act decisively and at once.

If Elliott will not go into an asylum then make Anna take the children and come home with you as soon as she can travel,

Yours always
Theodore Roosevelt

Source: *Letter from Theodore Roosevelt to Anna Roosevelt.* Theodore Roosevelt Collection, MS Am 1834 (319), Houghton Library, Harvard College Library.

Frances Perkins' Letter to Eleanor Roosevelt, December 17, 1928

Both Eleanor Roosevelt and Frances Perkins pointed to the Triangle Shirtwaist Factory fire of 1911 as a crystallizing moment in their lives. When these two labor reformers first met is debatable, but they interacted with each other through the Consumers' League and Al Smith's 1928 presidential campaign.

Eleanor recognized Perkins' expertise in labor policy and her visionary ideas on social safety-net programs. Other women in Eleanor's inner circle, Molly Dewson and Caroline O'Day, thought highly of Perkins. All agreed she would be an important resource for FDR. Eleanor also realized Perkins had the experience, temperament, and capability to work on an equal footing with men.

Perkins understood Eleanor's opinion carried great weight with FDR. She actively cultivated a relationship with "Mrs. Roosevelt."

In this letter dated two weeks before FDR's inauguration as governor of New York, interactions between Eleanor and Perkins are already apparent. Eleanor has facilitated a meeting between Perkins and FDR at Hyde Park.

Perkins is utilizing their relationship to send materials on farm relief to the governor-elect. Strategically, she compliments her new boss's wife. But Perkins also seems to envision that Eleanor's role in her husband's administration will be different than with previous governors. Eleanor Roosevelt and Frances Perkins built a working relationship that would last the rest of their lives.

FRANCES PERKINS
CHAIRMAN
STATE OF NEW YORK
DEPARTMENT OF LABOR
INDUSTRIAL BOARD
124 EAST 28th ST. NEW YORK CITY

December 17, 1928.

My dear Mrs. Roosevelt:—

This is the suggestion for a conference for farm relief which I talked to you about on the train the other morning. I talked about it briefly to Mr. Roosevelt, but the newspaper men arrived before we could go into it in detail. He asked me to send to him via you the memorandum which I had prepared. Therefore, I am burdening you with it. Thank you so much.

It was awfully nice to see you on Saturday and I enjoyed tremendously my glimpse of your lovely place. I thank you so much for asking me out. I had a very satisfactory talk with Mr. Roosevelt and under conditions which couldn't possibly have occurred otherwise. You will be very busy this next week or ten days, I know, but let me do anything I can to help you at any time.

I can't tell you how much the women of this State admire your prospective relationship to government; a new kind of a contribution is what you are going to make, I think.

Sincerely yours,
Frances Perkins

Mrs. Franklin D. Roosevelt,
49 East 65th Street,
New York City

Source: Perkins, Frances. 1928, December 17. "Letter, Frances Perkins To ER, December 17, 1928." Significant Documents Collection/Franklin D. Roosevelt Presidential Library & Museum. Series 2: Eleanor Roosevelt Significant Documents, Box 2. http://www.fdrlibrary.marist.edu/archives/collections/franklin/?p=collections/findingaid&id=510&q=&rootcontentid=144903.

Eleanor Roosevelt Campaign Strategy Memo, July 16, 1936

In 1936, Eleanor Roosevelt and Molly Dewson at the Women's Division of the Democratic Party felt FDR's reelection for president was far from guaranteed. With FDR away on vacation, Eleanor Roosevelt met with National Party officials—James Farley and publicity head, Charles Michelson—to ascertain how they intended to proceed with the campaign. Stephen Early was FDR's press secretary.

What she found underwhelmed her. By 1936, ER was a media professional. She had participated in and helped organize a range of campaigns for other candidates. While she frequently maintained she had little to no influence on her husband's political campaigns, this memo demonstrates otherwise.

She lays out organizational structure and specifically lists the range of media the campaign will need to address. She sets an agenda to identify responsibilities and, through specifically asked questions, provides a list of items that need to be addressed.

Her ground plan of coordinated messaging and data collection would benefit any modern political campaign. This private memo reveals Eleanor Roosevelt the organizer and tough politician; she has sources providing information on the opposition and advocates for an "aggressive campaign" against the Republican candidate—Alf Landon, governor of Kansas. Far from a political neophyte, Eleanor Roosevelt shows she had a depth of political experience and was very involved in the 1936 presidential campaign.

She also makes a groundbreaking suggestion to specifically employ members of the African American community to engage Black voters. (Her use of "negro" may seem distasteful, but the Black community in the United States preferred the term "Negro" until the 1960s Black Power movement.)

MEMO FROM MRS. ROOSEVELT   JULY 16, 1936.
TO: THE PRESIDENT
         MR. FARLEY
         MR. MICHELSON
         MR. HIGH
         MR. EARLY
         MISS DEWSON

I spent part of Tuesday afternoon and the morning of Wednesday at Democratic Headquarters. I had a conference with Miss Dewson and Mr. Farley; a conference with Mrs. Owen and Miss Dewson; and a conference with Mr. Michelson.

My impression is that the women are further along in their organization and more ready to go than any other unit as yet. I hear from outside sources that the Landon headquarters are set up and ready to work full time. They have continuity people writing for the radio, they have employed advertising people to do their copy, and the whole spirit is the spirit of a crusade.

My feeling is that we have to get going and going quickly, as I stated yesterday. I [sat] down and analyzed things which I thought necessary to organization. Some of the things I had in mind Mr. Michelson answered, a few things Mr. Farley answered for me at the time of the conferences. I am putting them down again simply as a matter of record to get the answers in black and white.

I hope the answers will be mailed to reach us at Eastport, Maine, on the 27th or 28th of July, when the President expects to be there.

1. At the meeting in Washington, the President said that Mr. Michelson[,] Steve Early, Stanley High and Henry Suydam would constitute the publicity steering committee, and I take it this must include radio, speeches, movies, pamphlets, fliers, news releases and trucks or whatever news goes out to the public. This committee is extremely important.

   Because of the importance of this committee, I hope a meeting will be held immediately for organizing and defining the duties of the members and that you will have the minutes kept at every meeting in order that a copy may go to the President and if the committee is willing, one to me as well so that I may know just what is done each time also.

2. Who is responsible for studying news reports and suggesting answers to charges, etc.?

3. Who is responsible, not for the mechanics of radio contracts for I understand you have a good man, but for the planning of a radio campaign, getting the speakers through the speakers' bureau, making the arrangements in the states for people to listen and getting in touch with Chester Davis, for instance on agriculture or any other people appointed as particular advisors on special subjects? In other words, who is making decisions under your committee on the above questions?

4. Who is in charge of research? Have we a department with complete information concerning all activities of the New Deal, and also concerning Landon and his supporters? If Miss Blackburn is in charge of this department as she was in the last campaign, have the heads of all campaign departments, men, women and young Democrats, been notified as to where to apply for information? This information should go out to the state committees also.

   I gather if the President o.k.'s [sic] it, the aggressive campaign against Landon's record will begin before Landon's acceptance speech. Who is to collect and maintain the complete data up to date and to check on all inconsistencies in Landon's pronouncement or those of his campaign managers as they relate to his former statements or record? Is there adequate material on this now at hand?

5. What definite plans have we made for tying in the other publicity organizations, both of men and women with the national publicity organization? I feel that anything of importance should go directly from a member of your committee and from the women in charge of national publicity to every publicity person in charge in the states.

6. Have you mapped out continuous publicity steps which will be taken between now and November? Is there any way at least of charting a tentative plan of strategy for the whole campaign, changing of course, as new things occur?

7. In the doubtful and Republican states what special attention do you plan to give and have you collected any data as yet on these states?

8. Who is handling news reels and will it be a committee or just one person and will your committee direct the activities?

9. Has your committee assigned as yet to each member definite fields for supervision?

10. How many people are now working on campaign speeches, both for men, women and young Democrats? Who is going over them for criticism so they cover all the necessary subjects?

11. Who is your man making contacts with newspapers all over the country?

12. Who is responsible for sending regular news to friendly newspapers? By this I mean feature stories, pictures, mats, boiler plate, etc.

I feel Mr. Rayburn should come at once to plan the policy and mechanics of the speaker's bureau. Then he could leave for a time.

I think it would be well to start some negro speakers, like Mrs. Bethune to speak at church meetings and that type of negro organization.

More and more my reports indicate that this is a close election and that we need very excellent organization. That is why I am trying to clarify in my own mind the functions at headquarters and have the President see a picture of the organization as clearly as possible in order that he may make any suggestions that he thinks necessary.

Eleanor Roosevelt.

Source: Roosevelt, Eleanor. 1936, July 16. "Memorandum, ER to FDR et al. re: 1936 Campaign Strategy, July 16, 1936." Significant Documents Collection/Franklin D. Roosevelt Presidential Library & Museum. Series 2: Eleanor Roosevelt Significant Documents, Box 2. http://www.fdrlibrary.marist. edu/archives/collections/franklin/?p=collections/findingaid&id=510&q=& rootcontentid=144903.

Executive Order 8802: Prohibition of Discrimination in the Defense Industry

Eleanor Roosevelt considered EO 8802 one of her most important contributions to racial equality. When African American labor unions and activists threatened a march on Washington, D.C., challenging the lack of opportunity for people of color in the military and defense industry employment, FDR sent the First Lady to negotiate. The result was a specific presidential act. For the first time, the U.S. government prohibited discrimination on account of race. EO 8802 opened the door for people of color in the U.S. military. It clarified that individuals could not be discriminated against to receive specialty military training. Companies fulfilling federal contracts in the defense industry were prohibited from discriminating against workers because of race or ethnicity.

Eventually, EO 8802 provided Japanese Americans in American internment camps a pathway to reclaim their family honor by joining the military and demonstrating they were loyal Americans.

Vital to the order's success, it included an enforcement element to investigate complaints of discrimination and follow-up with resolutions. The form and structure of the order shows the influence of Secretary of Labor Frances Perkins' successful labor reform legislation.

EO 8802 was an important first step toward antidiscrimination legislation and inclusivity.

Transcript of Executive Order 8802: Prohibition of Discrimination in the Defense Industry (1941)

Reaffirming Policy Of Full Participation in The Defense Program By All Persons, Regardless Of Race, Creed, Color, Or National Origin, And Directing Certain Action In Furtherance Of Said Policy

June 25, 1941

WHEREAS it is the policy of the United States to encourage full participation in the national defense program by all citizens of the United States, regardless of race, creed, color, or national origin, in the firm belief that the democratic way of life within the Nation can be defended successfully only with the help and support of all groups within its borders; and

WHEREAS there is evidence that available and needed workers have been barred from employment in industries engaged in defense production solely because of considerations of race, creed, color, or national origin, to the detriment of workers' morale and of national unity:

NOW, THEREFORE, by the virtue of the authority vested in me by the Constitution and the statutes, and as a prerequisite to the successful conduct of our national defense production effort, I do hereby reaffirm the policy of the United States that there shall be no discrimination in the employment of workers in defense industries or government because of race, creed, color, or national origin, and I do hereby declare that it is the duty of employers and of labor organizations, in furtherance of said policy and of this order, to provide for the full and equitable participation of all workers in defense industries, without discrimination because of race, creed, color, or national origin;

And it is hereby ordered as follows:

1. All departments and agencies of the Government of the United States concerned with vocational and training programs for defense production shall take special measures appropriate to assure that such programs are administered without discrimination because of race, creed, color, or national origin;

2. All contracting agencies of the Government of the United States shall include in all defense contracts hereafter negotiated by them a provision obligating the contractor not to discriminate against any worker because of race, creed, color, or national origin;

3. There is established in the Office of Production Management a Committee on Fair Employment Practice, which shall consist of a chairman and four other members to be appointed by the President. The Chairman and members of the Committee shall serve as such without compensation but shall be entitled to actual and necessary transportation, subsistence and other expenses incidental to performance of their duties. The Committee shall receive and investigate complaints of discrimination in violation of the provisions of this order and shall take appropriate steps to redress grievances which it finds to be valid. The Committee shall also recommend to the several departments and agencies of the Government of the United States and to the President all measures which may be deemed by it necessary or proper to effectuate the provision of this order.

Franklin D. Roosevelt
The White House
June 25, 1941

Source: Exec. Order No. 8802 dated June, 25 1941. General Records of the United States Government; Record Group 11; National Archives. Accessed December 4, 2020. https://www.ourdocuments.gov/doc.php?flash=true &doc=72.

United Nations Universal Declaration of Human Rights

Eleanor Roosevelt made handwritten notes in pencil during revisions of the Universal Declaration of Human Rights between January 1947 and its adoption by the UN General Assembly on December 10, 1948.

For comparison, the image of an early draft of the document containing Eleanor's handwritten notes has been provided following the final document text.

In the early draft, "Article 1" and "Article 2" reveal a focus on humans as part of and owing duty to a "community." The emphasis later changed toward the individual, and Eleanor lined out large sections. Compare the initial text of "Article 1" with the final text. You can see how conceptual ideas were winnowed down to their essence. The words "reason and conscience" were added, removed, debated, and finally included.

Eleanor Roosevelt championed clear concise language. Look for the origin of Article 3 (the final version) in the drafts of "Article 6" and "Article 7."

Under "Article 5" in the draft, Eleanor has written: "All are equal before the law." While she has lined it out, look for the phrase in the final version of Article 7.

Article 2 spells out expanded concepts regarding nondiscrimination, while Article 16 is groundbreaking as the first international statement of women's rights concerning marriage.

Unlike in the U.S. Constitution, socioeconomic rights are addressed: Article 23.

Creating such a document by committee, with comments from fifty-eight contributing countries, was a monumental challenge. The final document is a testament to Eleanor Roosevelt's management and the determination of people from different cultures and backgrounds to come together.

Universal Declaration of Human Rights (approved by the UN General Assembly December 10, 1948)

Preamble

Whereas recognition of the inherent dignity and of the equal and inalienable rights of all members of the human family is the foundation of freedom, justice and peace in the world,

Whereas disregard and contempt for human rights have resulted in barbarous acts which have outraged the conscience of mankind, and the advent of a world in which human beings shall enjoy freedom of speech and belief and freedom from fear and want has been proclaimed as the highest aspiration of the common people,

Whereas it is essential, if man is not to be compelled to have recourse, as a last resort, to rebellion against tyranny and oppression, that human rights should be protected by the rule of law,

Whereas the peoples of the United Nations have in the Charter reaffirmed their faith in fundamental human rights, in the dignity and worth of the human person and in the equal rights of men and women and have determined to promote social progress and better standards of life in larger freedom,

Whereas Member States have pledged themselves to achieve, in cooperation with the United Nations, the promotion of universal respect for and observance of human rights and fundamental freedoms,

Whereas a common understanding of these rights and freedoms is of the greatest importance for the full realization of this pledge,

Now, therefore,

The General Assembly,

Proclaims this Universal Declaration of Human Rights as a common standard of achievement for all people and all nations, to the end that every individual and every organ of society, keeping this Declaration constantly in mind, shall strive by teaching and education to promote respect for these rights and freedoms and by progressive measures, national and international, to secure their universal and effective recognition and observance, both among the peoples of Member States themselves and among the peoples of territories under their jurisdiction.

Article 1
All human beings are born free and equal in dignity and rights. They are endowed with reason and conscience and should act toward one another in a spirit of brotherhood.

Article 2
Everyone is entitled to all the rights and freedoms set forth in this Declaration, without distinction of any kind, such as race, colour, sex, language, religion, political or other opinion, national or social origin, property, birth or other status. Furthermore, no distinction shall be made on the basis of the political, jurisdictional or international status of the country or territory to which a person belongs, whether it be independent, trust, non-self-governing or under any other limitation of sovereignty.

Article 3
Everyone has the right to life, liberty and security of person.

Article 4
No one shall be held in slavery or servitude; slavery and the slave trade shall be prohibited in all their forms.

Article 5
No one shall be subjected to torture or to cruel, inhuman or degrading treatment or punishment.

Article 6
Everyone has the right to recognition everywhere as a person before the law.

Article 7
All are equal before the law and are entitled without any discrimination to equal protection of the law. All are entitled to equal protection against any discrimination in violation of this Declaration and against any incitement to such discrimination.

...

Article 14
1. Everyone has the right to seek and to enjoy in other countries asylum from persecution.
2. This right may not be invoked in the case of prosecutions genuinely arising from non-political crimes or from acts contrary to the purposes and principles of the United Nations.

Article 15
1. Everyone has the right to a nationality.
2. No one shall be arbitrarily deprived of his nationality nor denied the right to change his nationality.

Article 16
1. Men and women of full age, without any limitation due to race, nationality or religion, have the right to marry and to found a family. They are entitled to equal rights as to marriage, during marriage and at its dissolution.
2. Marriage shall be entered into only with the free and full consent of the intending spouses.
3. The family is the natural and fundamental group unit of society and is entitled to protection by society and the State.

Article 17
1. Everyone has the right to own property alone as well as in association with others.
2. No one shall be arbitrarily deprived of his property.

Article 18

Everyone has the right to freedom of thought, conscience and religion; this right includes freedom to change his religion or belief, and freedom, either alone or in community with others and in public or private, to manifest his religion or belief in teaching, practice, worship and observance.

Article 19

Everyone has the right to freedom of opinion and expression; this right includes freedom to hold opinions without interference and to seek, receive and impart information and ideas through any media and regardless of frontiers.

Article 20

1. Everyone has the right to freedom of peaceful assembly and association.
2. No one may be compelled to belong to an association.

...

Article 23

1. Everyone has the right to work, to free choice of employment, to just and favourable conditions of work and to protection against unemployment.
2. Everyone, without any discrimination, has the right to equal pay for equal work.
3. Everyone who works has the right to just and favourable remuneration ensuring for himself and his family an existence worthy of human dignity, and supplemented, if necessary, by other means of social protection.
4. Everyone has the right to form and to join trade unions for the protection of his interests.

...

Article 27

1. Everyone has the right freely to participate in the cultural life of the community, to enjoy the arts and to share in scientific advancement and its benefits.
2. Everyone has the right to the protection of the moral and material interests resulting from any scientific, literary or artistic production of which he is the author.

...

Source: The United Nations. 1948. Universal Declaration of Human Rights. https://www.un.org/en/about-us/universal-declaration-of-human-rights.

-2-

Organization and the Member States may constantly apply the
principles so declared; and

Have therefore adopted the following Declaration:

CHAPTER I   *General Principles*

Article 1 - Human beings ~~belonging to the community of Mankind are~~ free, of
equal dignity and rights and must consider themselves as brothers.

Article 2 - ~~It is the duty of every community to give~~ each of its members
equal opportunity for the full development of his physical, intellectual
~~and moral personality, without one being sacrificed to others.~~

Article 3 - As human beings cannot live and develop themselves without the help
and support of the ~~community~~, each one owes to ~~the community~~
fundamental duties which are: obedience to law, exercise of a useful
activity, ~~willful~~ participation in obligations and sacrifices
demanded for the common good.

Article 4 - The ~~rights of each one are~~ limited by the rights of others.

Art. 2 Sec.
Draft and U.S.

Article 5 - Law is equal for all. It ~~commands~~ to public authorities and judges
as well as to individuals. Everything that is not prohibited by law
cannot be legally prevented.

CHAPTER II

The right to life and physical integrity.

Article 6 - Everyone ~~has the right to life and physical integrity~~. No one,
even, when guilty, shall be subjected to torture, ~~to cruel
punishment or to indignity~~.

Articles 3 & 4
of Sec. Draft

CHAPTER III

Personal Liberties

Article 7 - Everyone has the right to personal liberty.

Art. 5 Sec. Draft.

An image of Eleanor Roosevelt's personal copy of an early draft of "Articles 1–7"
of the *Universal Declaration of Human Rights* with her notes written in pencil
(1946–1947).

Bibliography

Beasley, Maurine H. 1984. "Eleanor Roosevelt: First Lady as a Magazine Journalist." Paper presented at Annual Meeting of the Association for Education in Journalism and Mass Communication (August 5–8). https://files.eric.ed.gov/fulltext/ED246442.pdf

Beasley, Maurine H., and Paul Belgrade. 1985. "Eleanor Roosevelt: First Lady as Radio Pioneer." Paper presented at Annual Meeting of the Association for Education in Journalism and Mass Communication (August 3–6). https://eric.ed.gov/?id=ED258200

Binker, Mary Jo, ed. 2018. *If You Asked Me: Essential Advice from Eleanor Roosevelt*. New York: Atria Books.

Black, Allida M., ed. 1999. *Courage in a Dangerous World: The Political Writings of Eleanor Roosevelt*. New York: Columbia University Press.

Caroli, Betty Boyd. 1998. *The Roosevelt Women*. New York: Basic Books.

Cook, Blanche Wiesen. 1992. *Eleanor Roosevelt, Volume 1: 1884–1933*. New York: Viking Penguin.

Cook, Blanche Wiesen. 1999. *Eleanor Roosevelt, Volume 2: The Defining Years 1933–1938*. New York: Viking Penguin.

Cook, Blanche Wiesen. 2016. *Eleanor Roosevelt, Volume 3: The War Years and After, 1939–1962*. New York: Viking Penguin.

Downey, Kirstin. 2009. *The Woman Behind the New Deal: The Life of Frances Perkins, FDR's Secretary of Labor and His Moral Conscience*. New York: Random House.

Federal Bureau of Investigations. n.d. "FBI Records: The Vault; Eleanor Roosevelt." Accessed January 20, 2021. http://vault.fbi.gov/Eleanor%20Roosevelt

Franklin D. Roosevelt Presidential Library and Museum. n.d. "Eleanor Roosevelt." Accessed December 18, 2020. https://www.fdrlibrary.org/eleanor-roosevelt

Franklin D. Roosevelt Presidential Library and Museum. n.d. "Significant Documents Collection." Accessed December 18, 2020. http://www.fdrlibrary.marist.edu/archives/collections/franklin/?p=collections/findingaid&id=510&q=&rootcontentid=144903#id144903

George Washington University, Department of History, Columbian College of Arts & Sciences, Washington D.C. n.d. "Eleanor Roosevelt Papers Project; Online Documents." Accessed January 6, 2022. https://erpapers.columbian.gwu.edu/online-documents

Glendon, Mary Ann. 2001. *A World Made New: Eleanor Roosevelt and the Universal Declaration of Human Rights.* New York: Random House.

Goodwin, Doris Kearns. 1994. *No Ordinary Time: Franklin and Eleanor Roosevelt: The Home Front in World War II.* New York: Simon & Schuster.

Goodwin, Doris Kearns. 2018. *Leadership in Turbulent Times.* New York: Simon & Schuster.

Harvard Library, Cambridge, MA. n.d. "Women Working, 1800–1930: An Exploration of Women's Impact on the Economic Life of America between 1800 and the Great Depression." Accessed January 20, 2021. https://library.harvard.edu/collections/women-working-1800-1930

Johnson, Elizabeth Ofosuah. 2019, May 9. "Meet the Gallant All-Black American Female Battalion That Served in Europe During World War II." *Face 2 Face Africa.* https://face2faceafrica.com/article/meet-the-gallant-all-black-american-female-battalion-that-served-in-europe-during-world-war-ii

Lash, Joseph P. 1971. *Eleanor and Franklin: The Story of Their Relationship Based on Eleanor Roosevelt's Private Papers.* New York: W.W. Norton & Company, Inc.

League of Women Voters, New York. n.d. "Eleanor Roosevelt: First Lady, League Leader, Pioneer." Accessed January 20, 2021. https://www.lwv.org/eleanor-roosevelt-first-lady-league-leader-pioneer

Luscombe, Anya. 2014. "Eleanor Roosevelt as 'Ordinary' Citizen and 'Expert' on Radio in the Early 1950s." *SAGE Open.* July–September 2014:1–9. https://journals.sagepub.com/doi/10.1177/2158244014551712

McCullough, David. 1992. *Truman.* New York: Simon & Schuster.

McGuire, John Thomas. 2014. "Beginning an 'Extraordinary Opportunity': Eleanor Roosevelt, Molly Dewson, and the Expansion of Women's Boundaries in the Democratic Party, 1924–1934." *Women's History Review* 23 (6): 922–937. http://dx.doi.org/10.1080/09612025.2014.906841

Michals, Debra. 2017. *Eleanor Roosevelt.* Washington, D.C.: National Women's History Museum. https://www.womenshistory.org/education-resources/biographies/eleanor-roosevelt

Miller, Kristie, and Robert H. McGinnis, eds. 2009. *A Volume of Friendship: The Letters of Eleanor Roosevelt and Isabella Greenway 1904–1953*. Tucson: The Arizona Historical Society.

National First Ladies Library. n.d. "First Lady Biography: Eleanor Roosevelt." Accessed January 20, 2021. http://www.firstladies.org/biographies/firstladies.aspx?biography=33

New York Times. 1905. "President Roosevelt Gives the Bride Away." March 18, 1905. https://www.nytimes.com/1905/03/18/archives/president-roosevelt-gives-the-bride-away-his-niece-weds-his-cousin.html

O'Farrell, Brigid. "A Stitch in Time: The New Deal, The International Ladies' Garment Workers' Union, and Mrs. Roosevelt." *Transatlantica* 2006:1. http://journals.openedition.org/transatlantica/190

Perkins, Frances. 1946. *The Roosevelt I Knew*. New York: Viking Press.

Peyser, Marc, and Timothy Dwyer. 2015. *Hissing Cousins: The Untold Story of Eleanor Roosevelt and Alice Roosevelt Longworth*. New York: Nan A. Talese, Doubleday.

Quinn, Susan. 2016. *Eleanor and Hick: The Love Affair That Shaped a First Lady*. New York: Penguin Press.

Roosevelt, Eleanor. 1928, April. "Women Must Learn to Play the Game as Men Do." *Redbook* magazine, pp. 78–79, 141–142. https://erpapers.columbian.gwu.edu/women-must-learn-play-game-men-do

Roosevelt, Eleanor. 1935–1962. "My Day Index." *The Eleanor Roosevelt Papers Digital Edition* (2018). Edited by George Washington University. https://erpapers.columbian.gwu.edu/my-day-index

Roosevelt, Eleanor. 1960. *You Learn by Living*. New York: HarperCollins Publishers.

Roosevelt, Eleanor. 1961. *The Autobiography of Eleanor Roosevelt*. New York: HarperCollins.

Roosevelt, Eleanor. 1963. *Tomorrow Is Now*. New York: Penguin RandomHouse.

Roosevelt, Elliott, and James Brough. 1973. *An Untold Story: The Roosevelts of Hyde Park*. New York: G.P. Putnam's Sons.

Roosevelt, Theodore. 1910. "Nobel Lecture." Transcript of speech delivered at the National Theatre, Oslo, Sweden May 5. https://www.nobelprize.org/prizes/peace/1906/roosevelt/lecture/

Smith, Kathryn. 2016. *The Gatekeeper: Missy LeHand, FDR, and the Untold Story of the Partnership That Defined a Presidency*. New York: Simon & Schuster, Inc.

Smith, Stephen Drury, ed. 2014. *The First Lady of Radio: Eleanor Roosevelt's Historic Broadcasts*. New York: The New Press.

Streitmatter, Rodger, ed. 1998. *Empty Without You: The Intimate Letters of Eleanor Roosevelt and Lorena Hickok*. New York: The Free Press.

United Nations, New York. n.d. "Universal Declaration of Human Rights." Accessed October 16, 2018. http://www.un.org/en/universal -declaration-human-rights/index.html

Ware, Susan. 1981. *Beyond Suffrage: Women in the New Deal*. Cambridge, MA: Harvard University Press.

Woloch, Nancy. 2017. *In Her Words: Eleanor Roosevelt on Women, Politics, Leadership, and Lessons from Life*. New York: Black Dog and Leventhal Publishers.

Index

About the Author

Keri F. Dearborn, MA Education, is a nonfiction author and STEM education consultant in Southern California. She was a contributor to *Women in American History: A Social, Political, and Cultural Encyclopedia and Document Collection* (2017), recognized by the American Libraries Association in 2018 as a RUSA Outstanding Reference Source. She also contributed to *Technical Innovation in American History: An Encyclopedia of Science and Technology* (2019). She has written numerous biographies for young adult publications.